CRYING HANDS

CRYING HANDS

EUGENICS AND DEAF PEOPLE IN NAZI GERMANY

Horst Biesold

Translation by William Sayers

Introduction by Henry Friedlander

Gallaudet University Press

Washington, D.C.

Gallaudet University Press
Washington, DC 20002

Originally published as *Klagende Hände,*
©1988 by Jarick Oberbiel, Solms, Germany.

All the photographs of schools for the deaf are
used with permission from G. Lehmann, ed.,
*Taubstummenunterricht und Taubstummen-Fürsorge
in Deutschen Reich* (Dusseldorf, 1930). The author
wishes to thank Hartmut Rauer for supplying
reproductions of the original photographs.

Printed in the United States of America

Library of Congress Cataloging-in-Publication Data

Biesold, Horst, 1939–
   [Klagende Hände, English]
   Crying hands: eugenics and deaf people in Nazi Germany / Horst
Biesold; translation by William Sayers; introduction by Henry
Friedlander.
     p. cm.
   Includes bibliographical references and index.
   ISBN 1-56368-077-7 (alk. paper)
   1. Deaf—Government policy—Germany. 2. Deafness—Germany.
3. History of medicine, 20th century—Germany. 4. Eugenics—
Germany—History—20th century. 5. Social Darwinism—Germany.
I. Title.
HV2748.B5413   1999
362.4'2094309043—dc21   99-27291
                                                                       CIP

Jacket and interior design by Dennis Anderson.
The jacket art is from a woodcut entitled *Crying Hands* by
David Ludwig Bloch, who has graciously granted permission
for its use.

Contents

Publisher's Introduction   vii

Preface to the German Edition   xi

Acknowledgments   xvii

Introduction   1
  Henry Friedlander

1 From Social Darwinism to
  National Socialism   13

2 The Concept of Hereditary Deafness
  under National Socialism   28

3 Teacher-Collaborators   42

4 Forced Abortions   84

5 Deaf Collaboration: REGEDE   91

6 Deaf Resistance   109

7 The Jewish Deaf in Germany   130

8 Sterilization's Legacy   140

9 Euthanasia and Deaf Germans   160

Appendix 1: The Questionnaire   171

Appendix 2: Questionnaire Data   175

Appendix 3: Documents Written by
and in Support of Gertrud Jacob   184

Notes   189

Author's Bibliography   211

Selected Bibliography in English   219

Index   223

Publisher's Introduction

THE GERMAN deaf community's devastation by eugenics, educators, and National Socialism in the 1930s and early 1940s forms the subject matter of *Crying Hands*. Preparation of an American edition of this work, translated from Horst Biesold's *Klagende Hände*, presented Gallaudet University Press with serious challenges. The original text published in Germany essentially reproduced Biesold's dissertation in book form. A meticulous translation therefore yielded a manuscript crafted in a heavy academic style, replete with scores of documents in their original form and condition, organized as a research report, and containing sections written to influence contemporaneous German political discussions. While this presentation might appeal to a narrow audience of scholars familiar with German history, it presented too many obstacles for other readers.

Yet the book's evidentiary core and dramatic conclusions demand a wider audience. Interviews and survey data from deaf victims of Nazi eugenics practices exist nowhere else. In *Crying Hands* deaf voices bear witness to one of the horrifying results of Nazism; perhaps more importantly they call attention to a particular approach to disability that is not entirely foreign to American readers. The complicity of teachers in the forced sterilization of deaf children, captured in documents discovered by Biesold and interviews with deaf survivors, provides evidence of another kind of horror that needs to be understood, both for its historical significance and for its meaning in today's world, in which the medicalization of social problems and genetic engineering are becoming commonplace.

In order to make the new book accessible and relevant to American readers, therefore, we have altered the German text's presentation and organization while retaining Biesold's arguments and as much of his original language as possible. Henry Friedlander, a leading scholar of the Holocaust and author of *Origins of Nazi Genocide: From Euthanasia to the Final Solution,* has written a new historical introduction for the American edition, in which he frames the context for the particular experiences of deaf people that Biesold describes and analyzes in detail. In addition, a new compilation of references to English language books on related subjects has been added.

Some textual material from the German edition has been moved into the appendices of the English book. Biesold's questionnaire, which was distributed to deaf survivors, is no longer in the text; it now occupies appendix 1, along with Biesold's explication of various questions within the form itself. Similarly, the raw data from the questionnaires is now in appendix 2. A large collection of documents related to Gertrud Jacob, the subject of an interview in chapter 6, composes appendix 3. Other textual material has been moved into endnotes when it was believed to be more properly a reference than an integral part of the narrative.

Some sections that Biesold did not include in the main text have been integrated with it for the American edition. These parts, which the author had labeled "Excursus 1: Deaf Victims of the 'Euthanasia Action,'" and "Excursus 2: The Jewish Deaf in Germany," seemed essential to the text for an American audience. Segments of the manuscript that discussed sterilized deaf Germans' efforts to achieve compensation from the government, by contrast, were removed from the Gallaudet University Press version.

In the course of his research, Biesold gathered a huge quantity of original and photocopied documents to support his arguments. These items, which are referred to as "Biesold Archive" followed by a number in the endnotes to the American edition, became his personal property, and they were so indicated in the original publication. Happily, Biesold has released them so that other scholars may use them as well. They now can be found in the Biesold Archive, Library of the Institute for German Sign Language and Communication of the Deaf, University of Hamburg, Hamburg, Germany.

Crying Hands tells a painful story. The mutilation and suffering of children, adolescents, and parents, whose only crime was deafness, appears repeatedly in the documents and survivor testimony Biesold collected. Accounts of educators' complicity in atrocities against their own deaf students, moreover, is a second source of particular anguish for us in the Gallaudet University community. We hope that this translated and edited text will contribute to public understanding and debate about the troubling issues it raises.

Preface to the German Edition

THIS WORK could have been written only because there were more than twelve hundred deaf people who experienced and survived the most horrifying experiences and were willing to communicate them to a hearing person, despite the public silence that had been dictated.

One of my longtime friends who is deaf was the first to tell me about the persecution and suffering he experienced during the Third Reich and about the psychological torment that still afflicts him today. My friend had chosen the time and place for our conversation so that we were alone and could communicate without being disturbed. His greatest sorrow was the secrecy concerning his sterilization. I was deeply affected by his account of persecution and other forms of suffering, as well as by the emotion with which he told his story. Not once in the course of twelve years of living and working with deaf people, nor during a two-year preparatory program in deaf education, had I been confronted with the issue of the persecution of deaf people under the Nazi government that followed the passage of the Law for the Prevention of Offspring with Hereditary Diseases in 1933. Now I was suddenly made aware of the involvement of my fellow teachers in Nazi race ideology: the selection of several thousand deaf Germans, who were stigmatized as hereditarily diseased; the shameful truth that some deaf persons were reported on by others in the deaf community; the anguish and helplessness of most victims, but also the courage of some few who resisted; the long-term psychological and physical injury that many deaf people suffered as a consequence of compulsory sterilization; the exclusion and murder of mentally and psychologically impaired deaf persons; and the expulsion and elimination of deaf Jews.

I must admit that I was initially skeptical (my friend has since forgiven me). At that time (1979) I could not imagine that the tragic events that my friend had recounted could have occurred on such a dramatic scale without advocates for deaf people investigating and publicizing them after the Nazi dictatorship had come to an end.

The pastor to the Bremen deaf community, Herta Giesler, dispelled my skepticism. From her work with her congregation, she knew of the scope of the persecution and of the long-term effects that many of her deaf parishioners still experienced. She was also aware that hardly anyone among those who had been forcibly sterilized spoke openly of the injustice that had been suffered. Giesler encouraged me to act on my desire to try to liberate forcibly sterilized deaf people from the oppression of anguish and shame, and to make them fully aware that the compulsory operation they had undergone was an act of injustice by the Nazi state.

The method I chose for the project was determined by my wish to incorporate the biographies of victims in a work of historical reappraisal and explication. I believe that only through the acceptance of one's own destiny can the end of a historic injustice finally be recognized and internalized, and that only with this realization does there appear a way out of the darkness of disempowerment, degradation, and isolation.

After a few preliminary conversations with persons who had been affected by the law, it became clear to me that a biographical reappraisal of these persecuted lives could be undertaken only with circumspection and empathy. My knowledge of German Sign Language allowed me to develop a trusting relationship in interviews, conversations, and questions without communication barriers. In countless discussions and letters, I have again and again had to reassure forcibly sterilized deaf people that personal information about them would not be publicized. I have kept this promise, reinforced by legal requirements concerning the confidentiality of personal data. Also, I wanted to shield victims from the fresh humiliation of being scrutinized for a historical diagnosis after they had already been the subjects of "hereditary biology." In the following pages, personal data has been replaced by impersonal abbreviations (e.g., NN for a deleted personal name, XX for a place name). In my text, ellipsis (indicated by . . .) is at times employed for the same purpose. On other occasions, I have given explicit personal information at the express wish of the individuals involved or of their surviving relatives.

For the second category of those "involved," the perpetrators, I could not, out of consideration for the victims, accept the rationale for confidentiality of personal data.

In addition to my interviews with the victims, I also conducted research at many German schools for the deaf. The following stories exemplify some of the problems I encountered at these schools.

1. I informed the director of a northern German school for hearing-impaired students of my research project and requested access to the registry books of what was earlier the Institution for the Deaf. Permission to review materials was granted without comment. Administrative records for the period 1933 to 1945 were analyzed from the perspective of my project. Eight days later, I asked the director for access to the files of students who attended the institution between 1933 and 1945. With an expression of deepest regret, the director of the school explained that a few days earlier he had instructed government workers at the school to destroy all the old student records. Lack of space was given as the reason. An inquiry established that public service employees had indeed received instructions to destroy the records—the files were to be shredded and thrown into a waste container.

2. Some deaf victims of the sterilization law alerted me to offenses committed by the administration of a large church-run school in southern Germany during Nazi rule. These former students knew that their files from 1933 to 1945 were stored in the school archives. In a telephone conversation, a representative of

the present school administration showed a full understanding for my research and confirmed the statements of former students at the institution. A date for the start of my research work was agreed on. One day before the scheduled start of my work, I made a courtesy telephone call to inquire whether the date was still convenient. At this point the school administrator explained that it did not appear that the visit would be profitable, as scarcely any documents still existed. I was kindly asked to cancel my visit.

3. The principal of a western German deaf school, which administered the archives of one of the largest former German "institutions for the deaf," promised by telephone his assistance in the planned research work. He indicated great interest in the reappraisal of even this chapter of the history of German deaf education. When I showed up in the principal's office as we had agreed in order to begin my research, the impossibility of my request was explained to me. The principal stated that he had spoken with his head office in Münster and they had given him to understand that the research project was "too hot an issue"—if the media learned of it, he, the principal, "could get skinned." As I have since learned, eight days after this conversation, the archivists of the Westphalia-Lippe Regional Union came from Münster and removed all the documentation and student files of the former Provincial Institution for the Deaf. A telephone call to a staff member of the Westphalian Central Archives at the Westphalia-Lippe Regional Union in Münster corroborated for me that these school and student records were to be stored there. After an informal written request, I was told, an applicant could count on promptly beginning research. I made such an informal application on October 21, 1983, stating that I requested access to the records of former *deaf* students who had attended the institution between 1933 and 1945. By way of answer I was advised that I should know that a certain Professor NN was conducting research on the topic of euthanasia of the *mentally impaired* under the auspices of the Westphalia-Lippe Regional Union. I could then not be granted access to archival material at that time.

4. Various deaf victims of the sterilization law pointed out to me that there must still be a complete school archive in a large

deaf school in Rheinland-Pfalz. After several requests on my part to the director of this institution for permission to conduct research in his archives, the director declared that he was not authorized to make such a serious decision. The Ministry of Public Worship in Mainz was named as the appropriate agency to approach. At that time, the responsible director at the ministry had no knowledge of the existence of an archive in the deaf school that was under his supervision. He promised the speediest possible attention to the matter. After several vain promises over the telephone and a five-month waiting period, I made a written application on February 29, 1984, to consult the school archive. In a communication of March 29, 1984, the ministerial director answered that "the records of the former institution for the deaf . . . had been taken over for the time being by the Central Provincial Archives of Rheinland-Pfalz in Koblenz."[1]

But a very different picture emerges from the attitude of other institutions and school administrations in the Federal Republic of Germany and the German Democratic Republic. In the following archives, I was readily offered all rights of access and use and, beyond that, had the advantage of the sympathetic collaboration of the directors, teachers, and school community: The Hermann Schafft School, 3588 Homberg; the State Residential School for the Hearing-Impaired, 2380 Schleswig; the Pauline Home, 7057 Winnenden; the National Memorial Site, Ravensbrück; the Central State Archives of the German Democratic Republic, Potsdam.

AT THE writing stage of this project I faced a dilemma. On the one hand, research results ought to be written up with those personally affected in mind; on the other, the publication of findings and conclusions should meet accepted scientific standards. My deaf friends will forgive me that I eventually opted for scholarly publication. This decision was prompted by my recognition of new threats that are now signaled by genetic engineering and by

---

1. Letter from the Minister for Culture, Rheinland-Pfalz, 946-B-51271/32/3, March 29, 1984.

the attempts of "humane" genetics to promote sterilization on eugenic grounds. This book should also be understood as an urgent summons to oppose all such tendencies.

My decision to pursue this project as a work of social science meant that the literate testimony of deaf subjects had to be edited from the syntax of German Sign Language. I am a certified and sworn interpreter of the language of the deaf, authorized by the Ministry of the Interior. But the question remains whether, and how well, one can represent the feelings and perceptions of the deaf victims of the Nazis. Are suffering and accounts of pain scientifically quantifiable as data that can be fed into a computer and subjected to empirical representation in complicated analytical series and statistics? I wanted to expose, uncompromisingly, the role of deaf education and the complicity of educators in the illegal Nazi state. I owed this to the deaf victims, for they had placed boundless trust and hope for support in their teachers—in persons who for more than 150 years had been pledged to an ideal and to the right of deaf people to lives of human dignity realized through language, education, and humanitarian support.

Horst Biesold

Acknowledgments

THIS STUDY was accepted in 1986 by the University of Bremen as a dissertation qualifying the author for the degree of Doctor of Philosophy. Special thanks are due to the examiners, Professor Dr. Wilfried Wagner, Department of History, and Professor Dr. Wolfgang Jantzen, Department of Education of the Disabled.

A further word of thanks must be expressed in the name of the deaf victims of the Law for the Prevention of Offspring with Hereditary Diseases. This gratitude is directed to all true humanitarians in all political parties in the Federal Republic of Germany who, since the foundation of this state, have fought fiercely for the rehabilitation of the disenfranchised, and to those who provided the author with material support for the necessary research, through a grant from the Federal Ministry of the Interior.

The author also wishes to thank the following institutions, professional organizations, associations, and individuals, for their help and support for this research.

Chaim Apter, World Organization of Jewish Deaf, Tel Aviv, Israel
Archivum Panstwowe, Wroclaw, Poland
David Ludwig Bloch, New York
Central State Archives (*Zentrales Staatsarkiv*) of the former German Democratic Republic, Potsdam
Enzio Cramon and Francine Gaudray, producers of "Seeing Instead of Hearing" ("Sehen statt Hören"), Bavarian Television
Federal Association of Teachers and Social Workers for the

Hearing-Impaired, (*Bundesarbeitsgemeinschaft der Sozial-pädagogen und Sozialarbeiter für Hörgeschädigte*), Münster

Federal Mininster of the Interior (*Bundesminister des Inneren*), Bonn

Dr. Herbert Feuchte, Hamburg

Hannelore Feuss, Bureau of Parliamentary Representatives (*Büro der Bundestagsabgeordneten*), Bonn

Frau Fiedler, Association for the Advancement of the Deaf (*Gesellschaft zur Förderung der Gehörlosen*), Berlin

Gallaudet University, Washington, D.C.

Erich Gerber, Berlin

German Federal Archives (*Bundesarkiv*), Koblenz

Germania Judaica, Cologne

Herta Giesler, Bremen

Dr. M. Hauner, Department of History, University of Wisconsin, Madison, Wisconsin

Helen Keller Center, Tel Aviv, Israel

Margot Höxter, Hamburg

The Jewish Congregation of Berlin (Dr. H. Simon)

Körber Foundation (*Körber Stiftung*), Hamburg (Wolf Schmidt)

Gerd Leienbach, Bremen

Dr. Kikuji Nakanishi, Japan Hearing Handicapped Newspaper, Kyoto, Japan

National Memorial Site (*Nationale Mahn- und Gedenkstätte*), Ravensbrück

National Technical Institute for the Deaf, Rochester, New York

Parliamentary Archives, Federal Republic of Germany, Bonn

Marla A. Petal, Temple Beth Solomon of the Deaf, Los Angeles

Dr. Reiner Pommerin, Department of History, University of Cologne

Protestant Academy (*Evangelische Akademie*), Bad Boll

Hartmut Rauer, Oyten, Bremen

Dr. Erwin Reichmann, Bremen

Dr. Norbert Schmacke, Bremen

School archives in Bielefeld, Bremen, Dillingen, Homberg, Nuremberg, Schleswig and Winnenden

Waltraut Schulze, Bremen
Frau Siebert, Kassel
State Archives (*Staatsarkiv*), Bremen
State Archives (*Staatsarkiv*), Freiburg
Ina Tessmer-Glander, Bremen
Ernst Waltemathe, Representative of the Lower House, Bremen/
    Bonn
Otto Welker, Frankfurt
Yad Vashem, Jerusalem

CRYING HANDS

Introduction

Henry Friedlander

HORST BIESOLD'S *Crying Hands* treats a neglected aspect of the Holocaust: the fate of the deaf in Nazi Germany. His book covers a story that has remained almost unknown. In the United States, even in Germany, few are aware that during the Nazi era human beings—men, women, and children—with impaired hearing were sterilized against their will, and even fewer know that many of the deaf were also murdered.

The Nazi regime championed an ideology of human inequality designed to assure the health and purity of the German national community. Membership in the community was to be based on biology; race and not culture was to determine inclusion. It thus became the official policy of the German state to exclude those considered to be a threat to the nation's health and purity. This exclusion was based on biology and directed against groups of human beings considered alien or inferior; heredity determined the fate of groups and individuals.[1]

Although the campaign against supposedly alien influences was directed against large numbers of human beings classified as incompatible with the Nordic ideal of "Aryan" Germans—for example, persons of African or Oriental descent—only two so-called alien groups resided in Central Europe in sufficient numbers to require the intervention of the state: Jews and Gypsies. Against them the Nazi regime inaugurated a concerted policy of isolation, discrimination, and repression. Their isolation culminated in the Nuremberg racial laws of September 1935, which prohibited

1

marriages between Germans and members of the proscribed groups; it also made any sexual contact between them illegal and punishable by death. During the 1930s, the exclusion of Jews involved, in addition to isolation and marginalization, the drive to force them to leave the country, and exclusion of Gypsies—that is, Sinti and Roma—involved their incarceration in so-called Gypsy camps. During the war, the German state practiced a far more radical form of exclusion, the mass murder of all members of the excluded groups, applying the so-called final solution of the Jewish and Gypsy question in every European country occupied by or allied with Germany.[2]

A long tradition of anti-Semitism in Christian Europe had laid the groundwork for the popular acquiescence to the isolation of the Jews. But only the transformation of religious into racial anti-Semitism during the nineteenth century made possible the exclusion of Jews regardless of their commitment to German culture. Their heredity, and not their culture, determined their fate. The same applied to the Gypsies. As a result of the American and French revolutions, previously repressed minorities, including Jews and Gypsies, had been granted citizenship during the nineteenth century, but the equality engendered by emancipation had been challenged by the rise of scientific theories of race that opposed the absorption of the outsiders.[3]

The disabled made up the third target of the Nazi policy of exclusion. Alongside Jews and Gypsies, human beings with physical or mental disabilities—designated as "unfit"—were also to be eliminated from the German national community. They too faced a long tradition of prejudice, which in the nineteenth century had as well been transformed into a racially based theory of their inferiority.

The scientific movement responsible for this harsher view of the disabled was known as eugenics. The term had been coined in 1881 by the British naturalist and mathematician Francis Galton and described by the leading American eugenicist Charles B. Davenport as "the science of the improvement of the human race by better breeding." Eugenicists firmly believed that the increase of foreign and inferior populations prevented human advancement. To deal with so-called inferiors, eugenicists like Davenport called for the study of specific problems posed by "inferior" humans as, for example, "deaf-mutism, criminality, hereditary insanity, feeblemindedness, epilepsy."[4] At first eugenicists attempted to archive their goals through "positive" eugenics, that is, an increase of the birth rate of "superior" populations, but, as this approach did not yield results, the movement turned to "negative" eugenics, that is, sterilization and exclusion of "inferior" populations. The eugenicists in the United States thus argued that members of other races and ethnic groups must be prevented from entering the country; their campaign culminated with the enactment of the 1924 Johnson Immigration Restriction Act. The idea that mentally and physically disabled human beings must be excluded from the gene pool was a staple argument of the international eugenic movement, and this led to widespread sterilization of the disabled in various countries, including the United States.[5]

The eugenic movement in Germany was in the beginning, prior to World War I, relatively moderate. It emphasized "positive" eugenics and did not adopt the anti-Semitism popular on the German right. World War I radicalized the German eugenic movement. Not only did eugenicists begin to advocate "negative" eugenics, particularly sterilization, but many also adopted a racist viewpoint. German eugenicists agreed on "negative" eugenics but divided into a Nordic and anti-Nordic wing on the question of race. The proponents of the Nordic orientation subscribed to the belief in the superior qualities of the Nordic or Germanic peoples; moreover, the Nordic wing, centered in the Munich chapter of the eugenic movement, did not reject racial anti-Semitism and embraced this form of racism completely after the Nazis assumed power.

The Munich chapter was led by Fritz Lenz, who occupied the first chair in eugenics at the University of Munich; Eugen Fischer, director of the Kaiser Wilhelm Institute for Anthropology and professor of anthropology at the University of Berlin; Ernst Rüdin, director of the Kaiser Wilhelm Institute for Psychiatry; Hans F. K. Günther, who occupied the chair in racial anthropology at Jena University and later at Freiburg; and Otmar Freiherr von Verschuer, later director of the Frankfurt Institute for Hereditary Biology and Race Hygiene and thereafter Fischer's successor in Berlin. The opposition to the Nordic faction was centered in the Berlin chapter of the eugenic movement, led by the Social Democrat Alfred Grotjahn, who occupied the chair for social hygiene at the University of Berlin. The first battle involved the name of the movement. The anti-Nordic wing wanted to retain "eugenics," while the Nordic wing opted for "race hygiene." After Adolf Hitler's appointment as chancellor on January 30, 1933, race hygiene became the official designation for German eugenics.[6] The assumption of power by the Nazis assured the victory of the Nordic wing; the anti-Nordic wing disappeared. The new regime provided unlimited opportunities for the practitioners of race hygiene to implement their program. In turn, the race scientists provided the legitimacy the regime needed for its policies. Already in 1931, two years before Hitler's assumption of power, Lenz provided the Nazi leader with the following testimonial: "Hitler is the first politician with truly wide influence who has recognized that the central mission of all politics is race hygiene and who will actively support this mission."[7]

As soon as the Nazis had assumed power, they moved with alacrity to implement their racial and eugenic program. The disabled were among the first victims targeted by exclusionary legislation. On July 14, 1933, just four and a half months after assuming power, Hitler and his cabinet promulgated a sterilization law for persons suffering from a variety of mental and physical disabilities, and in the process defined the groups to be excluded from the national community. This law, issued with the cumbersome name of Law for the Prevention of Offspring with Hereditary Diseases, served as the cornerstone of the regime's eugenic legislation.[8] A sterilization law had already been prepared in Prussia, the largest of the German federal states, during the final years of the Weimar republic, but had never been passed by the legislature. The new German government simply adopted this

Prussian law, but, unlike the Prussian model, the new law included provisions for compulsory sterilization. Taking effect on the first day of 1934, the law eventually led to the sterilization of approximately 375,000 German nationals.[9]

The sterilization law was designed to deal with hereditary diseases and persons carrying such diseases. The opening words of the law proclaimed its content: "Any person suffering from a hereditary disease can be sterilized if medical knowledge indicates that his offspring will suffer from severe hereditary physical or mental damage." The law defined a person "suffering from a hereditary disease," and thus a candidate for sterilization, as anyone afflicted with one of the following disabilities: congenital feeblemindedness, schizophrenia, *folie circulaire* (manic-depressive psychosis), hereditary epilepsy, hereditary St. Vitus' dance (Huntington's chorea), hereditary blindness, hereditary deafness, severe hereditary physical deformity, and severe alcoholism, on a discretionary basis.

Official statistics collected by the Reich Ministry of Interior show that during 1934, the first year the law was in force, 32,268 men and women were sterilized against their will. This figure was still relatively low, because the capability to perform sterilizations was limited; the number increased during the following years. In 1934, persons judged feebleminded made up the largest group sterilized: 17,070, or 52.9 percent. The next largest group, 8,194, or 25.4 percent, consisted of persons diagnosed as schizophrenic, followed by 4,520, or 14 percent, of persons suffering from epilepsy. The group of the blind—201, or 0.6 percent—and that of the deaf—337, or 1 percent—was much smaller.[10] But these categories could all be expanded. The emphasis on the congenital nature of the disability was often disregarded, and intervention was often expanded to include persons whose disability was not severe; thus sterilization was not always confined to persons who were blind or deaf but was also applied to those with a more limited impairment in vision or hearing.

A 1935 amendment to the sterilization law attempted to close the loophole involving pregnancies that began prior to sterilization. The amendment authorized abortions performed to prevent births of children with hereditary disabilities; this would apply not only if the mother was disabled but also if the mother was healthy but the father suffered from a hereditary disability. Thus the law requiring sterilization for the so-called unfit had been expanded into a law also permitting abortion for the excluded group. At the same time, the amendment restated the prohibition under heavy penalties of sterilization and abortion for persons judged healthy. The expanded law was rigorously enforced. For example, in May 1940, the public health office in Feldkirch, Upper Austria, ordered an abortion for a pregnant young woman because "of concern that her offspring might suffer from congenital deafness."[11]

The next logical step in erecting a legal structure designed to exclude those judged biologically deficient was the passage of a law regulating marriages. The Nuremberg racial laws, prohibiting marriages and any sexual contact between Jews and Germans, was enacted in the middle of September 1935. One month later, on October 18, the German government enacted a similar law directed against the disabled: the Law for the Protection of the Hereditary Health of the German Nation. This so-called marriage health law prohibited a marriage if either party suffered from a mental derangement or had a hereditary disease specified in the sterilization law. Before marriage, a couple had to prove that no impediment existed under this law by securing a Marriage Fitness Certificate from the public health office.

An essential prerequisite for the exclusion of minorities was the ability of the state to define and identify members of the groups targeted for persecution.[12] For the disabled, the first step was simple, as the sterilization law listed the disabilities that would define the members of the excluded group. The second step—identification—required greater effort; although it too posed no serious problems, it was never totally successful.

No national register of disabled individuals existed in 1933. Still, the state could use some existing data at the start of the sterilization campaign: lists of persons committed to institutions or attending special schools. But this was not enough, and the authorities had to rely on denunciations. Their number was enormous in the beginning: 388,400 during 1934–1935. Of these, 21 percent were reported by physicians of the public health service, 20 percent by other physicians, and 35 percent by directors of institutions; only 20 percent came from the public. The overwhelming number of denunciations thus came from physicians, nurses, teachers, and social workers. The database on the disabled that was collected as part of the sterilization campaign was augmented by data gathered after passage of the marriage health law. The information thus collected by the public health service grew enormously. The ultimate aim, however, was a comprehensive system of registration to provide eugenic information on all individuals. The state wanted to establish an inventory on race and heredity, which would have enabled the authorities to identify every disabled person and, equally important, their suspect relatives. War and defeat, however, did not permit completion of this task.

The coming of war in 1939 radicalized the exclusionary policies of the Nazi regime. In the winter of 1939–1940, the regime initiated a killing program targeting disabled German nationals, euphemistically labeling this mass murder as "euthanasia," but also designating it "the destruction of life unworthy of life."[13] To implement the decision to kill the disabled, Hitler appointed two plenipotentiaries: Dr. Karl Brandt, his escorting physician, and Philipp Bouhler, who headed the Chancellery of the Führer. The two plenipotentiaries appointed Victor Brack, a senior official of the Chancellery, to organize and direct the killings. Brack created various front organizations designed to hide the involvement of the Chancellery; these were located in Berlin on Tiergarten Street No. 4, and the killing enterprise was therefore known as "Operation T4." But neither the Chancellery, whose participation had to remain secret, nor T4, which masqueraded as a nongovernmental organization, had the power of enforcement. Therefore, the Reich Ministry of Interior, especially its health department, had to serve as enforcer to ensure cooperation. Dr. Herbert Linden, the official in charge of the department dealing with state hospitals, race, and heredity, served as the ministry's liaison to the T4 operation.

Hitler labeled the T4 killings as "euthanasia" or "mercy death," although this term did not apply to these killings; the victims did not suffer from a painful terminal condition and could have continued to live painlessly for many years. The scientific and medical community did not oppose Hitler's radical decision to murder the disabled, in part because the idea had circulated since 1920, the year the legal scholar Karl Binding and the psychiatrist Alfred Hoche published a polemic advocating such a radical step with the title "Authorization for the Destruction of Life Unworthy of Life." They had argued that "if one thinks of a battlefield covered with thousands of dead youth . . . and contrasts this with our institutions for the feebleminded with their solicitude for their living patients—then one would be deeply shocked by the glaring disjunction between the sacrifice of the most valuable possession of humanity on one side and on the other the greatest care of beings who are not only worthless but even manifest negative value." [14]

The killings started with the murder of infants and young children born with mental or physical disabilities. For this purpose, Brack created his first T4 front organization, equipping it with the impressive-sounding name of Reich Committee for the Scientific Registration of Severe Hereditary Ailments. Physicians, midwives, and hospitals reported disabled infants and young children to the public health service, which transmitted the reporting forms to the Reich Committee. Using these forms, physicians working for the Reich Committee selected the children for the killing program. The children were transferred to children's wards for expert care, which T4 had established at selected state hospitals. Parents often voluntarily surrendered their children because they were deceived through promises that new medical procedures would lead to a cure. Against those who refused, the Reich Ministry employed various forms of coercion. In the wards the children were killed through the use of medication, usually overdoses of standard barbiturates, but sometimes also through starvation. The physicians and nurses in the children's wards continued the killings, often accompanied by self-serving experiments, throughout the war.

Children with hearing impairments were included among those killed in the children's wards. After the war, the psychiatrist Hermann Pfannmüller, director of the Eglfing-Haar state hospital in Munich as well as the physician in charge of its children's ward, testified at the Nuremberg medical trial about the disabilities that brought children to his killing ward, including among them those suffering from "congenital blindness, deafness, dumbness." [15] Pfannmüller's postwar successor as director of Eglfing-Haar reported that surviving case histories showed that deaf children were among those killed by his predecessor. He reached the following conclusion about "ten deafmutes from the Ursberg institution" killed at Eglfing-Haar: "Almost all were active, a few were mildly feebleminded, but others—considering their skill at work—possessed normal intelligence." He added that even when they were diagnosed as moderately feebleminded, that diagnosis was not reliable because it was probably due to their hearing and speaking disability. [16]

Even before the murder of the children had been fully implemented, Hitler also ordered the killing of disabled adults, and gave this job as well to Brandt and Bouhler. The larger task to kill disabled adults was both easier and more complex. It was easier because only the institutionalized disabled were to be included. Unlike the far smaller number of infants and young children, the far larger number of adults could not be enticed to commit themselves. Further, any attempt to conduct roundups of the disabled, taking them from their homes by force, would have breached the wall of secrecy surrounding the killings and would have caused popular unrest in the middle of the war. In any event, the number of institutionalized adults judged disabled was sufficiently large to satisfy the killers; the rest could be dealt with after victory.

The system of selecting the disabled victims followed the scheme applied to disabled children. Backed by the authority of the Reich Ministry of Interior, T4 requested that all state hospitals complete a questionnaire for each handicapped patient. T4 approached the public through newly created front organizations, including the Reich Cooperative for State Hospitals and Nursing Homes and the Charitable Foundation for Institutional Care.

Teams of psychiatrists serving as consultants selected the victims on the basis of these questionnaires. The disabled patients were never even seen, much less examined, by the psychiatrists deciding their fate. At first, victims were selected only from state and private mental hospitals, but soon the search for victims was widened to include psychiatric clinics, nursing homes, old age homes, as well as specialized homes as, for example, Zieglers Institution for Deafmutes in Wilhelmsdorf, Württemberg, a residential school.

The task of secretly killing large numbers of human beings and disposing of their bodies posed additional problems. The method used to kill the children—medications in regular hospitals—was deemed too slow to accomplish the job. T4 decided to use gas as the killing method, and created for this purpose the "killing center," an invention that Nazi Germany has bequeathed to the world. T4 established six killing centers—Brandenburg, Grafeneck, Hartheim, Bernburg, Sonnenstein, and Hadamar—equipped with gas chambers and crematoria. There the T4 operatives killed their victims in assembly-line fashion in the gas chamber and burned their bodies in the crematorium. And prior to cremation, they looted the corpses, taking from the corpses gold teeth for the enrichment of the German state and body organs for the research of German scientists. Later they exported their invention to the East, where killing centers like Treblinka and Auschwitz applied the same method to kill Jews and Gypsies.[17]

On August 24, 1941, Hitler ordered an end to the gassing of the disabled. In the preceding twenty months, about eighty thousand disabled human beings had been murdered. A change of heart did not cause Hitler to issue this order. Instead, he was reacting to the growing popular opposition to the killings. The secrecy surrounding the murders had not lasted, and the outrage of relatives of victims had become too public. Catholic and Protestant church leaders, who for more than a year had privately petitioned the government without success, finally spoke out in public. The regime could not afford such public disquiet in the middle of the war.

Hitler's order, which applied only to the killing centers, did not end the murders. The T4 centers were thereafter used to kill concentration camp prisoners, and underemployed T4 operatives were posted to Poland to operate killing centers for Jews and Gypsies. The killing of the disabled continued unabated in Poland and the occupied Soviet Union where public opinion did not matter. Even inside Germany, where the murder of disabled children had not been stopped, the murder of disabled adults soon resumed. But henceforth they were killed in selected state hospitals through starvation, overdoses of medication, or deadly injections. As these killings occurred in regular hospitals and were spread over a longer period of time, public knowledge was limited and popular opposition was muted. The T4 operatives used the term "wild" euthanasia to describe these decentralized killings; the number of victims was just as large as before.

As the war continued, the decentralized killings became even more arbitrary and the killing hospitals came to resemble concentration camps. In the Pomeranian state hospital Meseritz-Obrawalde, one of the leading killing institutions of "wild" euthanasia, the staff not only killed those unable to work, but in addition also patients "who increased the workload of the nurses, were deafmute, sick, or disobedient."[18]

After the war, disabled victims were not recognized as persons persecuted by the Nazi regime. Survivors received no restitution for time spent in the killing hospitals; neither did they receive restitution for compulsory sterilization. Although the sterilization law had been declared invalid by the Allies, the postwar German state did not recognize sterilization under the Nazi era law as racial persecution, and postwar German courts held that compulsory sterilization under the law had followed proper procedures. Disabled persons challenging such rulings lost their cases in court when they could not prove that the finding that led to their sterilization had been medically wrong. The appeal of a sterilized deaf person was thus denied in 1950 after two court appointed physicians certified that the original finding of congenital deafness had been accurate. In 1964, the appeal for restitution from a sterilized person, who during the Nazi period had been a student at the former Israelite Institution for the Deaf in Berlin, was denied. The postwar German court found that while the appellant as a Jew belonged to a group recognized as persecuted under the restitution law, his sterilization as a deaf person did not constitute Nazi persecution.[19] To this day, the German state has not fully recognized and compensated the disabled, including the deaf, for their persecution during the Nazi period.

H. F.
Bethesda, Md., May 1998

1

From Social Darwinism
to National Socialism

THIS BOOK reconsiders deaf education during the era of National Socialism.[1] A leading historian on the education of hearing-impaired children in Germany has written that "German deaf education was set back decades as a consequence of National Socialism and the war," but this is hardly an adequate explanation for the monstrous events of this period.[2] Before reviewing the historical record connecting deaf education to the sterilization of deaf men and women, forced aborting of deaf women's fetuses, and killing of deaf people's children that characterized the Nazi period, I will discuss how the positive, humanitarian achievements of deaf education degenerated into the degrading form it took under Nazism in the 1930s—what must be called the deaf education of National Socialism.

In 1861, a prominent teacher of deaf pupils, Friedrich Hill, noted a growing tendency among German physicians to speculate on hereditary biology. Hill saw this as a threat to deaf people, whose basic human rights could be violated without justification. He suspected that "physicians in general were quite unqualified to provide well-founded assessments" of deaf people. In particular, Hill was concerned about doctors who denounced congenital deafness as a "moral deficiency." He wrote that these doctors were incompetent to judge the significance of the impairment they designated as "heritable." "These moral deficiencies [of deaf people] are simply illusory and exist only in the minds of such persons as do not recognize the nature of the infirmity under discussion and its consequences for the temperament of those so afflicted," Hill wrote.[3]

Hill believed that the medical establishment's political stance was conservative and aligned with the confused, irrational, racist ideas of the French philosopher of history, Joseph Arthur de Gobineau, that were popular among the German nobility and upper middle class in the late nineteenth century. Gobineau wrote in "Essay on the Inequality of the Human Races" that racial variability and inequality determined the course of every social development. He defined revolutions as "social diseases," supported demands for unrestricted one-class rule, and characterized claims for social equality as contrary to both law and nature.[4]

Following the nobility and *haute bourgeoisie,* the German middle class also became increasingly interested in theories that justified the existing power structure and the unequal distribution of property in the face of growing social opposition to such privilege. Charles Darwin's theories, as well as the laws of heredity published by Gregor Mendel in 1865, became handy instruments in these interpretations. Darwin had taught that evolution was possible only through the principle of natural selection, as the result of a struggle for existence that would eliminate weak and helpless individuals. Yet Darwin rejected the idea of the extermination of humans, since the preservation of the weak was a necessary aspect of the human instinct of sympathy.[5]

Within this milieu, in 1895 physician Alfred Plötz first used the concept of "racial hygiene" as he sought to develop an ideal of "Germanness" in human beings. Plötz believed that political and economic measures were insufficient to create a society based on "Germanness," but he thought that medicine offered hope for creating a new society. Plötz gained acceptance from the mainstream medical establishment after founding the Archive for Racial Science and Social Biology in 1904 and the Society for Racial Hygiene in 1905.[6] Interested parties in the growing German steel industry also supported Plötz's argument that the medicalization of social problems, regulated by the government, could produce an ideal society, and large industrial corporations provided substantial financial support for research and public information on racial hygiene. These commitments enhanced the subsequent acceptability and feasibility of the National Socialists' eugenics program.

Plötz was not alone in his thinking on eugenics. As early as 1889, Paul Naecke, the public health officer in Colditz, had recommended the sterilization of "degenerates."[7] The psychiatrist, eugenicist, and later leading National Socialist Ernst Rüdin proposed the sterilization of alcoholics, among others, in 1903.[8]

Economic efficiency was the ultimate goal of German eugenicists, who believed that the "social burden" created by people with disabilities could be decreased through racial hygiene. Thus accounts from Switzerland of the sterilization of long-term female inmates were criticized as hardly sensible in economic terms because the program was voluntary. German eugenicists believed that only legally regulated compulsory sterilization would lead to effective measures, and they looked to the United States for a model.

In the *German Medical Weekly (Deutsche Medizinische Wochenschrift)*, the physician O. Juliusburger described the sterilization program of an American prison doctor, H. Sharp, who sought to cure young men of excessive masturbation through sterilization. The alleged "good results," 456 sterilizations in nine years, led to legislation in the state of Indiana in 1907 that authorized the sterilization of "criminals, idiots, and the feeble-minded" without their consent. By 1911, Indiana had carried out this procedure on 873 men, "mostly criminals," according to Juliusburger.[9]

An essay by the German physician G. Hofmann, "Eugenics in the United States of America," gave this topic greater publicity.[10] Hofmann praised the United States "as a shining example in the matter of sterilization," but passed in silence over the fact that the legislatures of several states had decisively rejected bills that proposed the forced sterilization of persons with hereditary afflictions; only California and North and South Dakota had passed such bills.[11]

In 1911, the German Parliament passed an important law concerning the schooling of blind and deaf children.[12] This law did not mention the central tenet of the racial hygienists that "inferior" people need to be sterilized, but appended to the legislation was a sample questionnaire that devoted considerable space to eugenic matters. Eight of the twenty-nine questions specifically targeted the heritability of deafness. Nazi directors of schools for deaf children later utilized this questionnaire as a model to refer pupils suspected of hereditary disease to the health authorities and hereditary health courts.

German teachers of deaf students were aware of racial hygiene theories and often linked eugenics with their professional responsibilities. One of the most eager advocates and instigators of the Nazi sterilization law of 1933 was Herbert Weinert of Dresden. In an essay that appeared in 1934, he wrote that "educators of the deaf were and still are interested in eugenics problems," and he stated that under the provisions of the Law for the Prevention of Offspring with Hereditary Diseases "much practical work has already been accomplished," that is, "drawing up genealogical charts, which even before [World War I] had been initiated on a tentative and trial basis in Leipzig and probably also at other institutions."[13] As early as March of 1923 the executive committee of the Union of German Teachers of the Deaf demanded in the *Journal for Deaf Education (Blätter für Taubstummenbildung)*, their professional organ, that deafness be seen in the light of the modern science of genetics.[14] In the May 1923 issue, teacher G. Neuert raised the question "Should deaf-mutes marry?" He allowed that "medical science and statistics do not offer sufficient evidence to give a positive yes or no to the question."[15]

In the same year, the district physician of Zwickau, Gustav Boeters—and later other racial hygienists—publicized results of their own investigations that gave a negative answer to Neuert's question. Boeters' draft of a law for the sterilization of "inferiors," which he presented to the government of Saxony in 1923, carried the title "The prevention of unworthy life through operative measures." Boeters promoted the *Lex Zwickau* (Zwickau Law), as it was called, in the editorial section of several newspapers. He also sent a selection of his newspaper pieces to the federal health authorities with the request that they take a stand on the matter.[16]

When the authorities did not respond, Boeters urged prompt attention to the issue and explained that he and his medical colleagues were already sterilizing disabled persons against their will. In a letter of December 3, 1923, he argued that "keeping down the numbers of poorly endowed offspring" promised great success for racial hygiene.

> To my knowledge [Boeters continued], I am the first German medical official who has dared to translate the aims of practical racial hygiene into action in his area of professional responsibility. We in Zwickau have undertaken sterilization operations on mental defectives and others, under the aegis of our highest public authorities . . . since in many cases the consent of parents and others is not to be had at any price, even though the necessity of an operation is clearly evident for anyone not himself a mental defective, I urge the introduction of legislative coercion.[17]

Although the federal health authorities also failed to answer Boeters' second communication, he lobbied the government of Saxony and the federal government ceaselessly.[18] Boeters' pressure on the medical profession and on the state, his growing support among professional colleagues, his many press releases, and the media articles about him made the topic of racial hygiene a matter of great public interest in the 1920s. In order to provide a basis for future decisions, therefore, the federal ministry finally commissioned the Public Health Department to test Boeters' case.

In one of the first public comments about Boeters' proposals, the chairman of the Federal Health Department, Professor Bumm, stated in 1923 that his office did not reject the argument that "a reduction in the useless and unserviceable elements in the people" was in principle desirable. Bumm contended that forcible sterilization for eugenic reasons had certain financial advantages, but such an action would have to stand up to rigorous legal, economic, social, and theological testing. The federal ministry was instructed to defer the introduction of a forced sterilization bill until an empirical review had been completed. Boeters' goal, to bring the draft to legislative deliberation, had been achieved.[19]

Still, the federal Public Health Department was not ready to accept Boeters' basic claim for racial hygiene. A committee of the Prussian Provincial Health Board on December 1, 1923, reached the conclusion that Boeters' proposals were "not suitable, at present," although the committee also said that experience in the United States and Switzerland revealed the "innocuousness of the operation . . . and the absence of negative consequences for the patient."[20]

By February 1925, the federal Public Health Department still showed no willingness to approve Boeters' principles, despite the fact that they had been expanded in the interim and had been praised in numerous commentaries by eugenicists and racial hygienists. Bumm objected that "in more than a few cases heredity was wrongly claimed as cause [for a disability], while the true reason was the unfavorable effects of upbringing and environment."[21]

The reservations of the public health authority could not check further developments, however. The National Socialist movement was becoming stronger, and in it were the most eager proponents of the Lex Zwickau principles. Professor of medicine Fritz Lenz, for example, expressed his concern for the Germans "without space . . . the at least 20 million capable persons," for whom he wished to find room within Germany's borders. Lenz recommended that more space could be found by reducing the population through the "sterilization of all the unfit and inferior."[22] Lenz believed about 30 percent of the population to be bearers of unsound hereditary traits who should have no right to reproduce.

Among German teachers of deaf children, growing support for racial hygiene and thus for sterilization was apparent in the 1920s. Teachers subscribed to the views of authors Bauer, Fischer, and Lenz in *Outline of Human Genetics and Racial Hygiene (Grundriss der menschlichen Erblichkeitslehre und Rassenhygiene)*, which was published in two volumes (Vol. 1, *Human Genetics*; Vol. 2, *Human Selection and Racial Hygiene*). A book reviewer for the *Journal for Deaf Education*, a teacher identified only by the letters *W. J.*, noted in 1926 that Lenz had devoted a chapter to hereditary causes of deafness and gave great currency to the term "hereditary." On the whole, he "especially wished to recommend" the first volume. He also praised the second volume as "quite interesting," for "here the theme and objective of the entire work are revealed to the reader: an earnest and thoroughly justified exhortation to racial hygiene."[23]

Writing in the same journal, teacher A. Abend had asked in 1925, "What does racial hygiene have to say to the teacher of the deaf?" He insisted that all deaf educational efforts were failures, and that "the schooling of the deaf constitutes contra-selection." While he agreed that persons deafened from "accident or illness are genotypically [hereditarily] sound," persons with hereditary deafness should not be allowed to marry. His concluding thesis marked a strong endorsement of racial hygiene programs applied to deaf people. "The severely, genotypically degenerate deaf constitute a burden on the people. The people's need can demand the prevention of their reproduction."[24]

Abend's essay represented a change of course for German deaf education that would last until 1945. His central assertion, that "deafness represents nothing desirable, nothing worth striving for," marks the turning point. Abend reinforced his statement with an admonition to deaf education: "As teachers of the deaf, we too must adopt this [the eugenicist's] position."[25]

In 1929, teacher P. Schumann wrote about the causes of deafness and made clear that he, too, judged eugenics favorably. He granted heredity "a very important role" in deafness, and he noted with regret "that the influence of heredity is often underestimated." On the other hand, he warned against exaggerating the heritability of deafness, "lest there arise a demand for the sterilization of all the constitutionally deaf."[26] In the concluding part of his essay, Schumann returned to his approving assessment that "direct genetic transmission . . . to a certain and not inconsiderable extent is to be assumed as the cause of deafness."[27] Since genetic inheritance was "not, however, the rule," Schumann suggested that "in general, legal intervention would not be useful relative to the elimination of reproduction among the deaf and dumb."[28]

Schumann's conclusions thus were ambiguous. It was not clear whether he rejected laws permitting forced sterilization, or whether he believed all legally deaf people were to be classified as hereditarily diseased according to the law. Schumann gave no opinion of his own about evaluating whether deafness was hereditary in individual cases, but deferred to the racial hygienists, since "the science of genetics . . . has drawn significant conclusions of both theoretical and practical worth from the material available for study."[29]

Herbert Weinert's 1934 pamphlet on "The Sterilization Law" also illustrates the spread of eugenics ideology among teachers of deaf children.[30] Weinert welcomed the Law for the Prevention of Offspring with Hereditary Diseases as "the fulfillment of years of publicly stated proposals and wishes, above all from eugenicists."[31] As proof that "the cadre of teachers of the deaf was and is interested in the problems of eugenics," he supplemented his essay with "an inventory of works on the theme of deafness and eugenics that have appeared in the professional press."[32]

The titles in Weinert's bibliography (here in English translation) also show the extent of the dissemination of eugenic thought and its potential:

Abend, A. "What Does Racial Hygiene Have to Say to the Teacher of the Deaf?" *Journal for Deaf Education* [hereafter, *JDE*] (1925).
Schumann, P. "The Zwickau Law and the Deaf." *JDE* (1926).
Lindner, R. "Marriage Counseling for the Deaf." *Commemorative Volume of the Leipzig Institution for the Deaf* (1928).
Weinert, H. "On the Hereditary Transmission of Deafness." *JDE* (1928).
Handbook on Deafness (1929), 16–20.
Hild, H. "On the Elimination of Deafness in the German State." *JDE* (1929).

Weinert, H. "Hereditary Deafness and Its Suppression." *JDE* (1930).

Schumann, P. "Dangers for the Deaf and Their Education." *JDE* (1932).

Schumann, P. "Biological Considerations in External Affairs." *JDE* (1932).

Richter. "Hereditary Deafness of the Mentally Defective Type." *JDE* (1932).

Weinert, H. "Marriage Counseling and Genealogical Research on Behalf of the Deaf and Hard of Hearing." *Journal for the Welfare of the Deaf* (1933).

Schmähl, O. The Deaf-mute. *Congress Proceedings* (1933).

Gower, E. "Genetic Considerations in the Education of the Deaf." *JDE* (1933).

Hild, H. "Sense and Mission of the School for the Deaf in the New State." *JDE* (1933).

Schumann, P. "The Law for the Prevention of Offspring with Hereditary Diseases and Its Basis." *JDE* (1933).

Such publications by teachers, and their activities in support of race hygiene programs, fed the anxiety of students at deaf institutions. They feared that their instructors would report them under the sterilization law. Schumann wrote, for example, that "German teachers of the deaf . . . were well disposed to eugenic measures because of fresh daily experiences with their distinctive and difficult material."[33] In 1933, a teacher of the deaf urged the inclusion of individual teachers' associations in the larger organization of the National Socialist Teachers Confederation, calling for "a change in the work of welfare, whose mission . . . extends to serious genetics questions. We shall have to take a stand on these issues and, by our incorporation in the National Socialist Teachers Confederation, will do so unequivocally in the sense of National Socialism."[34]

In a 1933 essay on marriage counseling and genealogical research, Weinert proposed the establishment of "marriage counseling centers at individual institutions for the deaf."[35] He also promoted questionnaires on heredity and "a card registry of all the hereditarily diseased" at the deaf schools, for, in his opinion, "the facts of heredity force us to practical counter-measures." He characterized the questionnaires, though, as innocuous, "more like preparatory, facilitating measures. They are an extension of the files established on all families with hereditary hearing impairment."[36]

Weinert also commented on the effectiveness of "practical counter-measures" to deafness in the same essay. "The surest is sterilization," he wrote, raising the question of what the true goal of his "marriage counseling centers" was to be. He proudly announced that eight hereditarily hearing-impaired persons had submitted to sterilization between 1930 and 1932. In all, "through the offices of the marriage counseling center [in Dresden under Professor Fetscher] 65 sterilizations have been effected since 1929."[37]

Weinert pursued his program in consistent fashion. The model of "marriage counseling" that he had conceived in 1933 was followed by the model of a larger "marriage agency." In an essay, he gave an account of a trial marriage agency for hearing-impaired Germans, established along racially hygienic lines, which he set up at the request of the Federal Committee for Public Health Service and the Race Policy Authority in the province of Saxony.[38]

In another essay, Weinert described the success of the race-hygienic care of hearing-impaired people in Saxony.[39] He particularly emphasized the value of the explanatory lectures that had been given by officials of the Race Policy Authority. In support of his "enlightening activity," he was allocated 1,000 marks by the Federal Committee for Public Health Service, for which he presented on February 14, 1935, an account of expenditures totaling 722.63 marks. The expense account noted that with these resources a total of fifty-one lectures had been given under the direction of the senior teacher of the deaf, "Herr Weinert of Dresden."[40]

The primary purpose of the talks and explanations was "to make the idea of sterilization popular among the relevant hereditarily impaired"[41] and to deflect "further criticism of sterilization."[42] Weinert believed that intensive efforts to influence deaf people were urgently required because "some of the sterilizations that have been carried out so far have had an unfavorable effect, in that the subjects have claimed that their health has been negatively affected by them."[43]

The experts Weinert hired to counsel deaf people included officials from the schools for deaf children in Dresden and Leipzig. In addition to Weinert, Dresden provided a teacher named Heidrich, and the school principal, named Conrad. Dr. Becker (with Sandig, the deputy provincial head of the Reich Union of the Deaf of Germany [REGEDE], as interpreter), senior teacher Lindner, and teacher Eymann were from Leipzig.[44] "Almost 3,000" persons attended the lectures. The following topics were addressed:

1. The Law for the Prevention of Offspring with Hereditary Diseases
2. The German People and the Family
3. The German and the Jews
4. The Life and Death of Civilized Nations
5. Practical Experience in the Cultivation of Hereditary Health
6. The Marriage Health Law
7. Hereditary Value—Performance Value
8. All Life Is a Struggle, a Struggle for Existence
9. Race-hygienic Marriage Mediation
10. German Pre-history[45]

Weinert was still not satisfied with these activities, however, and thus he also informed on deaf people he believed were hereditarily afflicted: "In about 300 cases, information and expert opinions were furnished to the health authorities, the hereditary health department of the Ministry of the Interior of Saxony, the hereditary health courts, as well as the race and morals authority of the SS," Weinert wrote. In addition, he provided the hereditary health authority of Saxony with genealogical charts for more than two hundred deaf families.[46]

Weinert's activities challenge the argument of one German historian who has stated that teachers of disabled students, such as those who were blind or mentally impaired, only reluctantly supported the coercive nature of the 1933 sterilization law or complied with it with a bad conscience.[47] This thesis can also be tested against the further examples of the teachers of deaf pupils, Otto Schmähl, Hans Hild, and Schumann.

In 1930, the director of the Educational and Training Institution for the Deaf of Breslau, Dr. Otto Schmähl, had vehemently denied that "the congenitally deaf were to be categorized with the mentally ill, idiots, epileptics, dipsomaniacs."[48] He also rejected the demand that "all the congenitally deaf, who . . . could never be determined with certainty and in whose identification some hereditarily sound would also be included, should be forcibly sterilized."[49] He "could not justify such measures, either ethically or socially." Yet three years later, Schmähl expressed no reservations about "voluntary sterilization in the case of hereditary deafness." He now cited page 8 of Weinert's essay of 1933, which assured him to his satisfaction that "in the case of the deaf, too, such voluntary sterilizations had already been effected."[50]

Schmähl attended the National Socialist Teachers Confederation program at Birkenwerder training camp from January 7 to January 15, 1935, as did several other teachers of deaf pupils. In 1937, Schmähl made public his change of opinion. He now accorded deaf people "the *right to a modest place*" * in the German community, but he reminded hereditarily deaf people of their duty to agree to sterilization "with full understanding to the racial policies and measures of the state."[51]

Fully subscribing to Abend's thesis, Schmähl represented deafness as a physical defect, "which, like all defects, was undesirable in society." Concerned with the degradation of the race by the "hereditarily unfit," Schmähl justified the sterilization law, since

---

*Emphasis in the original.

it sought to "eliminate this diseased strain." In his estimation, hereditarily deaf individuals constituted "about 35 percent of all German deaf."[52]

Schmähl also proposed collaboration between deaf education and Nazi medicine:

> The necessity of cooperation with the district doctors lies not just in the fact that they complete the questionnaires for the subsequent education of deaf children; collaboration is above all also necessary in the interest of implementing the Law for the Prevention of Offspring with Hereditary Diseases.[53]

A pamphlet Schmähl wrote on continuing education courses for the vocational training of deaf adults proves that in the end he unconditionally followed the Nazi racial policy program. In the commentary to the pamphlet, he said that "not the least of the objectives of" vocational training "would be the ideological and racial-political instruction of the deaf."[54] When he, a fellow-director from Liegnitz, and a senior teacher from Breslau were named advisors to the race policy authority, Schmähl enthusiastically shared the news of his professional advancement with the readers of a journal, for the most part teachers of deaf children.

In 1932, Camberg teacher Hans Hild appeared to oppose racial hygiene policies. He published a pamphlet at his own expense on the topic of "Special Education and Youth Welfare in the Context of National Defense."[55] He gave it the subtitle "A defense against unilateral practical politics (*Realpolitik*) and unbounded eugenics proposals." In the pamphlet, released just before the Nazi assumption of power, he rejected "the tendency toward radical racial betterment as it might affect the deaf." Hild called on his colleagues to defend "the respect for the life of another person . . . at a time when political incitement and social confusion are playing with the fate of the German people."[56]

But in August of 1933, Hild also shifted course to the Nazis. The same man who one year earlier had leveled sharp criticism at the contempt for humanity behind the Nazi sterilization law now congratulated the Nazis on their rise to power, on "the great awakening of the German nation," which would also assign new responsibilities to teachers of deaf pupils in the national state.[57]

Chapter 2 of Hild's 1933 essay laid out what the National Socialists might expect of deaf education, stating that "even the schools for the deaf have to train their pupils as Germans." He cited Minister of the Interior Frick's contention that the general task of education was "to form the political person, who in every thought and deed had his roots in the people whom he served, for whom he sacrificed, and who was linked in his heart to the history and destiny of his nation."[58]

Hild explained his sudden ideological about-face in his chapter "Race Cultivation." He accorded it "particular attention in the new state." He wrote that hereditary deafness did not make "our charges inferior," yet he believed that because of deaf people's "biological inferiority . . . a legal distinction . . . of a mere 5 percent of all deaf" would be justifiable. The racial hygienists, once Hild's opponents, had become his "friends of compulsory sterilization."[59]

Schumann also made a public display of his integrity and loyalty toward the Nazi regime. He familiarized his readers with the Law for the Prevention of Offspring with Hereditary Diseases and expressed his confidence that "German teachers of the deaf approve of the law with inner conviction," since their responsibilities would be enhanced under it. Teachers of deaf pupils would profit by the new law: "The compulsory implementation of the law would, and must necessarily, advance our knowledge of deafness."[60] In his own reflections on the advancement of knowledge in this sphere, he developed concepts that a future program of race cultivation would promote—concepts to the disadvantage of deaf people and their education.[61] Among these notions, "genealogy, . . . the administration of genetic questionnaires, and the creation of a card catalog of all the hereditarily deaf in every district and province" were requirements that both supported arguments that deaf people who wished to marry each other should be sterilized and concurred with Weinert's demands.[62] Two quotations illustrate Schumann's opportunism and invite the conclusion that his efforts strengthened the fascist racial fanatics in deaf education.

Early in 1933, Schumann was still engaged in "the right to life of the deaf" and warned of the intention to divest deaf persons of "the right to pass on their life to the future."[63] Seven years later, however, in his account of the "History of the Deaf from the German Perspective," he fully adopted fascist terminology and thereby established himself as a Nazi race ideologue:

> But neither training nor welfare [of deaf persons] should be promoted to the detriment of the people as a whole, in that they might create the possibility of founding families and thus through heredity transmit the affliction, thereby contributing to the degeneration of the race. The educational and extra-educational care for the deaf will be acceptable to the people only in conjunction with eugenic and race-hygienic measures, as stipulated in the Law for the Prevention of Offspring with Hereditary Diseases of July 14, 1933.[64]

The majority of educators of deaf children perhaps greeted the Nazi regime "with the same enthusiasm and hopes as the conservative-nationalist faction generally," as has been said of the teaching staffs of the special schools for mentally impaired children.[65] A 1933 essay entitled "Transformation!" in the *Journal for Education of the Deaf* provided a description of the intellectual milieu that enveloped German teachers of deaf children at the beginning of the Nazi era. The author wrote of the "unfortunate tragedy . . . of deaf-mutes deprived of hearing and speech." This "tragedy," he continued, "forces us to a conviction—generally characterized as conservative in the past"—that is "a correctly oriented party position." The teachers' patriotic line, the author claimed, would prevent "the association [of German Teachers of the Deaf] from ever being yanked towards the left." The author knew of the "hate-filled" and "very strident" protests of the "left-leaning deaf" who, however, generally could change nothing in the hopeless situation of their fellow-sufferers, "for the great majority of teachers of the deaf stood on the right."[66]

2

The Concept of Hereditary Deafness under National Socialism

SCIENTIFIC literature on the incidence of hereditary deafness was inconsistent in the years preceding Nazi rule.
Moreover, Nazi race hygienists distorted what little evidence
there was about the frequency of hereditary deafness (as well as
its applicability to particular individuals) to fit their ideological
goals and preconceived beliefs.

The first German records on the heritability of deafness date
from 1836, when an ear, nose, and throat specialist by the name
of Kramer addressed the question. He noted that "until now, no
case is known where deaf parents produced deaf children."[1] Much
later in the nineteenth century, in volume 1 of the *Journal for Deaf
Education* of November 15, 1888, an anonymous author wrote
that "both physicians and teachers of the deaf . . . have been deeply
engaged in the question of whether deafness is hereditary." The
author concluded that "this question must, in general, be answered in the negative," but he also added that "this file is not yet
closed."[2]

The first German statistics collected on hereditary deafness
are found in a 1902 study by F. Bezold, an ear doctor and professor of otolaryngology at the University of Munich.[3] Among the
196 congenitally deaf persons this specialist examined, "there was
not a single case in which one could posit an assured direct genetic transmission from father or mother or even, skipping a generation, from the grandparents."[4] After citing a colleague who
had found among 6,133 deaf persons investigated only six with either a deaf father or deaf mother (three of whom were from a
single marriage), Bezold came to the conclusion that "transmis-

sion from deaf parents or grandparents to their direct offspring" was rare.[5] Bezold accorded greater importance to "indirect transmission," that is, "deafness in the collateral lines of families." He calculated a figure of "6.1 percent of cases in which one or more of the relatives suffered from deafness or extreme hearing loss."[6] A study published in 1924 presented similar findings: "The genetic transmission of deafness in a direct line from parents or grandparents is very infrequent, and even in the case of deafness in both parents it occurs only exceptionally."[7]

The statistics of the state census of impairments from 1925 estimated "about 45,000 deaf-mutes" in Germany. The genetic factor supposedly accounted for "about one third."[8] In 1935, M. Werner believed that hearing individuals carrying a single, recessive gene for deafness were much more numerous than those deaf persons with two recessive genes. He wrote that the number of "recessive homozygotic carriers of deafness would have to number from 13,000 to 14,000, while the number of heterozygotic carriers who spoke and heard normally, would number 1.5 million."[9] Schumann's 1926 essay "The 'Lex Zwickau' and the Deaf" concluded that "opinions on the percentage of hereditary deafness are widely divergent" and mentioned studies claiming anywhere from 15 percent to two-thirds of all deafness to be hereditary.[10]

By the 1930s, research devoted to racial hygiene was reaching its own conclusions. In 1931, Otmar von Verschuer, director of the Frankfurt Institute for Racial Hygiene, made public "his careful and scientifically conducted investigations into the extent of genetic affliction in the German people."[11] In his view, 15,000 persons suffered from hereditary deafness. Eugen Fischer, director of the Kaiser Wilhelm Institute for Anthropology in Berlin, reached similar conclusions in 1933. He claimed that of the "45,000 deaf people in Germany, 23 to 30 percent" would be hereditarily deaf, "i.e., about 10,000 to 13,000."[12]

After 1935, there was a flood of publications and academic dissertations concerning the heritability of deafness. At this time it was politically correct to produce evidence in support of the notion of a high percentage of "genetic inferiors." The dissertation of K. Wördehoff illustrates the specious arguments that were used. He investigated forty-five cases for "the significance of heredity in the etiology of inner ear hearing loss." In twelve of these cases, he established a "hereditary defect and constitutional inferiority." In his calculation, this amounted to 26.67 percent. This percentage did not suffice for his argument, though, so he added a further "nine cases whose genesis was unclear" to his twelve genetically flawed examples. He assumed that these nine cases were due to a genetic predisposition. From this he drew his conclusion: "It then follows that in 21 cases, i.e., 46.7 percent or almost half of the total patient population at the Würzburg audiology clinic, deafness is revealed to have been occasioned by heredity and predisposition."[13]

Another dissertation also deserves to be mentioned, since it was supported by a leading member of the Reich Union of the Deaf of Germany (REGEDE).[14] In 1939, W. Wilcke presented a "Contribution to the Investigation of Deafness in the Administrative District of Wiesbaden."[15] His primary objective was "to acquire a better basis for research into deafness, especially the hereditary variety," and he concluded that "the figures in the state census [of 1929] on impairments for feeblemindedness in conjunction with deafness are set far too low." In the 66 cases investigated by Wilcke, "the number of instances identifiable as hereditary amounts to only 14." Like Wördehoff, though, Wilcke claimed that "in a further 21 cases classed as unexplained . . . additional instances of hereditary disease cases could be separated out."[16]

Even a dissertation on dental science concerned itself with "investigating hereditary hygiene," although this particular eugenic study by dentist Josef Wesendahl encountered sharp criticism and decisive rejection by educators. In 1937 an anonymous article in the *Journal for Deaf Education* castigated Wesendahl for dealing in an unscientific manner with Fischer's published figures indicating that "the number of hereditary carriers of deafness was to be estimated at 1.55 million."[17] Wesendahl had asserted that 72 percent of all deaf individuals would intermarry, and from this he concluded that "there was an especially high risk that the children would be born deaf." Wesendahl was accused of wanting to create the impression "that 72 percent of 1.55 million persons were going to intermarry and produce deaf children."[18]

Further criticism was directed at Wesendahl's tabular presentation, in which he tried to show that a hereditary defect afflicted 36.98 percent of the 173 students at the Provincial Institution for the Deaf in Soest. It was imputed that he had taken the data for Soest from the list of those suspected of hereditary disease and had counted some instances more than once. This procedure led the reviewer to the following emphatic summary: "As desirable as inquiries into matters of hereditary hygiene may be at the special schools, there is still a great danger in investigations of this nature. The schools for the deaf must decisively reject the study of the dentist Josef Wesendahl of Hamm."[19]

The medical thesis of a former teacher of the deaf provides a final example of doctoral dissertations on the subject of hereditary deafness. In her 1941 study "Audiological Studies of Deaf Twins,"[20] S. Seidenberg presented as the objective of her research an insight into the "value of twin studies as a method of determining the relative shares of heredity and environment in the development of physical and mental life."[21]

She reported that until the time of her publication there were few research results available on deaf twins in the scientific literature, and she made no references to any studies outside of Germany. Her treatment of German research results on deaf twins refers first of all to Albrecht, who purported to give an account of "a pair of identical twin sisters with dominant deafness."[22] She names other German deaf twin researchers, such as Emmerig, Glatzel, Langenbeck, and Schmaehl. For her own work, Seidenberg proposed that "the same traits, in general, appear as hereditary in twins, [thus] hereditary factors will be the most relevant for the study of deafness among them, especially among identical twins."[23] In her calculation of how many deaf twins there were in Germany she accepted without question the race hygienist

Verschuer's figure of "about 40 percent of the hereditary kind."[24] This led her to the assumption that there must have been 165 pairs of hereditarily deaf twins.

Seidenberg made audiological examinations of seven pairs of twins and came to the conclusion that they represented "four recessive and three dominant instances of deafness." In her actual audiological investigations, she noted in audiometric comparisons of hearing curves that

> no characteristic differences could be observed between the curves of single- and double-egg twins, between recessive and dominant, hereditary and possibly adventitious deafness. Without information on the medical history of the families and individual medical histories, it is not possible to give a sure diagnosis as to the cause and nature of deafness in twins, although in the case of uniovularity the evidence points in the direction of heredity.[25]

In her descriptions of individual cases Seidenberg closely followed the eugenic line, as can been seen in her discussion of a pair of male twins from Westphalia. Seidenberg's recreated family history indicated that the twins, born in 1919, were descended from a hereditarily sound family.

Yet she discovered that the father of the twins, because of his work as a stonecutter (eight years of daily work with a drill and stone-dressing machine) had experienced noise-induced hearing difficulties at the age of fifty. Seidenberg used this vocational injury, the hearing loss in advanced age of the grandfather of the twins, and late acquisition of speech by the grandfather's brother, to formulate her diagnosis: "Thus one might consider the deafness of the twins as dominant."[26]

The annual reports of the institutions for the deaf were similarly ready to publicize figures and percentages on the presence of "hereditary defects" among their "charges." In 1937, E. Emmerig published reports on the Provincial Institution for the Deaf in Munich for the years 1927 to 1937. Statistical information concerning the assumed causes of deafness was highlighted. For example, the following breakdown is found:

Of the 120 students enrolled in the academic year 1936–37, 26 or 21.7 percent were born deaf as a consequence of a hereditary flaw. Not demonstrably proven as hereditarily diseased were 34 students or 28.3 percent. Unknown causes accounted for 11 cases or 9.2 percent, illness and the like after birth for 49 cases or 40.8 percent.[27]

Two years later, on the occasion of a lecture on "the results of hearing tests, evaluated from the perspective of hereditary biology,"[28] Emmerig published further data on the causes of deafness in students enrolled from 1932 to 1939. Now there was a substantial difference from the 1937 numbers as concerned students in the "hereditary" classification. Emmerig now claimed that 30.04 percent of his 223 students were deaf because of heredity.[29]

The Institution for the Deaf in Leitmeritz also released a comprehensive report for the year 1936.[30] Among the reasons for deafness, heredity was the most prominent and was claimed in the case of 150 charges at the school. Thirty-three of these cases (22 percent) were classified as hereditarily defective.

The most definitive account was presented by Pfefferle in 1937, with the publication of "Examinations of the Children at the Institution for the Deaf in Heidelberg." Here, the high percentage of cases of deafness attributed to heredity was prominently mentioned. For the first time, the results of extensive research into hereditary flaws in students' families were also presented. Pfefferle examined the etiology of deafness in 118 children from 113 families and found that heredity could be identified as the most probable cause in 40 children (33.9 percent); it was not assured in 23 children (19.5 percent); and the cause of deafness was unexplained in 55 children (46.6 percent). Pfefferle also looked at the families of the children to determine whether the children's deafness was due to hereditary causes (see table 2.1). If one accepts Pfefferle's figures, only 46.02 percent of the 113 families examined can be classified as absolutely hereditarily healthy according to Nazi racial ideology, and thus entitled to produce a further generation.

Data I gathered from Heidelberg and a comparison group of three other institutions suggest that publication of investigative

Table 2.1 Family Health Statistics of 118 Students at the Institution for the Deaf in Heidelberg

Family Health	Number of Families $N=113$	Percentage
Both parents healthy	109	96.4
Both parents deaf	2	1.8
One parent hard of hearing	2	1.8
One grandparent deaf or hard of hearing	6	5.3
Collateral relatives deaf or hard of hearing	13	11.5
Consanguineous marriage (in half the cases no flaw is discernible in earlier generations)	16	14
One or more siblings deaf	22	19.5

Data from Pfefferle35

results like Pfefferle's were exploited by overzealous proponents of sterilization, in the spirit of "better one too many sterilized than one too few."[31] Each of the comparison schools met three criteria: (1) geographical location within the Federal Republic of Germany; (2) student bodies of approximately the same size; and (3) as far as can be determined, no statistics on hereditary biology, similar to those of Heidelberg, were published by the school.

The questionnaires I distributed showed that at least thirty-two, or 27 percent, of Heidelberg's students were sterilized. Comparable data from the other schools show that an average of 11 percent of the student body from 1931–1932 were sterilized (see table 2.2).

The Sterilization Law

With the passage of the Law for the Prevention of Offspring with Hereditary Diseases on July 14, 1933, the Nazi race ideologues signaled the initiation of the program of heredity and race cultivation that was later to be to so monstrous in its scope.[32] The fascist rulers could now finally realize "their racist plans as an integral part of their ideology through legislative and administrative

Table 2.2 Comparison of Sterilization Rates in Four Schools for the Deaf

Location of School	Number of Students 1931–1932	Number Known Sterilized	Percentage of Total Enrollment
Heidelberg	122	32	27
Osnabrück	121	17	14
Straubing	110	12	11
Würzberg	108	7	7

Data from *Statistisches Jahrbuch*[37]

measures," as one historian has written.[33] Equally important, for the Nazis the sterilization law represented "an important connecting link between . . . the objective of maintaining and improving racial purity, and the extermination of life."[34]

The National Socialist Democratic Workers Party plans for genetic and race cultivation evolved over several years. The first legislation in their program was introduced on April 7, 1933: the Law for the Restoration of the Professional Civil Service, under which "non-Aryans" and Democrats were dismissed from government positions, and others were transferred, demoted, or promoted.[35] The sterilization law followed in July of 1933 and was amended and extended on June 26, 1935. Section 10a was added, which authorized forced abortions in women who were otherwise subject to sterilization. On September 15, 1935, the Nuremberg race laws were passed, the so-called Blood Protection and Reich Citizenship Laws, and on October 18, 1935, came the Marriage Health Law.

Section 1 of the Law for the Prevention of Offspring with Hereditary Diseases defined its parameters. First, it stated that "a person who is hereditarily diseased may be sterilized by a surgical operation, when the experience of medical science indicates a strong likelihood that the offspring will suffer from severe hereditary physical or mental defects." The "defects" that could lead to sterilization were (1) congenital feeblemindedness, (2) schizophrenia, (3) *Folie circulaire* (manic-depressive psychosis), (4) hereditary epilepsy, (5) hereditary St. Vitus' dance (Huntington's chorea), (6) hereditary blindness, (7) hereditary deafness, (8) severe hereditary physical deformity, and (9) severe alcoholism.

Application of the Sterilization Law to Deaf People

Historical studies from the postwar period have not dealt substantively with the implementation of the sterilization law and its effects on deaf people. Occasional references exist, and one German historian has suggested that more than fifteen thousand congenitally deaf persons must have fallen victim to the law.[36] As the author of this book and in my capacity as a teacher of deaf pupils and a sign language interpreter, however, I was confronted with the victimization of deaf people under the law's provisions and sought sources to substantiate it.

Isolated references by victims led me to the archives of the deaf schools. There I sought to obtain detailed knowledge of the process by which the "hereditarily diseased" were subjected to prosecution under the sterilization law. This turned out to be difficult, however, for there were still in the 1980s parties in the Federal Republic of Germany that discouraged research into, and discussion of, the persecution and extermination of deaf persons under National Socialist rule. As I mentioned in the preface, the student files that I requested from one school were suddenly destroyed after I asked for them. At other schools I was at first told I could examine archival materials and then later denied access to them with a variety of excuses.

Interviews with the Victims

The lack of written source materials for this subject led me to a biographical approach that would interweave oral history data with other documentation. I considered the possibility of personally questioning persons affected by the sterilization law concerning their experiences.

Preliminary conversations with deaf individuals indicated that gaining the active collaboration of the majority of deaf persons who had been forcibly sterilized would be problematic for two reasons. First, race hygienists' claims that the hereditarily diseased were inferior created a self-perception of worthlessness among congenitally deaf people, leading to a sense of shame and agonizing isolation. Second, legislators during the 1930s, supported by other institutions, agreed to remain silent on the subject of persecution under the sterilization law, and deaf persons and their families were warned not to speak of their sterilizations.

The letter in figure 2.1 illustrates the pressure put on deaf people to keep their sterilizations secret. Cynically invoking God and pseudoreligious tactics to support racial hygiene, it was written and distributed to congregations by the Reich Union of Pastors of the Protestant Deaf. The letter insisted that "no one may speak about sterilization" and urged those who were ordered to be sterilized to "obey the authorities."

In order to gain the cooperation of the deaf victims of sterilization in reevaluating a portion of their own history, I made an appeal in publications that deaf people read, hoping to overcome their natural reluctance to discuss this subject.[38] The response was overwhelmingly positive. The first eighty replies, which were accompanied by numerous documents, formed the basis for a personal documentary archive.[39] This further strengthened my belief that it was both important and possible to introduce the deaf victims of the Nazis to the idea of a biographical account and to request their cooperation in reaching a common objective.[40]

After these preliminary considerations and the steps that were taken to make the research project known to deaf people, I began the process of gathering information.[41] In collaboration with some of those concerned and with the help of a pastor of the deaf, a questionnaire* was developed.[42]

I relied on various organizations and institutions with which I was already in contact through my professional and extraprofessional activities to distribute the questionnaires. I also used announcements in deaf newspapers published by the two main churches in Germany and in the publications of the German

*The questionnaire and Biesold's comments about it appear in Appendix 1. *Pub.*

Ein Wort an die erbkranken evangelischen Taubstummen.

Die Obrigkeit hat befohlen: Wer erbkrank ist, soll in Zukunft keine Kinder mehr bekommen. Denn unser deutsches Vaterland braucht gesunde und tüchtige Menschen.

Viele Menschen haben von Geburt an ein schweres Gebrechen oder Leiden. Die einen haben keine gesunden Hände, Arme oder Füße. Die anderen sind am Geiste so schwach, daß sie die Schule nicht besuchen konnten. Wieder andere sind blind. — Und Du selbst, lieber Freund, leidest an Taubheit. Wie schwer ist das doch! Du bist oft traurig darüber. Du hast wohl oft gefragt: „Warum muß ich taub sein?" Und wie traurig sind wohl auch Deine Eltern gewesen, als sie merkten, daß Du nicht hören konntest!

Es gibt taubstumme Kinder, deren Vater oder Mutter auch taubstumm ist. Es gibt auch Taubstumme, deren Großeltern ebenfalls taubstumm waren. Sie haben das Gebrechen ererbt. Sie sind **erbkrank.**

Zu diesen Menschen sagt die Obrigkeit: **Du darfst Dein Gebrechen nicht noch weiter auf Kinder oder Großkinder vererben; Du** mußt ohne Kinder bleiben.

Wenn Du an ererbter Taubheit leidest, bekommst Du wohl eine Vorladung vor das Erbgesundheitsgericht. Da geht es um die Frage, ob Du auch niemals Kinder haben sollst. — Vor allem eins: Nichtwahr, Du wirst **die Wahrheit sagen,** wenn Du gefragt wirst. Denn **so will es Gott von Dir!** Du wirst die Wahrheit sagen auch dann, wenn das unangenehm ist.

Vielleicht bestimmt das Erbgesundheitsgericht: Du sollst durch eine Operation unfruchtbar gemacht werden. Du wirst traurig. Du denkst: „Das möchte ich nicht. Ich möchte heiraten und Kinder haben. Denn ich habe Kinder lieb." Aber nun überlege einmal: Möchtest Du schuld daran sein, daß die Taubheit noch weiter vererbt wird? Würdest Du nicht sehr traurig werden, wenn Du sehen müßtest, daß Deine Kinder oder Enkelkinder auch wieder taub sind? Müßtest Du Dir dann nicht selber schwere Vorwürfe machen? Nein, das möchtest Du doch wohl nicht. **Die Verantwortung ist zu groß.**

Sieh, da will die Obrigkeit Dir helfen. Sie will Dich bewahren vor Vererbung Deines Gebrechens.

Aber, sagst Du, unangenehm, sehr unangenehm ist das doch. Denn die Menschen klatschen darüber, wenn ich unfruchtbar gemacht bin. Sie verachten mich. — Nein, so mußt Du nicht denken. Die Obrigkeit hat befohlen: **Niemand darf über die Unfruchtbarmachung sprechen.** Du selbst auch nicht. Merke wohl: Du darfst zu keinem Menschen darüber sprechen! Auch deine Angehörigen nicht! Und der Arzt, der Richter, sie alle müssen darüber schweigen!

Gehorche der Obrigkeit! Gehorche ihr auch, wenn es Dir schwer wird! Denke an die Zukunft Deines Volkes und bringe ihr dieses Opfer, das von Dir gefordert wird! Vertraue auf Gott und vergiß nicht das Bibelwort: **„Wir wissen, daß denen, die Gott lieben, alle Dinge zum Besten dienen."**

Reichsverband

der evang. Taubst.-Seelsorger Deutschlands.

Figure 2.1. Letter from the Reich Union of Pastors of the Protestant Deaf to Their Congregants. The translation appears on the opposite page.

A Word to the Hereditarily Diseased
Protestant Deaf

The authorities have ordered that whoever is hereditarily diseased shall have no more children in the future, for our German fatherland needs healthy and sound persons.

Many persons, from birth onwards, have severe disabilities or afflictions. Some have defective hands, arms or feet. Others are so weak mentally that they cannot attend school. Still others are blind. And you, dear friend, you are afflicted with deafness. How burdensome it is! You are often sad because of it. Certainly you must often have asked, "Why do I have to be deaf?" And how unhappy your parents must have been, when they first learned that you could not hear!

There are deaf children whose father or mother is also deaf. There are deaf persons whose grandparents were deaf, too. They have inherited this affliction. They are hereditarily diseased.

To such persons the authorities say: You should not transmit this affliction to your children or grandchildren. You must remain childless.

If you suffer from hereditary deafness, you will receive a summons from the hereditary health court. The court will judge whether you should ever have children. One thing above all others: You must tell the truth when you are asked. God wishes this of you! You must tell the truth even if it is disagreeable.

Perhaps the hereditary health court will decide that you are to be made sterile by an operation. You will be unhappy. You will think: "I don't want to have that done. I want to get married and have children. Because I love children." But think it over for a moment: do you want to be responsible for deafness being inherited even further in the future? Would you not be very unhappy to see that your children or grandchildren were also deaf? Wouldn't you harshly blame yourself for this? No, you would not want to do this. The responsibility is too great.

Now, this is where the authorities want to help you. They want to protect you from transmitting your affliction.

But, you will say that this is unpleasant, very unpleasant. Because people will talk if I am sterilized. They will scorn me. No, you should not think in this way. The authorities have ordered: No one may speak about sterilization. Not even you yourself. Take note: You are to tell no one about this! Not even your relatives. And the doctor and the judge, they too must keep silent.

Obey the authorities. Obey even when it is difficult for you. Think of the future of your people and make the sacrifice that is asked of you. Trust in God and don't forget the words of the Bible: We know that all things turn out for the best for those who love God.

Reich Union
of Pastors of the Protestant Deaf.[37]

Association of the Deaf, as well as in some social services publications for hearing-impaired people and a television program for this same public, to contact deaf victims of the Nazis in the hope that they would be willing to complete the questionnaire.

Conventions of deaf groups at which I gave talks provided another way to reach victims of the sterilization law. I distributed almost five hundred questionnaires during such gatherings and in the ensuing conversations when I made myself available to the public, not least for inquiries concerning compensation. The meetings of the large deaf associations in Berlin, Hamburg, Kassel, Munich, and Bremen were especially well attended. Through them news about the project traveled quickly to other more distant areas, and smaller deaf clubs and deaf individuals were sent questionnaires by mail. In addition, social service agencies for hearing-impaired citizens in all parts of the Federal Republic of Germany participated in the distribution of the questionnaire.

During the Congress of the German Evangelical Church, held June 8–12, 1983, in Hanover, I was invited to speak with those persecuted by the Nazis, and to set up interviews. In this way, almost three hundred more questionnaires were distributed to the persons who had suffered under the law. Additional questionnaires were completed during interviews with victims or during private visits.

IN THE course of the inquiry, 1,215 questionnaires were completed by forcibly sterilized deaf persons. Findings from this research that require extensive description or analysis, or that can be illustrated by case histories, are presented later.* A summary of the data, however, reveals the following.

1. Slightly more than half (54 percent) of the surviving victims of forced sterilization are female.
2. Nearly all deaf sterilization victims (95 percent) were born between 1901 and 1926.

*The tabulation of raw data appears in Appendix 2. *Pub.*

3. The youngest deaf person sterilized was nine years old when the operation was performed; the oldest was fifty. The most common age (over 35 percent of the total) for sterilization was between twenty-two and thirty.

4. The victims named 104 institutions for deaf students as their home school. The largest number of sterilized deaf people attended the school at Soest (60) and City of Berlin school (54).

5. Sixty percent of the deaf persons who were sterilized stated their occupations as dressmakers, tailors, artisans, or unskilled workers.

6. Sterilization victims were turned in, or reported on, by a variety of groups and individuals. Most often this was the local health authority (46 percent), but the Nazi party (30 percent) and their school (22 percent) were also named frequently.

7. Sterilizations took place throughout Germany but particularly in cities that contained schools for deaf children. The largest number of respondents (104) listed Berlin as the site of their sterilizations, but twenty-nine other cities were named by ten or more respondents. Seventeen of these contained schools for the deaf.

8. Sterilizations occurred every year from 1933 through 1945, but a majority (54 percent) occurred during a three-year span from 1935 through 1937.

3

Teacher-Collaborators

THE TESTIMONY I gathered suggests that educators in Germany's special schools actively supported racial hygiene measures against deaf people; they did not share the "rescue mentality" claimed by historians for special education teachers.[1] It is worthwhile to begin this discussion by reviewing the influence of the director of the German training institute for teachers of the deaf and the directors of regional institutions for the deaf on teachers' beliefs and actions.

The Training Institute for Teachers of the Deaf in Berlin-Neukölln

The State Institution for the Deaf at Berlin-Neukölln is the oldest institution for deaf pupils in Prussia.[2] It was founded in 1788 by the son-in-law of Samuel Heinicke, the founder of German deaf education.[3] In 1811 it also became the training institute for Prussian teachers.[4] Over time, other provinces began to send their teacher trainees to Berlin-Neukölln. The school's principal also served as director of the teacher training program.

Gotthold Lehmann assumed this dual position in 1924. Six years later he reported that the training program had twenty-eight candidates and that "the admissions register, which was begun in 1874," had reached candidate number 487.[5] Lehmann was responsible for making proposals for future university courses to the Prussian State Ministry for Science, Art, and Public Education, and for supervising payments to the institute's faculty.[6] The financial accounts for fiscal year 1930 and for second-year students during the winter term of 1931–1932 provide information about "special lectures" on professional themes. For example, a Professor Flatau lectured on the physiology of voice and speech.[7]

Early during the period of the Nazi Party's expansion of power and the initiation of its race policies, Lehmann proposed eugenics-related topics for participants in the first-year program, such as "Introduction to the Theory of Heredity" and "Exercises in the Science of Heredity." Course topics proposed for the years 1932–1938 "for the scientific instruction of participants in the program for the training of teachers of the deaf" illustrate Lehmann's

State Institution for the Deaf in Berlin-Neukölln

indoctrination of a generation of teachers with National Socialist racial ideas. Among the courses listed were the following:

- Eugenics
- The science of human heredity and German race cultivation
- Contemporary problems in the maintenance of public welfare (heredity, eugenics, sterilization, conservation)
- The theory of heredity and race hygiene
- Hereditary diseases
- General studies of deafness, the collaboration of the schools for the deaf in the implementation of the Law for the Prevention of Offspring with Hereditary Diseases
- Environment and hereditary predisposition
- Views on race hygiene
- The theory of human heredity as the basis for race hygiene[8]

Evidently, Lehmann's proposals were accepted by the Prussian State Ministry for Science, Art, and Public Education, although the training programs were canceled by the Ministry for 1933–1935 and 1938–1940.[9]

Reich Professional Group of Teachers of the Deaf and Hard of Hearing (with Reich Professional Group Leader and Party Member Maesse). Reprinted by permission from *Die Deutsche Sonderschule*, 1935, p. 159.

The alignment of the teacher training institute's curriculum with National Socialist goals was intentional. Lehmann was a member of the National Socialist Teachers' Confederation even before the Nazis' coordination and integration of the Union of German Teachers of the Deaf, and, according to a colleague from Berlin, he shared the National Socialist point of view.[10] Furthermore, Lehmann encouraged the implementation of the sterilization law among the students of his institution. There are reliable accounts from those affected that he took the initiative in informing authorities about them and that he sought to influence parents.[11]

The latter charge is substantiated by the case of a deaf woman, born in 1921 and ordered to be sterilized when she was fifteen. Lehmann's letter to the girl's mother is reproduced in figure 3.1.

The Director

State Institution for the Deaf   Berlin-Neukölln   April 14, 1936
and   Mariendorfer Weg 47/60
Training Institute
for Teachers of the Deaf

Log No. 544

To Frau NN

The health authority of Berlin-Neukölln has informed me by a letter of April 6, 1936, that a judgment concerning the sterilization of your daughter has been delivered in accordance with the law and that NN is to be conducted within two weeks to the Neukölln Municipal Hospital for the performance of the operation. I would ask you to sign the enclosed declaration and to return it to me. We will then convey NN to the hospital.

I would point out that thus far fourteen sterilizations have been completed on our children and that in no case have negative effects occurred.

Heil Hitler!

[signature][13]

Figure 3.1. Letter from Gotthold Lehmann Requesting a Parent's Authorization on a Sterilization Order

The Director

State Institution for the Deaf   Berlin-Neukölln   August 25, 1936
               and   Mariendorfer Weg 47/60
         Training Institute
      for Teachers of the Deaf

         Log No. 930

                    Dear Frau NN,

NN was released from the clinic in good health on August 16. The operation proceeded normally. NN has already written you about this.

The law stipulates that in the case of persons above fourteen years of age, the operation may be performed without the consent of parents and guardians. You could not then have changed anything in this regard. I believe that it will be quite a good thing for NN that she has no children. Her life will likely be hard enough as it is.

                  With best regards, Heil Hitler![14]

Figure 3.2. Letter from Gotthold Lehmann Informing a Mother of Her Daughter's Sterilization

Her mother protested the sterilization order in a letter to Lehmann on April 15, 1936. At the close of her letter, she wrote: "I cannot sign this [the consent form]."[12] In the end, however, the deaf girl was sterilized anyway. Lehmann's letter (see fig. 3.2) reminded the mother that parental consent was not necessary.

One of Lehmann's former students has described how force was used when pupils resisted sterilization. Just turned fourteen, he was to be sterilized at the Rudolf Virchow Hospital in Berlin in November of 1938 on the recommendation of his teacher, Schürmann. On his third attempt to escape from the school, he was apprehended by the police, put in handcuffs, beaten, and delivered to the hospital.[15]

The example of senior teacher Schürmann illustrates Lehmann's personnel policy. Schürmann had been a teacher at the Provincial Institution for the Deaf in Soest since 1929. He had

particularly distinguished himself during the Nationalist Socialist training camp for officials of the Nazi teachers' confederation
in Birkenwerder/Havel by giving a report on "hereditary biology
in the schools for the deaf."[16] Two years later, in a letter to the
Reich and Prussian Minister of Science, Art, and Public Education,
Lehmann nominated Schürmann for a university-level teaching
position.[17]

Schürmann was to assume responsibility for the areas of general deaf studies and race cultivation. In his recommendation,
Lehmann presented Schürmann as especially qualified for these
duties, since "he has for some time been active as a consultant in
the Reich Union of the Deaf of Germany." Lehmann particularly
emphasized that Schürmann had been a member of the Nazi party
since August 1, 1932. As a result, Schürmann was appointed
professor of race cultivation, with the written authorization of
the Reich and Prussian Minister for Science, Art, and Public
Education.[18]

Lehmann selected candidates for teacher training according to
political criteria. In one case, he rejected an applicant because the

Participants at the National Socialist Teachers Confederation Training Camp II at
Birkenwerder in 1935

individual had been a member of the Social Democratic Party of Germany before the "seizure of power."[19] Another applicant, on the other hand, was particularly recommended by Lehmann, since he was "an old fighter, a member of the Nazi Party since 1932."[20]

Higher authorities noticed the director's support for Nazi objectives. After an unannounced inspection of his school's training program, the inspector appointed by the Reich and Prussian Minister for Science, Art, and Public Education, Dr. Schaefer, stated in the summary of his investigative report that Lehmann worked "with the greatest skill and exemplary conscientiousness" and that he had "tangibly stamped the overall image of the Institution with his educator's zeal."[21]

Director Wegge—The Provincial Institution for the Deaf in Soest

The crimes of Wegge, director of the Provincial Institution for the Deaf in Soest, who according to accounts of former students carried out his educational duties in an SS uniform, have until today remained concealed by institutional interests. The student register of the Soest school, however, offers a close look at Wegge's attention to selecting students for sterilization.

The headings of the register, created by Wegge himself in the absence of any printed form, reveal the thrust of his activities. His handwritten entries state that the students were "examined for hereditary health." Those whom Wegge determined should be sterilized had next to their names the code *A*, meaning "referral [*Anzeige*] to the Health Authority."[22]

The register begins with entering student number 1210, admitted to the Soest institution on April 15, 1925, and discharged on March 30, 1933, and concludes with student number 1779, admitted May 2, 1944, and discharged June 2, 1944. There are check marks in either blue ink or pencil next to the names of 338 of the 569 students Wegge recorded in the register. The blue ink definitely indicated that a student had been examined for "hereditary health," and the pencil may have had the same meaning. Wegge may be assumed, therefore, to have examined about 60 percent of his students for hereditary health reasons. However, this figure masks the diligence with which Wegge sought to "construct" the desired numbers of "hereditarily diseased deaf students."

The register indicates that Wegge referred 85 students to the health authority who had been admitted to the school from 1926 through 1934 (student numbers 1235 to 1471). This represents 36 percent of the 236 students covered by these register years, including 28 students transferred to Soest on January 8, 1934, from the Provincial Institution for the Deaf in Petershagen. Particularly heinous is the fact that Wegge informed against children aged eight to ten years old.

The register is not clear for the years after 1934, but it may be that Wegge reported on nearly every student. For students with entrance numbers between 1472 and 1779, under the column headed "Remarks," there is a handwritten addition, "A–Z: Reported to the health authority." With six exceptions, this reference is found for each child in this group. Occasionally, there is the name of a place and a date. The code letter *A* is missing. One can only speculate whether Wegge did, in fact, refer for sterilization 98 percent of all entrants to the school between 1935 and 1944.

Wegge attempted to cover the tracks of the policies that he initiated, as figure 3.3 shows. He recommended to the municipal health authority in Dortmund that the sterilization operations be carried out during the summer holidays to prevent student unrest and to avoid circulation of details of the sterilization among the deaf clubs. The second letter in figure 3.3 indicates that the health authorities agreed with his request.

Documents from the Soest institution demonstrate that many of this school's pupils were forcibly sterilized, and that Wegge not only personally made the notification to authorities, but also arranged the transport of his students to the clinics where the operations were performed (see fig. 3.4). In one such case, Wegge reported to authorities on a ten-year-old student; the school apparently arranged to transport her to the municipal hospital in Hamm, and her parents were informed only after the operation had been performed (see fig. 3.5).

The Director
of the Provincial Institution for the Deaf
Soest, April 26, 1935

Your letter of April 12, 1935 File 32/K-II

To the State Public Health Authority:

For the sterilization of NN, the Municipal Hospital in Hamm will be used. I would ask you, if possible, to arrange that the operation be performed there during the summer holidays, which last from July 25 to September 2. By carrying out the operation in her hometown during the holidays, the sterilization can be kept from the other students more readily than if the girl were sent from here to Hamm.

Wegge

State Health Authority of the Minden District

The Public Health Officer   Minden, Westphalia, May 29, 1935

To Fräulein NN of XX
c/o the Director of the Provincial Institution for the Deaf Soest

In accordance with the application of the director of the Provincial Institution for the Deaf in Soest of May 28, 1935, the procedures for your sterilization operation pursuant to article 7 of the third decree of the Law for the Prevention of Offspring with Hereditary Diseases of February 25, 1935 (*Reich Law Gazette,* I, p. 289) will be postponed until the beginning of the summer holidays (July 24, 1935).

In accordance with this letter and with the order to undergo the operation that was sent to you by the public health officer on May 25, 1935, you will present yourself at the Municipal Hospital (Dr. Kopischke) or at the private clinic of Dr. Strempel in Bad-Oeynhausen, promptly after July 24 so that the entire process can be completed in timely fashion by the end of the holidays (September 3).

Public Health Officer

Figure 3.3. Correspondence from Director Wegge and a Public Health Officer Regarding a Student's Sterilization

The Director of the Provincial Institution for the Deaf

Soest, October 12, 1936

Herr NN

XX, Westphalia

On the orders of the Public Health Authority of the city of Gladbeck, your daughter Traudchen was conducted to the municipal hospital in Hamm in order that the decision of the Hereditary Health Court of Essen might be carried out.

Wegge

Figure 3.4. Letter Describing Transport to a Clinic for Sterilization

The Director of the Provincial Institution for the Deaf

Soest, February 8, 1936

Your letter of January 19, 1936

To Herr NN

Your daughter Anneliese was conducted to the municipal hospital in Hamm on the 6th of this month to have the operation performed. I inquired about her condition by telephone today and received the following information from the nurse in charge: the operation was performed yesterday; Anneliese is doing well. She is already quite friendly with the nurse and could make herself well understood.

Wegge

Figure 3.5. Sterilization Operations Often Took Place Without Parents' Knowledge

Provincial Institution for the Deaf, Soest, Westphalia

February 19, 1935

To Frau NN

Your letter of February 15, 1935

Dear Frau NN,

Since I was on leave, I am only today able to respond to your letter. The Hereditary Health Court will point out that in your husband's family there is a consanguineous marriage. His great-grandparents were first cousins. Such a consanguineous marriage, even so far in the past, justifies the suspicion of hereditary disease. Proof that NN incurred deafness as a consequence of an illness in her early youth would then be difficult for you to advance, since you previously indicated that the deafness was innate. Your husband may withdraw his application. The process will, however, proceed. In the event that the Hereditary Health Court decides in favor of sterilization, you may file an appeal. The matter will then be dealt with by the Superior Hereditary Health Court. If it confirms the decision for sterilization, this will be carried out, with force if required. In the case of children, recourse to such coercion will not be made until they are 14 years of age.

The sterilization of girls is not performed in Soest but in a hospital in Hamm. As far as I have heard, the subjects all recover quite promptly.

If you cannot prove that NN became deaf as a result of illness, your appeal will scarcely have a chance of success. If hereditary disease is indeed present, it would be appropriate that NN not have children. There are no other negative effects from the procedure.

Figure 3.6. Wegge Used Intimidation and Coercion to Fulfill the Sterilization Laws

One more document from Soest further illustrates Wegge's attitude and tactics. In an attempt to intimidate parents who had protested an order to sterilize their daughter, he used the specious argument that consanguinity in the child's paternal great-great-grandparents "justifies the suspicion of hereditary disease." He warned that the parents' appeal of the sterilization order would not be successful, that the operation would be performed "with force if required," and that, in any case, "if hereditary disease is indeed present, it would be appropriate that [their daughter] not have children" (see fig. 3.6).

Provincial Institution for the Deaf in Königsberg, Prussia

SS Director Bewer—The Provincial Institution for the Deaf in Königsberg

Four former students of the Institution for the Deaf in Königsberg, Prussia, indicated on their questionnaires that SS Director and Senior Teacher Bewer reported them to the authorities, and there is other evidence indicating Bewer's complicity in Nazi crimes.

Alexander Hundertmark, who was chairman of the Deaf Refugees until his death in 1980, gave a deposition in 1957. His statement naming Bewer was written on behalf of a former fellow student who applied for remuneration under the Federal Compensation Law. She had been forcibly sterilized, Hundertmark said, "through the offices of Senior Teacher of the Deaf, Bewer," who was "known to have been a fanatic Nazi."[23]

I also questioned a former student at the Institution in Königsberg concerning Bewer's activities. Frau T. was not sterilized, as she argued successfully that she had lost her hearing due to a childhood accident. Frau T. said that Bewer wore his SS uniform in the course of his school duties. He remained faithful to the Nazi regime up to the last day of the war. In 1945, when the Soviets were already outside Königsberg, Bewer ordered all forty-eight students in the vocational school at the institution to remain at the facility. This order resulted in the loss of thirty-six girls' lives.

Director Edwin Singer—The Institution
for the Deaf in Heidelberg

Similar practices also reportedly occurred at the Institution for
the Deaf in Heidelberg, which distinguished itself by following
the party line and publicizing "hereditary biology" data on its students. The director of the Heidelberg school, Edwin Singer, col-
laborated closely with the head of the university ear, nose, and
throat clinic, Professor. K Beck, and with the resident physician
at the Institution, Dr. W. Hoffmann.[24]

Former Heidelberg students answered the question "Who informed on you?" with "the institution" or "the teacher."[25] To the
question, "Did the police come and take you to the hospital?"
one person answered, "Director Singer, removed by force!" This
individual was fifteen at the time of his sterilization in 1936. He
described it this way:

> While the other students from the Residential School for the Deaf
> in Heidelberg went on holidays, I and a few other deaf students were
> taken away on the orders of the principal for compulsory sterilization.
> I wanted to run away, but I knew that I didn't have a chance. They
> threatened to have me brought back by the police. Just before the op-
> eration I cried a great deal because I felt so powerless.

Two other informants specifically named Singer as the person
who reported them to the authorities. One of these men applied
for compensation in 1951 and sought the assistance of the Baden
Association of the Deaf in Heidelberg. The chairman of the association was the same Edwin Singer, their informer. He wrote back
to the sterilized deaf man: "We can confirm from our own knowledge of the exact circumstances that in 1936 (March 19) you were
a victim of the Law for the Prevention of Offspring with Hereditary Diseases. The sterilization operation was performed at that
time in the surgical clinic in Heidelberg."[26]

For Singer, as for many other Nazi followers, there was no reason after the collapse of the Third Reich to reflect on and analyze
the failures of German deaf education during the previous twelve
years of fascist rule. In 1946, Singer turned to the new agenda, just

The St. Joseph Institution for the Deaf in Swäbisch Gmünd

The Institution for the Deaf in Heidelberg, Viewed from the East

as if it were a question of clearing away rubble. He expressed no concern for the disenfranchised, those former deaf students who had been robbed of their basic human rights, degraded, and exterminated.[27] In a 1946 article he wrote that it was "not seemly for us to dwell on the ruins." Rather, teachers of deaf children should "teach them to speak, and warm their hearts so that they too become human beings."[28]

Singer's inability to value deaf people and their lives, and the irony of his role as superintendent of a school for deaf children and then the head of an association for deaf people's welfare, merits one more comment. A man born in 1919 and sterilized in 1935 exchanged letters with Singer, his former principal, in 1960 and 1961. This deaf pressman told Singer of his suffering and of his deep sense of violation. He was angry that Singer had never told him that he was to be made infertile, and he asked why he had to be sterilized. "You did not really understand what a human being is," the deaf man wrote to his former teacher (see fig. 3.7). Singer, then eighty-one years old, replied with a haughty letter, saying, "The fact that you have no children should not be seen as a misfortune. Better to have no children than one who is blind or deaf or epileptic" (see fig. 3.8).

Dear Director Edwin Singer, I must first ask you to pardon me for writing to you so openly and for requesting your response. The time is long since past when on September 16, 1926, I was admitted to the school at the Institution for the Deaf in Heidelberg. At the school I was taught by Herr Kaspar Derr, and was promoted and discharged on April 10, 1936. I was afterwards astounded by your earlier letter, which my mother had kept. My class teacher, Herr Derr, and my mother knew about it. What did my mother and the Lord God do to me, a poor child, that they didn't let me know about this when I left my home town for the last time on March 8, 1935, in the direction of the institution for the deaf in Heidelberg? On March 31, 1935, I was confirmed in the Castle Church in XX. It was a beautiful confirmation ceremony. It was wonderful to

---

Figure 3.7. Letter from a Sterilization Victim to Edwin Singer, August 15, 1960

celebrate God's holy victory. At once, my father received a registered letter from the District Court in XX (Nazi Party). When I came to the city hospital on Wednesday, April 10, 1935, I did not know what I was doing there. Then I lay in bed for only two days, until Friday, when the National Socialist doctor, Herr Karl Gamstäder, said that I would be operated on at 10 A.M. that same day. This assistant doctor sterilized my abdomen in the cruelest fashion and made me infertile. On April 20, 1935, I was released from the city hospital. On the way home I was faint with weakness. I felt so tormented and cruelly treated because I hadn't been told anything. Why did you keep silent and not tell me that sterilization would mean killing my body and that it is a wrong and a crime that I cannot have any children? You also abused my brother NN and Frau NN and NN. You didn't warn us. We are not content with you professionally because of your offenses and disregard. Sterilization makes a body worthless. I no longer feel like a real person. It was not right and it was a tragedy. A very great and serious crime has been committed. God sees everything with a stern eye. He said, "Thou shalt not kill." Since that time I have suffered great misery. I am innocent. I can't have any children. Why did I have to be sterilized? For a long time I have been very dissatisfied with your actions, because I am unhappy that in 1933 [the formation of the Reich] you were already the Führer of the Hitler Party in the Heidelberg deaf school. You would rather kill my belly and have me sterilized and keep silent, than let me know openly that I could not have a child. Fortunately God can save me. He punishes the grave sins that were done to me with the killing and sterilization. . . . A great deal has been lost from my life, because there can never be any happy love. I can no longer trust you or accept the idea of how unjustly you treated people. For you, the word human is no longer applicable, because you gave me no help. You are guilty of a crime toward me. You abused me. You had me sterilized, killed, and destroyed me so that I can't have a child. You did not really understand what a human being is. I know from my own experience what Hitler was up to. He was a cheater, a liar and a serious criminal. I was not born defective and I am not feebleminded. It was all deceit and lies and tricks of the Hitler party. Hitler was clearly feebleminded himself. Otherwise he wouldn't have behaved like such a monkey, wouldn't have had such a big mouth and been so dishonorable. He was godless. . . .

Figure 3.7—*Continued*

Edwin Singer, Director (ret.), Heidelberg, August 18, 1961

Herr NN,

Dear NN, To deaf adults I usually speak formally, but in this letter I will be more informal, as in the past, so that you understand me better. You wrote me that you were sterilized 26 years ago. I did not know that. But I am hardly surprised. At that time, all the hereditarily diseased were to be made infertile. You ask: Who is guilty? Who is responsible that you were sterilized? Many hundreds of thousands of people can ask the same question, all of whom were sterilized. My answer is: the government of the day. It was the National Socialist German Reich. At the head of the ruling party stood Hitler, Himmler, Göbbels, Frick, and others. They are all dead now. Do you want to carry your complaint down into Hell? Then they will answer in turn: Parliament, the duly elected representatives for the people, passed the Law for the Prevention of Offspring with Hereditary Diseases. The doctors had to obey and carry out the law. Dear NN, such complaints are useless. You are not badly off, but you are not content. But compare yourself to others. Several million fell in the war or were killed. You are still alive. You can work and earn a satisfactory living. The fact that you have no children should not be seen as a misfortune. Better to have no children than one who is blind or deaf or epileptic. Even as a youngster you were often unhappy. But when I talked to you and you thought things over, you were happy again. That's the way it should be now too. So, NN, keep your chin up. And good luck!

With best regards,

Edwin Singer

Figure 3.8. Edwin Singer's Reply to His Former Student

Oskar Rönigk—Homberg Institution

The Electorate of Hesse founded the Homberg Institution on May 1, 1838, as a training college for teachers of deaf students. Hermann Schafft served as its first principal, and he sought to implement Moritz Hill's reforms for German deaf education at the school.[29] In 1933, a staff of sixteen taught eighty-eight deaf students.[30] Nazi Party member Oskar Rönigk was the principal;

Table 3.1. Students Reported to the Health Authority by Oskar Rönigk

Research Corpus	Year of Discharge	Number of Files	Reports under the Sterilization Law	Percentage of Students Reported
Student records	1933–1934	70	29	41.43
Student records	1920–1932	34	21	61.76
Total research corpus		104	50	48.08

former students report that he ran a very strict school and also informed on students to the health authorities under the sterilization law.[31]

An examination of the remaining records of this school allowed me to document Rönigk's actions. They revealed that the director not only reported his current students to the health authorities for sterilization, but also reported former pupils. From 1920 through 1932, thirty-four students were discharged from the Homberg school. Rönigk reported twenty-one of these, 62 percent, to the authorities. Twenty-nine of the seventy students discharged during 1933 and 1934 were reported by the director of their school (see table 3.1).

My research at the Homberg school had three goals:*

1. To verify the accuracy of the information received earlier through the questionnaire and interviews
2. To determine whether students were reported on after being discharged from the school
3. To evaluate the effects of Rönigk's racial hygiene views on individual students

The student registers available to me contained information on 593 Homberg students, 104 for the period 1920–1934. Red and

---

*Research work in the school archives of the Provincial Institution for the Deaf of Homberg was substantially supported and facilitated by the school administration and teaching staff.

blue marks were below or next to some students' names in the register. The same marks also appeared in various student files. The student records marked with red and blue proved to be those of students whom Rönigk had referred to the health authorities for sterilization. For such reporting, Rönigk employed a form letter that he had developed.

Rönigk's decisions about children to report were determined by entries in the school register under the headings "Physical Condition" and "Cause of Deafness." The notation "hereditary deafness" always led to a referral. But it is also possible to identify fifty-three students whom Rönigk also reported on for whom illness had occasioned their deafness or where the cause was entered as "not determined." Only by proceeding in this way could Rönigk achieve such a high number of "hereditarily diseased" students.

Rönigk also worked in the spirit of his fellow party member, Maesse, the leader of the Reich professional group, who tried to

Provincial Institution for the Deaf at Homberg, Main Entrance

> Director of the Provincial Institution for the Deaf,
> Homberg, December 20, 1934
>
> The respected parents of our deaf and hearing-impaired students are *urgently* requested to complete the enclosed genealogical charts conscientiously and to return them to the Institution by Easter 1935 at the very latest.
>
> Heil Hitler!
> signed Rönigk

Figure 3.9. Oskar Rönigk's Letter Requesting Genealogical Charts from His Students' Families

use genealogical charts of his pupils' families to conduct research on "hereditary diseases and on the conditions of genetic transmission in families."[32] For this purpose, Rönigk wrote to the parents of students, as seen in the letter transcribed in figure 3.9.

The headings on the inner pages of Rönigk's genealogical charts show the relevance of the questions to racial hygiene. For example, they deal with hearing impairment, consanguinity, and other perceived ailments.

Rönigk believed that it was necessary for school principals and doctors to collaborate in the implementation of the sterilization law, and that one or the other should make the report to the public health officer.[33] An example demonstrates this practice, and it provides more evidence of a school administrator's enthusiasm for sterilization of deaf people, as he released student files that had not even been requested.

On July 21, 1935, the chairman of the district council of Korbach inquired into the behavior, during her school years, of a deaf girl who had been discharged from the institution. His letter of inquiry stated that the girl "has already begun to fool around," and he asked, "Were any steps taken at that time in the way of sterilization? Since it is unquestionably a case of hereditary deafness, making an application is an urgent matter."[34]

Rönigk's reply on July 29, 1935, indicates collaboration between the school and Nazi medicine. He wrote that "notification [for sterilization] is made in cases of this kind in the course of the student's last year at the institution," but this girl had not been scheduled for discharge until the following year. Rönigk nevertheless was more than willing to comply. "I enclose NN's student file with the request that you take cognizance of it and return it," he wrote.[35]

Director Heidbrede at the Schleswig Institution for the Deaf

Georg Pfingsten founded the Schleswig Provincial Institution for the Deaf in 1787. By 1931, the school had 14 staff members and 121 deaf pupils.[36] After the Nazi takeover, a Nazi Party member and teacher of the deaf named Heidbrede was appointed director. He immediately made efforts, in part based on his experiences at the Nazi Training Camp I, to enlist the support of parents and teachers for Nazi racial hygiene policies.[37] To that end, he developed the following letter to send to parents:

Schleswig, ... 1934

The agencies responsible for the implementation of the Law for the Prevention of Offspring with Hereditary Diseases of July 14, 1933, (*Reich Law Gazette* 1, 1933, No. 86) may expect accurate information from us concerning the deaf children who fall under the provisions of the law. In accordance with section 1, paragraph 2, of the law, these are persons suffering from *hereditary* deafness.

Our personal and medical questionnaires give us only scanty information on the *cause* of deafness, since they aim only to determine the educability of the child, and in this regard the distinction between inherited and adventitious deafness is of little consequence.

We would then request you to help us complete the missing information on the enclosed questionnaires with answers as detailed as possible. The information is unconditionally required for the complete and successful implementation of the law.

We know that we have set you no light or welcome task, but we hope that you will gladly take this opportunity to collaborate in the improvement of the German people, which is the ultimate objective of this law.

Your cooperation will be of value in completing the work of our Führer Adolf Hitler; in his vision, as we know, race hygienic thought is a cornerstone in the formation and expansion of the Third Reich.

"We must," as Professor Eugen Fischer, Director of the Kaiser Wilhelm Institution, says, "sharpen the focus of our ethical responsibilities and of our consciences with regard to coming generations. In addition to the love of our neighbors, we must add a love of our successors, who will be our grandchildren and great-grandchildren. We must not only love the people of which we are now a part but also those who we shall one day become."

We then count on your valuable assistance and request the prompt return of the questionnaire.

Heil Hitler!

The Director of the Provincial Institution for the Deaf

Kindly return the questionnaires to Lutherstrasse 14, Schleswig.

Residence of the Provincial Institution for the Deaf, Schleswig

Table 3.2. Students Reported to the Health Authority by Heidbrede

Research Corpus	Year of Discharge	Number of Files	Number Reported under the Sterilization Law	Percentage of Students Reported
Student records	1926–32	23	5	21.74
Student records	1933–35	77	21	27.27
Student records	1936–43	20	10	50
Total research corpus		120	36	30

The questionnaires that were sent to parents of his deaf students with this letter—responses to which Heidbrede characterized as "absolutely necessary for the comprehensive and successful implementation of the law"—had been reworked by Heidbrede in keeping with the beliefs of his Nazi colleagues.[38] Heidbrede used not only Questionnaire B of the Nazi authority for public health, Schleswig Holstein district, but also a questionnaire that he himself had developed.[39] The primary objective of his questionnaire was "research into family trees" on the "sound basis of the genealogical charts of the Heidelberg Institution for the Deaf."[40]

Heidbrede's complicity in racial hygiene policies is also evident from data in the pupil discharge records for the academic years 1926–1943. The school director reported on five of his former students who were discharged between 1926 and 1932. Furthermore, on his own authority Heidbrede informed on almost one-third of his students, and thus delivered them to sterilization authorities (see table 3.2).

Individual cases indicate Heidbrede's enthusiasm for his racial hygiene work. He wrote the following comment in one student file and forwarded it to the relevant heredity health authorities:

The mother of NN and the father of the twin brothers NN and NN are siblings. In the case of these cousins it is then a question of hereditary deafness in the family, which falls under the provisions of the Law for the Prevention of Offspring with Hereditary Diseases.[41]

In another example, in which the hereditary health authority in Heide requested information on the "hereditary deficiency" of a female student as part of its investigation into large families, Heidbrede entered a remark on a transcript that was sent on March 10, 1936.[42] There he expressed the opinion that the student was "totally deaf and very weakly endowed, as well as not beyond ethical reproach (suffers at times from kleptomania)." Furthermore, he wrote, "In consideration of the circumstance that there is an additional deaf child in the family, I would certainly assume that NN does indeed suffer from a hereditary defect."[43]

Yet another case demonstrates Heidbrede's attitude. In a confidential letter of May 24, 1939, the district public welfare authority in Ratzeburg inquired about a former student of the Schleswig Institution who had been discharged from the school in 1936. The letter inquired "whether the preconditions for sterilization had been identified or whether this procedure had already been implemented."[44] Heidbrede replied, also confidentially, that he did not know whether "in the meantime the law of 14.VIII.1933 had been applied" in the case of his former student. He regretted that the file did not permit him to say "whether in the present case it is an instance of hereditary or adventitious deafness," and he complained that "no sure information was available from relatives." Heidbrede apparently wished to indicate that genetic deficiency could be assumed and sterilization warranted, however, for in his reply he wrote: "In any case three brothers of the paternal grandfather died of tuberculosis."[45]

The Schleswig Institution's willing cooperation "in the improvement of the German people" and "valuable assistance in completing the work of our Führer Adolf Hitler," in Heidbrede's words, are also illustrated in figure 3.10.[46] They indicate that Nazi authorities, with the complicity of the school, wanted to streamline the process of identifying supposedly "defective" persons.

Race Political Authority of the   Reich Union for the
Nazi Party and Office of the Leader   German Family
Reich Administration

Berlin W 15, Sächsische Strasse Nr. 69.

To the Leader of the School for the Deaf in Schleswig

Re: Hereditary biology screening (Strictly confidential)

For the purposes of the race biology screening of the Reich Union for the German Family I would request, in the interests of saving time, that in the place of the previously requested copies of affidavits concerning the family named below you complete the information on the next page about members of the family who attended or are attending school there. The family must under no circumstances know of this. Please accept my grateful thanks in advance for a fully completed response.

Kindly send replies to: Reich Union for The German Family
                    Schleswig-Holstein Provincial Administration
                    Kiel, Sophienblatt 23

                                Heil Hitler!
                                (signed) I. A.

Encl: Postage-paid return envelope

To families to be judged:
Name of the head of the household: NN
Residence: XX
1. Child NN born xxxx

1. Which children attend a special school (schools for the feebleminded, for the deaf, for the blind) Name and location of the school:	*NN* *Provincial School for the Deaf Schleswig, since 1936*
2. Were the objectives of the school not reached or is there a prospect that they will not be reached? By which student?	*NN is a student in a weakly endowed class in which it is foreseen that he will achieve the objectives of the school.*
3. Have you noted in the children signs of bodily malformation or defects such as epilepsy, feeblemindedness or unhealthy inclinations?	*No*

Figure 3.10. Letter and Questionnaire Sent to Families of Children in the Schleswig Institution for the Deaf

4. In the event of poor performance, do you consider the children nonetheless of average gifts? How do you explain the poor performance?	*No*			

5. Please rank the children (by the numbers assigned them on the next page) in these categories of natural endowment:

Weakly endowed	Below average endowment	Average endowment	Above average endowment	Highly endowed
No. 1				

6. Have you observed signs of character-related inferiority? In which child? Which signs?	*No*
7. Does the family home provide for the well-being of the child? (Physical care and clothes, supervision of household tasks or other positive upbringing by parents and siblings, any abusive exploitation of the child as a domestic servant?)	*Not known*
8. Are other family members or blood relatives inmates in a school for the retarded, reform school, nursing home, preventive detention center, etc.? Who?	*Not known*

9. Final numerical grades, as well as the grading system employed

	Child 1	*Legend*
Language	4	1 = very good
Counting	4	2 = good
Phys. Ed.	3	3 = satisfactory
Manual work	3	4 = adequate
		5 = not adequate
		6 = unsatisfactory

Place and Date: Schleswig, June 22, 1943
Signature of the school leader:
Director of the Provincial School and Residence for the Deaf
signed Obrecht

Figure 3.10—*Continued*

Collaboration in Private Institutions

Franz Schmid and Georg Schmid—St. Joseph Private Institution for the Deaf

Even private Roman Catholic schools were unable to protect their students from the hands of Nazi teachers. A sixty-year-old former resident of the St. Joseph Private Institution for the Deaf in Schwäbisch Gmünd wrote on his questionnaire that he and about forty classmates, including two of his brothers, were taken for sterilization immediately after being discharged from the school.[47] Another former student described the same incident, adding that none of the boys knew what was going on at the time. "Only later," he wrote, "did I learn just what kind of hospital stay I had made. What kind of a body do I have now?"[48] A third victim has identified Franz Schmid, the institution's director, and senior teacher Georg Schmid as the informers who turned the boys in for sterilization.[49]

District Instructional and Vocational Institution for Deaf Girls

Two concluding examples are drawn from the District Instructional and Vocational Institution for Deaf Girls in Dillingen, a Catholic school founded in 1847 at the suggestion of J.-E. Wagner, professor of dogmatics at the university in Dillingen. Wagner was also the pastor and spiritual director of the Franciscan convent in Dillingen. In 1931, ninety-eight Catholic girls attended the convent school. They were taught in eight classes by twelve trained nuns.[50]

In 1936 a thirteen-year-old deaf baker's assistant, who was living at the institution, received a letter telling her to submit voluntarily to the sterilization operation. She refused on the basis of section 6, paragraph 4, of the ordinance for the implementation of the law from December 5, 1933. This section reads:

> If the subject has been admitted at personal expense to a private institution that offers a full guarantee that reproduction will not occur, the law stipulates that on the subject's application the completion of the operation may be deferred as long as the subject is living in this or a

Students at the District Vocational and Instructional Institution for Deaf Girls in Dillingen Embroidering Church Vestments

similar institution. If the subject is legally incapacitated or has not yet reached eighteen years of age, the legal guardian is authorized to make such an application. If a deferral occurs before the eighteenth birthday, the subject may after that date make a personal application for further exemption.[51]

The ordinance thus indicates that the girl was within her rights in refusing to allow the operation to be carried out. She was clearly in a private institution. Since she had not yet passed her eighteenth birthday, however, she had to ask her guardian to apply for the exemption from the operation.

The mayor of the city of Dillingen, Dr. Hogen, dismissed the regulation related to private institutions in his decision (see fig. 3.11). He claimed that as he was the girl's legal guardian, article 6 of the ordinance justified his use of coercive measures. He apparently followed the case closely, and wrote on the back of his decision, "Matter settled. NN was committed to the Günzberg Hospital on December 14, 1936."[52]

A particularly dramatic case study is offered by the record of another student at the Dillingen Institution. Her guardian was Conrad, the Nazi director of the State Institution for the Deaf in Dresden. The June 18, 1937, entry in her student progress record

Re: Sterilization of NN, baker's assistant in the Institution for the Deaf of Dillingen, born xx in XX, resident in Dillingen at the Institution.

Decision

It is hereby ordered that NN born on xx in XX shall be forcibly conveyed to the hospital in Günzburg for a sterilization operation, unless she immediately goes there of her own accord.

Grounds

NN is to be sterilized in accordance with the decision of the Hereditary Health Court of the Augsburg District Court of October 20, 1936, No. XIII 414/36. The decision has been drawn up by the court clerk in the office of the Hereditary Health Court with the mention that it becomes final on November 13, 1936, and that the sterilization operation may also be performed against the will of the subject. This decision was delivered on November 19, 1936, to the legal representative of NN, NN a farmer in XX, with the order of the public health officer that NN present herself for the operation at either the municipal hospital in Augsburg or in Günzburg within two weeks.

Since NN did not submit to sterilization voluntarily nor did her legal representative provide any further explanation, forcible sterilization at the hospital of Günzburg is to be effected in accordance with the prescription of the state health authority in Dillingen with the assistance of the responsible police authorities (Mayor of the City of Dillingen) (article 6 of the Ordinance of December 5, 1935, *Reich Law Gazette* 1, 1021, section 2, Ordinance of July 8, 1933; Referral No. 222/36).

Dillingen, December 10, 1936
District Police Authority, Dillingen
signed Dr. Hogen

Figure 3.11. Dr. Hogan's Decision to Override Article 6 of the Law for the Prevention of Offspring with Hereditary Diseases

shows that Conrad requested that the administration of the Dillingen institution permit the sterilization of his deaf ward. In doing so, he angered the Catholic administration there, since the Vatican had issued the encyclical "Casti connubi" on December 13, 1930, stating that "authorities do not have direct power over the bodily organs of their subordinates."[53] The orthodox Catholic view was to reject all motives for violating the integrity of a human being, especially eugenic motives.[54] This unambiguous stand by the Holy See against eugenic efforts serves as the background for a letter from the directress of the institution, the Franciscan nun and senior teacher, Mother Agreda Dirr. She wished to save the trainees entrusted to her from the grasp of the Nazis. Conrad's answer was not long in coming. Although Conrad was the girl's guardian, the young deaf woman nevertheless attempted to prevent the sterilization. Mother Dirr supported her by writing another letter to Conrad. However, Conrad's response again emphasized that he was not moved by the arguments concerning negative psychological consequences on his ward. Then, as before, he did not agree to the deferment, and the victim was forced to submit to the operation against her express will (see fig. 3.12).

June 21, 1937

Dear Director Conrad,

Our letters concerning NN have apparently crossed in the mail. To be on the safe side, we must not neglect to call your particular attention once again to the possibility of article 6, paragraph 4, of the implementation ordinance for the hereditary health law. . . .

The Institution for the Deaf of Dillingen qualifies as such a private institution in the sense of the law according to the decree of the Reich Minister of the Interior of January 11, 1936, No. 5348 e 133. This would then offer a legal possibility that NN would not have to undergo the operation, since there is no charge against public funds on her behalf. In any case, she would then have to renounce holidays with her grandparents or anywhere else outside a private institution. We have a wealth of girls here who have taken advantage of this ruling. I would request you to communicate to me whether you will make an application on behalf of your ward under the provisions of article 6, paragraph 4. This must occur within the prescribed fourteen-day period. I look forward to hearing from you. With German greetings,

Mother Agreda Dirr
Directress of the Institution

Figure 3.12. Correspondence Between Mother Agreda Dirr and Herr Conrad, Director of the State Institution for the Deaf, Dresden

Dear Madame Directress, article 6, paragraph 4, of the Law for the Prevention of Offspring with Hereditary Diseases, which you cite, is known to me. Nonetheless, I should like to have the operation carried out, firstly, to permit NN to go on holiday to her relatives and acquaintances and, secondly, since the sterilization would in any case have to be performed if NN left the institution or got married, and the operation is *then, in my experience, much more unpleasant than if it had been performed at a younger age* [emphasis added].

Institution for the Deaf, Dillingen/Danube July 3, 1937

Dear Director,

I have just received 50 marks for NN and have had them deposited in her savings account until she needs the money.

At the same time I must inform you that NN was not prepared to go to Günzburg on July 1 and it then happened that I went with her to the district physician instead of the hospital so that she could herself request that the operation be postponed. I supported her urgent request and accompanied her later that same evening to the public health officer who stated that the operation could very easily be postponed, since NN lives in a private institution. All that needs to be done is that her guardian submit an application to the relevant district physician for a postponement of the decision. That is the present state of things.

I was more than a bit surprised at NN when she stood up for herself with such firmness. That has not often happened earlier. I believe that if NN is not permitted to go on holidays again this year, she will finally make up her mind on her own and it would probably be best to sit back and wait for this. For this girl, who from a psychological point of view is rather fragile, formal coercion would not have good results, and I would be of the opinion to wait until she leaves the institution, whether on holidays or for good. I look forward to your decision and eventual application on her behalf.

With German greetings,
Mother Agreda Dirr

Extracts from NN's Student Progress Record

September 28, 1935: The guardian states that he agrees with the above proposal and will send 50 Reich marks quarterly. Agreement: Three years of apprenticeship—three years unremunerated supervised work is to continue.

Figure 3.12—*Continued*

April 21, 1936: A. started her instruction in plain needlework at the beginning of the school year. Inquiry concerning hereditary disease.

July, 1936: A. cannot travel to her relatives for the holidays. Director Conrad proposes to take her to the summer camp at a country place near Dresden, but since the investigation into hereditary disease is still ongoing, he considers it better that A. remain in Dillingen for the time being.

June 18, 1937: A. has received an order to present herself for sterilization within fourteen days. At the same time her guardian also sent the decision and the legal order with the request that A. should comply with the order on July 16, 1937.

June 21, 1937: We have reminded the guardian of the possibility of a postponement of the decision by reason of entry into a private institution.

June 23, 1937: Nonetheless, the guardian urges the completion of the sterilization; grounds:

1. A. can then go home to her relatives for the holidays;
2. Sterilization would still have to be performed when she left the institution or if she married and would then be much more unpleasant than now.

July/August, 1937: A. was to have been brought on July 1, 1937, to Günzburg but she refused and applied to the district authorities for a postponement of the operation. The latter required that her guardian submit an application for a suspension of the decision. The guardian is not in agreement with the deferral. A. was taken to the hospital in Günzburg on July 22, 1937. After the completion of the sterilization operation she returned to the institution on August 6, 1937.

Figure 3.12—*Continued*

The Pauline Home in Winnenden

The primary objective of research at the Pauline Home was to determine from the evidence of resident files the number of persons referred to the health authorities.* As in other cases of archival

---

*The administration of the Pauline Home (an institution of the Home Mission) permitted unimpeded access to the archives. Their supportive attitude stands out in comparison with that of other institutions in the Federal Republic of Germany.

work, this was a matter of testing and verifying the responses given to the question "Who informed on you?"

Two criteria guided the selection of resident files: (1) The person in question must have been a resident of the Asylum for the Deaf at the Pauline Home in Winnenden between 1933 and 1945 and (2) he or she must have reached reproductive age. Forty-nine residents met these requirements. Twenty-six were reported on in accordance with section 3 of the sterilization law. The superintendent's office of the Pauline Home submitted recommendations on its own initiative for the sterilization of wards in sixteen instances. In ten others the application was made by the provincial youth health officer in Stuttgart or by the health authorities with the cooperation of this office. Twenty-three students were not reported for sterilization.

A vocational school also was associated with the Pauline Home in Winnenden. Thirty-three students attended and received training as basketmakers, tailors, shoemakers, and brushmakers.[55] I sampled twenty-seven student files from the vocational school to determine whether the superintendent's office reported on young persons who were only temporarily lodged at the institution. The files showed that fifteen vocational students were reported on, and twelve were not. In six cases, the superintendent's office made the notification; in eight cases the provincial youth health officer stepped in; and in one case the health authority in Waiblingen instigated the report.

The figures are complemented by an official list drawn up by the Pauline Home in Winnenden concerning the application of the sterilization law. This list contains the names of fifty-nine deaf people, and in the diagnosis of "Hereditary Disease" lists "feeblemindedness" and "deafness" indiscriminately. Only nine of the forty-one cases identified through my research appear on this list as reported under the sterilization law.

In summary, the seventy-six student records examined in Winnenden show that a total of forty-one children, about 54 percent, were reported on under the terms of the sterilization law. These figures do not reveal the effect this process had on its victims, however, or of the rigor with which the superintendent of the Pauline Home, Pastor Müller, transferred the young people entrusted to him to the machinery of the Nazi race fanatics. Müller was an adherent of Nazi race ideology and a member of the Nazi Party. The "Troop Orders" for April 9, 1938, state that he was a storm trooper, Leader of Nazi 6/121 Second Troop.[56]

Even before the implementation of the sterilization law, Müller had advocated the application of racial hygiene measures to a person living in the Asylum for the Deaf in Winnenden. In response to an August 2, 1933, inquiry of the district welfare office in Schwäbisch Hall as to whether continuing educational efforts at the home had good prospects for success, Müller wrote on August 4 as follows: "As it now is, it cannot be commended in good conscience to anyone. It will pose a constant threat to public welfare, unless *the principals of eugenics* are applied" [emphasis added].[57]

The case history of a fourteen-year-old student illustrates Müller's close working relationship with Nazi institutions engaged in the application of the hereditary health law, although he presented himself as the guardian of his underage ward. After the "due process" of prosecution in the hereditary health court, which passed sentence on January 19, 1939, Müller renounced his right to object to the decision for the sterilization of his ward.[58] This removed any possibility of an appeal and cleared the way for the operation. Just how eager Müller was to have the sentence carried out is apparent in a remark added to his letter to the Hereditary Health Court in Stuttgart: "I am requesting the prompt transmission of the definitive verdict, so that the sterilization can be completed as soon as possible before the confirmation ceremony."[59]

In four additional cases that have come to my attention, Müller demonstrated a similar eagerness. In one instance, the Hereditary Health Court in the District Court of Stuttgart noted in its judgment of September 17, 1935, that "the leader of the institution requests the completion of the sterilization operation, since the girl is not reliable in sexual matters."[60] This evidence led to a ruling favoring sterilization for a resident of the Pauline Home.

Superintendent Müller's judgment was crucial to the fate of his students, as can be seen by comparing his comments with those used by the court to justify sterilization. In December of 1936, Müller wrote to the State Health Authority of Waiblingen about a particular student. He said that she was "suspected of congenital feeblemindedness." This was his "evidence":

> NN was enrolled at our institutional school on April 22, 1922. . . . Her school performance was unsatisfactory; see the enclosed report card. After confirmation, the girl worked in various positions, but always came back to us. The chief characteristic of her behavior is defiance to the point of open impudence; toward men, on the other hand, she behaves in a very forward manner. She is a resident in our asylum at the Pauline Home and helps with the housekeeping. Her performance is poor and requires constant supervision.
>
> Office of the Superintendent

The Hereditary Health Court's decision on February 26, 1937, employed Müller's language almost word for word as the grounds for its decree:

> NN has been at the Pauline Home in Winnenden since April 22, 1922. Her school performance is unsatisfactory, as her discharge certificate from the Spring of 1927 shows. After confirmation, the girl worked in various positions, but returned to the Pauline Home in Winnenden. The chief characteristic of her behavior is defiance to the point of open impudence; toward men, on the other hand, she behaves in a very forward manner. She is a resident in the asylum of the Pauline Home and helps with the housekeeping, but her performance is poor and requires constant supervision.[61]

Müller's eagerness to have his pupils sterilized is evident also from the case of a young girl who was about to be discharged after successfully completing training at the Pauline Home. The provincial youth health officer in Stuttgart, a Dr. Eyrich, examined her case. He judged initially that the girl's mother was "physically and mentally inferior." Müller had indicated that the father was "of modest mental endowment," but the physician disagreed. "The father . . . does not make an unfavorable impression on me, but is *very hard of hearing*" [emphasis added].[62]

The parents had stated that the child was born hearing and was deafened at seven years of age as the result of a traffic accident ("on July 6, 1932, she was run over by a beer wagon"). Eyrich dismissed this testimony with the remark that "the child bears the signs of *lues congenita*" (congenital syphilis), and apparently Müller was not convinced either.[63] Eyrich's examination indicated that the girl was not feebleminded: "For example, she can complete an intelligence test without difficulty, can read and write, do written sums quickly, and has also learned to sew at the Home . . . and has passed the apprenticeship examination." Müller's evidence, though, influenced the physician: "But according to the report of the director of the institution she is not a good worker and is very frivolous, is out after men, has an acquaintanceship with a deaf man in Feuerbach, but also flirts with the deaf in the institution."[64]

Eyrich's ultimate conclusion in favor of sterilization is bizarre, but it achieved the goal he and Müller desired:

Diagnosis: congenital deafness. The question of whether deafness is of a hereditary nature cannot be unequivocally answered. In all probability, it is a question of deafness as the consequence of congenital *lues.* Consequently, the girl is not to be characterized as hereditarily diseased in the sense of the law. Nonetheless, I recommend sterilization since our findings suggest that *lues* is probably not the single cause of her inferiority and, in addition, the father is extremely hard of hearing. Both father and mother are mentally inferior. It must be concluded that the risk in NN having children is very great and that, in the event of reproduction, one must certainly reckon with inferior offspring. In addition, she would be completely incapable of raising a child in proper fashion.[65]

Public health officer Eyrich's "expert opinion on proposed sterilization" was submitted along with his recommendation to the Stuttgart I District Court on December 7, 1934.[66] Further inquiry scarcely need be made as to the decision reached by the Hereditary Health Court of Stuttgart I.

The case history of a sister and her surviving brother, who could still be questioned during my investigation, demonstrates that Müller went far beyond the duties that were incumbent on him under the sterilization law. A basketmaker who lived at the Pauline

Home in Winnenden reported that "the institution" informed on him.[67] The chief medical officer of the State Health Authority, Schwäbisch Hall, Dr. Walter Gmelin, in a letter of November 28, 1934, requested "information whether hereditary disease was present" in the case of the basketmaker, who was then thirteen years old. The doctor continued: "The subject's sister has been reported to me on the grounds of hereditary (?) epilepsy."[68]

Müller's reply makes clear that he reported on the brother and sister, and that he tried to persuade their parents that they should "voluntarily" apply for the sterilization operations (see fig. 3.13).

Winnenden, February 11, 1935

To the Chief Public Health Officer, Schwäb. Hall,

Re: Hereditary health cases of NN, born xx, and NN, born xx, children of the farmer, NN, in xx.

Until December 23, 1934, NN was a charge in our vocational school for the deaf. In due course, she was reported by us to the provincial youth health officer responsible for the institution, Dr. Eyrich, as hereditarily diseased. He examined her and came to the decision that an application for sterilization should be made. Meanwhile, the time came for her discharge from the institution. This occurred in agreement with the provincial youth health officer. He had previously been in contact with the parents and had requested their agreement to the sterilization. Since I do not know whether the youth health officer has informed you as senior public health officer in Schwäb. Hall of this, I am so informing you now, so that if necessary the father can be prevailed upon to make the application voluntarily.

Her younger brother, NN, is also with us and will likely stay for a few more years. The youth health officer has also been notified about him. Since Karl is still rather childish, a recommendation about him can be deferred for some time. We will report again on him during his last year of training so that a decision can be made about an application for sterilization.

Office of the Superintendent
Müller

Figure 3.13. Letter from Superintendent Müller Notifying the Chief Public Health Officer of Two Siblings' Sterilization Status

Just one year later, on January 30, 1936, a judgment was passed on the fourteen-year-old boy by the Hereditary Health Court of Öhringen: "NN is to be sterilized, because in the official medical assessment of the Provincial Youth Health Officer of Stuttgart he suffers from hereditary feeblemindedness (section 1, paragraph 2, point 1, of the Law for the Prevention of Offspring with Hereditary Diseases of July 14, 1933)."[69]

As noted earlier in this chapter, the two diagnoses—"hereditary deafness" and "hereditary feeblemindedness"—were used indiscriminately, and they were prominent in the official list of conditions that called for the application of the sterilization law. In the case of this individual, as well as others, considerable doubt must be cast on the accuracy of the diagnosis "congenital feeblemindedness." Several factors suggest that the label of "feeblemindedness" is incorrect—the boy's four years of attendance at an elementary school; his residence since 1931 at the School for the Deaf in the Pauline Home at Winnenden, and his successful completion of training in basketmaking.[70] Moreover, the official register of the Pauline Home lists under the heading "Ailment" only "congenital deafness" for the boy and his sister.[71]

Research in the archives of the Pauline Home in Winnenden gives no indication of any effort by Müller to appeal sterilization decisions, although he could have done so according to section 9 of the sterilization law. Rather, he was an active proponent of sterilization and tried to intimidate parents into giving up their right to appeal decisions to sterilize their children, as shown by the following letter:

February 5, 1936

Dear Herr NN,

The Hereditary Health Court has decided on the sterilization of your son, NN. If you raise no objection to it before the District Court in Öhringen, the judgment will enter force on February 14. The sterilization operation will be performed in the Waiblingen District Hospital. We urge you, however, not to raise any such objection, since the matter will not be dropped because of this measure, but only deferred to a later date. With best regards.

Office of the Superintendent

In another case the parents of a fourteen-year old girl, who was being trained as a clothesmaker, were not notified by Müller until three days after the girl's admission to the hospital and after the completed operation:

June 27, 1936

> Dear Herr NN. We should like to inform you that by order of the hereditary health court your daughter has been in the Waiblingen District Hospital since Wednesday for a sterilization operation. It is anticipated that she will return to us by the middle or end of next week. With best regards and Heil Hitler! Signed for (signature)[72]

Müller was inconsistent on the question of whether the Pauline Home qualified as a private institution, and thus did not have an obligation to inform on its wards, while eagerly and voluntarily identifying children to be sterilized, and often for reasons that seemed to have little to do with their potential for transmitting hereditary deafness. An inquiry from the Esslingen District Welfare Authority, asking whether a resident of the institution ought to be discharged and returned to his mother, led Müller to answer negatively on November 3, 1938, and then to notify the health authorities of the child's eligibility for sterilization. He told the Welfare Authority, "NN is lame on one side so that he is very impaired when walking and working. He is completely deaf and dumb, and also very weak mentally. In addition, he has a very difficult character and is not easy to handle. The question of sterilization could be put off as long as he was at the Institution. Notification has been made to the health authority of suspected hereditary disease."[73]

In the case of a fifteen-year-old deaf girl, who was being trained in needlework at the Pauline Home, Müller informed the district public welfare authority in Saulgau on April 17, 1936, that "her gifts are not sufficient to promise success in needlework training." He added in conclusion that "such pitiable children are best raised in an institution" and advised the welfare authority and the girl's father to let her stay on at the Pauline Home "in the girl's interest." Müller's chief argument for the "ongoing necessity of institutional care" for the girl was "the constant danger of moral abuse."[74] He also found grounds for notification according to section 3 of the sterilization law. "We must also notify the provincial youth health officer about her because of hereditary deafness and congenital feeblemindedness; in all likelihood the sterilization operation will also have to be carried out. (Until this matter is resolved she must definitely not be discharged from the Institution.)"[75]

In the case of a fifteen-year-old boy, Pastor Müller told the Superior Hereditary Health Court in Stuttgart on April 8, 1936, that the "sterilization operation" was "urgently necessary." Müller wrote that the child's "debility is of moderate degree," and his performance was satisfactory in civics, reading, arithmetic, singing, and physical education. Müller found grounds for sterilization, however, because of "defects of character." He described the deaf boy as "extremely restless, very excitable, completely unreliable, rebellious, recalcitrant," with asocial behavior. Müller finally recommended a deferral of the operation for one to two years.[76]

Müller not only used criteria other than deafness to justify sterilization, but he also seemed unconcerned about establishing any proof of genetic causes. Thus he wrote about one boy that "our documents provide no information" concerning the cause of deafness. Nevertheless, he wrote that "we have notified the appropriate district health officer of his suspected hereditary disease." Müller believed the child would need to be sterilized before he left the institution, but he told the State Health Authority in Ehingen, in a letter of October 20, 1936, that he would prefer the sterilization recommendation to come from them.

Pastor Müller's attitude, and the sterilization law itself, must have created anxiety and unrest among the deaf residents of such an institution as the Pauline Home in Winnenden. Indeed, on March 23, 1934, the youth health authority for Nürtigen-Urach discussed the case of a nineteen-year-old shoemaker's apprentice who was hard of hearing. The writer of the letter informed the Pauline Home that the boy's father said the youngster "has become very upset, as were other wards of the Pauline Home, on learning about the sterilization law. He is reported to have had thoughts of suicide at the prospect of sterilization." The letter

---

April 13, 1934

To the Youth Authority in Nürtingen-Urach
Re: Care for NN, born xx, 1915, in XX.
Document M.F. 294

NN is one of our most promising charges. He is making very good progress in shoemaking. His behavior is also good. He will take his apprentice's exam in the fall and will probably pass with a good grade. Then it will be a matter of finding a position for him, and he will be well able to earn a living on his own. The sterilization law has, however, caused some anxiety among our charges. They read far too much about it in the newspapers. I have talked to him myself and calmed him down. I scarcely believe that his thoughts of suicide are to be taken very seriously. Our people talk a lot about it, especially since a severely psychopathic student took his life last year. Whether sterilization is necessary in NN's case is beyond my judgment to say. The hereditary health court must first determine whether his defective hearing is hereditary or not; the decision lies with this court.

We have only the responsibility to make reports. So far nothing at all has happened in this case.

Office of the Superintendent

Figure 3.14. Müller's Reply Regarding Student Concerns about the Sterilization Law

concluded with the following statement and question for Pastor Müller: "I do not believe that in the case of NN there exist the preconditions for sterilization. Is the administration of the institution at all aware of these difficulties?" [77] Müller's ambiguous reply appears in figure 3.14.

Summary

The central question addressed in this chapter was whether the stand taken by educators of the deaf toward the sterilization law and their acquiescence in the implementation of that law support the claim of some German scholars that there was a "rescue mentality" among special education teachers. They do not.

In the mind of Reich leader Maesse, teachers of deaf students were "true defenders of the state and people" and functioned not

Table 3.3. Summary Data on the Number of Students Reported
by School Authorities

School	Number of Files Reviewed	Number Reported under Sterlization Law	Percentage of Students Reported
Provincial Institution for the Deaf, Homberg	104	50	48.08
Provincial Institution for the Deaf, Schleswig	120	36	30
Pauline Home, Winnenden	76	41	53.95
Total research corpus	300	127	42.33

only as "convinced advocates and collaborators" but as the "keenest agents in the great work of preventing diseased offspring."[78] Furthermore, 349, or 28.72 percent, of the respondents to the questionnaire reported that they had been sterilized before reaching their eighteenth birthday, in part with the permission or active participation of their own schools, teachers or principals. Some 34 percent were informed on by their teachers (see table 3.3).

The close collaboration of deaf education, medicine, jurisprudence and other Nazi institutions made possible the extensive selection of "hereditarily diseased" deaf children and their referral to the Nazi race hygienists. The collective silence surrounding these events could have been circumvented by persecuted deaf people through their own communication system, but this was of no advantage in mounting a strong, more active resistance movement. Contributing greatly to this powerlessness was the unification and harmonization policy of the Reich Union of the Deaf of Germany (REGEDE), whose Nazi leadership clique fully endorsed the ideology of Nazi eugenicists and race hygienists.

Under these circumstances, the various expressions of passive resistance, including the "noncompliance" of almost one-third of the deaf people prosecuted under the sterilization law, and individual efforts toward active resistance must be recognized as admirable acts of courage.

4

Forced Abortions

THE FASCIST rulers and their accomplices from medicine, jurisprudence, and education intended the Law for the Prevention of Offspring with Hereditary Diseases to block the creation of "impaired" life, in keeping with their view of race ideology. They took the first step toward the elimination of life, however, with the passage of the Law to Amend the Law for the Prevention of Offspring with Hereditary Diseases.[1] This expansion of the original act gave physicians the legal means to terminate pregnancies by force. Race hygienists and advocates of sterilization argued for it after a number of women defied public policy and became pregnant. As one scholar has stated, "The amendment to the law was . . . a consequence not only of an immanent and expansive race-hygienic 'logic,' but also of the opposition of 'inferior' women."[2]

Of the 662 deaf women who reported compulsory sterilizations, 57 also reported being forced to terminate their pregnancies. This data surely understates the actual number of women sterilized and the number of pregnancies forcibly terminated. It may be assumed that some of the forcibly sterilized deaf women did not wish to reveal something that many considered a deep degradation. Unmarried women may have kept silent about their abortions out of shame about their pregnancies. Statements by clergy and follow-up questions to respondents support these assumptions about the limitations of the data.

All fifty-seven women who were willing to admit the termination of their pregnancies stated consistently that their abortions

Table 4.1. Month of Pregnancy in Which the Abortion
Was Induced

Month	Respondents N=57	Percentage
3rd month or earlier	8	14.04
4th month	9	15.79
5th month	10	17.54
6th month	10	17.54
7th month	4	7.01
8th month	2	3.51
9th month	7	12.28
No month given	7	12.28

were carried out under coercion and that they had never given their consent. This information is confirmed by the data in table 4.1, from which it can be adduced that at least twenty-three women had their pregnancies terminated during or after the sixth month.

The physician's report reproduced in figure 4.1 provides bureaucratically detailed and medically objective information on a grave crime, and provides a view of other practices that involved induced abortion even after the sixth month, in violation of the law.

This doctor's report deserves further comment. First, I had an opportunity to speak with the woman in question in the Pauline Home in Winnenden. Seventy-six years old at the time of the conversation, she was mentally alert, and she continued to perform housekeeping duties. She could still recite the first and last names of schoolmates who had shared her experience and who had been removed from the Pauline Home and murdered under the "euthanasia" action (see chapter 9). Her diagnosis as "hereditarily feebleminded" seemed, forty years later, to have been subjective and incorrect.

Second, the abortion and sterilization were not made with the subject's consent. Rather, Harsch, the senior controller appointed as legal guardian of the "feebleminded," gave his consent to a surgical intervention that was in violation of the law, and to a murder, since the fetus was viable.

It is impossible to measure statistically the many accounts of suffering that respondents gave in answer to the question about

Physician's Report
(in accordance with section 11, paragraph 2 of the Law
for the Prevention of Offspring with Hereditary Diseases)

...., who suffers from

(Name, date and place of birth)

feeblemindedness and is a resident of the Pauline Home in Winnenden ,

was sterilized by me on   August 23, 1941 , pursuant to the decision

of the Hereditary Health Court of   Stuttgart   of July 22, 1941 (docu-

ment code   119/41   ).

Type of sterilization: In the course of the operation, the Fallopian tubes were
tied off, a two-centimeter-long portion excised, the ends tied off, and treated
against peritonitis.

The operation proceeded   normally   .

The incision healed in   10   days without complications.

The patient was released on   September 1 , 19 41 , in good health, in

accordance with the legal requirement.

In addition, pregnancy was terminated on July 11, 1941, with the authorization
of the guardian, senior controller Harsch.

Type of operation: drug-induced premature labor with subsequent rupture of
the sac.

Length of the fetus: 42   centimeters.   Particularities of the fetus

(malformations): — —

Sex of the fetus: female

Other observations (twins): ....

The patient was released on .... in good health.

Place: Waiblingen   September 2 , 19 41

To the Medical Officer in ⎤
To the Offices of the   ⎬   Waiblingen
Hereditary Health Court in ⎦

(signature)

Figure 4.1. Physician's Report from September 2, 1941

other horrible experiences they endured. They can be summarized only with difficulty since a wide range of subjective criteria underlay the experiences of the respondents. Two statements by deaf women, however, permit some insight into the procedures used in this form of persecution, and its psychological and physical effects on the victims. One respondent, born in 1914 and now both deaf and blind, recounted that her fiancé and the father of the aborted child—she was six months pregnant—was of Jewish origin. In her opinion, this was the reason for the prompt termination of the pregnancy. In detail, Frau NN wrote:

> My subsequent marriage to Herr NN was very sad, since we could have no children. And I continued to experience terrible pain during intercourse. Even today I am still very unhappy to be without children, since I have been completely blind since 1961. A child of my own would have been a great help. Killing my baby and the sterilization operation that was carried out at the same time took from eight o'clock in the morning until one in the afternoon. I will never forget the screaming and swearing of that awful woman doctor; it is stamped into my memory. I also had problems with my breasts; each time I had my period they swelled up and were very painful. In 1943, my right breast had to be removed, at the Walburg Hospital in Meschede. I had operations on both armpits. No part of my body has been spared.[3]

Frau Fanny Mikus was sterilized against her will in 1936. When she later became pregnant, she was forced to have an abortion and then undergo a second sterilization procedure. The following statement was made by Frau Mikus during the filming of the television program "Nazi Injustice Toward the Deaf" in Munich. The scriptwriters had originally planned a programmed interview with Frau Mikus. While the camera was running, a spontaneous outburst arose from her painful memories, and we chose not to interrupt. The result was the following statement, here in transcription. It is a witness to the times.

> For being what I am, I too was sterilized by the Nazis. [In 1935], my parents received a letter from the health authorities, that I was unconditionally to be sterilized. But my parents and relatives were against it, and formally rejected it in a letter to the district court. Then there was

a legal summons. We all went, and there I was sentenced to sterilization despite our objections. My mother was also supposed to be sterilized. But she was already in menopause. She had to sign a statement
that she would not have a fourth child. We signed it. But I didn't want
to be sterilized. I cried a lot. Then I received a summons for the operation. I went there as requested. If I hadn't gone, they would have taken
me in a police car. My parents wanted to avoid that. So [in 1936] we
had to go. The nurse had to lock me in the room I was brought to because I kept trying to get away. I just didn't want to go through with it.
There were also two other deaf women in the other beds, and they
cried too. The next night the nurse gave me four shots, because I was
restless. After I fell asleep, I was taken from the room. I felt that I was
being moved. I was only partially anesthetized. After the sterilization
operation, I was in the intensive care ward and the nurses came to me
and they cried too. Pointing to the picture of Hitler, they said "not good,
but we have to keep quiet." After the operation, I went to the health
insurance office and applied for medical benefits. There they told me,
"What do you want medical benefits for? Now you'll have a lot of fun,
you don't need to be careful any more that you'll get pregnant." I was
worried that my fiancé would leave me, because I had been sterilized.
He said, "No."

Then in 1938, we wanted to go to the registry office and give notice
that we planned to get married. The registry official opened a book and
looked in it and said that I was to be sterilized again. Well, when I was
released from the hospital after the sterilization, they told me that I
would not have any children. I didn't believe it. I still didn't have much
of a clue. Then in 1938, I got pregnant. I didn't believe that I could have
a child. My mother wasn't there; she was away. When she got back she
was horrified that I was pregnant. She said, "You have to go to the gynecologist." Then we went to the gynecologist and had me examined. The
doctor was friendly and he congratulated me. He said that I really was
pregnant. I told him that I had been sterilized and my mother told him
the same thing. Then the doctor got scared and stopped treating me.

My stomach continued to swell. Then I got a letter from the gynecology clinic; it was a summons. I went there. The nurses took my
stockings, my panties and all my clothes. They examined me. Then I
left the examination room. I wanted to get dressed again, but all my
clothes were gone. So then I asked the doctor, "Where are my clothes?"
The doctor said, "No. You're staying here." They wanted to test my
urine for three days. I said, "I don't believe it. I want to go home. I can
also be examined at home." The doctor said, "No, you are to stay here."

So I stayed there. I was locked up again in my room on the fourth floor. I kept waiting for the moment when the nurse would come and open up, and then I ran down the hall. But they grabbed me and pushed me back in the room. I cried so much. During those three days I was not able to pass any urine. This was never investigated. After three days the doctors came on their rounds and simply said "Out with it." I asked, "What do you mean?" They said, "It has to come out." I said "No!" I wanted to run to the window. But they caught me. Then I had to be moved to another room, where the windows had bars. I can't forget it. I was desperate. The nurses and the doctor went away. Then I quickly wrote a postcard and ran quickly down the hall, then down the stairs. Then I saw my friend. She was just making a visit. Quickly I gave her the card. But I had been seen. The card was confiscated. I wanted to write to my friend that I'd had to have an abortion. Then I went back into the hospital room. That night I cried a lot, an awful lot. I got a shot to tranquilize me. The next day I was rolled away. I saw the operation room in the half-light—basins, instruments, the table. I cried out again and then I passed out. After the operation, I woke up in the intensive care ward. I felt that my stomach was still swollen. I asked the nurse whether the baby was still in there. "No, it's already gone." The nurses cried too. They felt sorry for me. They said, "It was a boy; he was normal." "Hitler is crazy," the nurse said. But she had to keep quiet. Then I cried and told the doctor that it burned and burned down below. I wanted to pee, but the doctor said "No, the dressing is still in there." On the third day the dressing was taken out. A whole mountain of blood. I asked the nurse whether I could have visits. The nurse said I could. My baby's father had already been there but he had his working clothes on. The nurse asked me, "Who is Christian?" I said, "My boyfriend, we're engaged." What's his last name?" "Mikus." "Good."

That afternoon my boyfriend came to the intensive care ward. He had received special permission from the nurse. He was in total shock. He let his presents drop because I was so pale. I was worried that he wouldn't want me anymore because I no longer had the baby. But he said, "We're in the hands of the state. We can't do anything, but we'll stay with one another."

In 1938, after the abortion, I went to the registry office. Now we wanted to get married without any more fuss. The registry official took out a paper from the health authorities where it said that I had to be sterilized again—I forgot to tell you. From the clinic that performed the abortion I got a paper that said that I was to come back again in ten weeks. But I didn't go back. I just couldn't. I put it off for a long time.

Until when? 1938. Then the registry official said, "I'm sorry." Then I went home and told my parents about it and asked them what I should do. I said then that I would rather enter a convent to wait until Hitler had lost the war. But my boyfriend said that they did the same things to people in church homes: sterilizations, abortions, and so on. What was I to do? So I said, "Then we won't get married." But my boyfriend wanted to marry me. Then, with a heavy heart, I let myself be sterilized again. But this was much worse than the first time. My stomach was cut up horribly. For the first sterilization, the incision was horizontal but the second time they made a long vertical cut in my belly. I've often had a rupture when I got up during the night when I was upset. It just bursts. I was out of my mind. And again I didn't get any sick benefits. My uncle cursed a lot about Hitler. Then he was summoned by the Nazis to Berlin, then Munich, Berlin, Munich. It was really bad. Then in 1940 or 1941, he was arrested because he had said so much about Hitler and he had wanted to help the deaf and do everything he could. It was a bad time. Then we went to the registry office in 1941. We got the marriage papers because I had been sterilized. But afterwards, our marriage was so unhappy, no children and our lovemaking was not as complete as before. It was really bad.

Years later, in the cold language of medical bureaucrats, the double process of forced sterilization and forced termination of pregnancy reads as follows:

Gynecology Clinic and Midwifery College
of the University of Munich
Munich, February 27, 1952

Physician's Certificate

On the orders of the Hereditary Health Court of Munich, file No. 16 XIII 12/36, the sterilization of Fräulein Franziska Schwarz, born on November 27, 1918, was completed on March 21, 1941, by means of laparotomy, wedge-shaped excision of both tubes, and extirpation of the tubes, since the sterilization operation of May 7, 1936, had been unsuccessful. In August of 1938, Fräulein Schwarz's pregnancy was terminated in the fourth month.

This is confirmed by an examination of the file.

Dr. Hollenweger-Mayr
Assistant Doctor

5

Deaf Collaboration: REGEDE

THE REICH UNION of the Deaf of Germany
(REGEDE) was a social organization of and for deaf Germans
founded in Weimar in 1927. It lost its independence under the Nazi
regime. REGEDE was incorporated into the National Socialists'
public welfare program at Easter of 1933, along with all deaf advocacy and support agencies and other self-help organizations,
such as the deaf welfare associations and the National Union for
the Welfare of the Deaf.[1] By 1934, REGEDE's 3,900 registered
members, including deaf activist Karl Wacker, found themselves
to be members of the Nazi Party.[2] Apparently the organization's
head, Fritz Albreghs, had applied for Party membership for everyone in REGEDE.[3]

Albreghs described this action in May of 1937 in Breslau, on
the occasion of the tenth anniversary of REGEDE's founding:

> Shortly after the Party Congress in Nuremberg in 1933, I put REGEDE
> under the supervision of the National Socialist party, national direc-
> tion, central authority for public welfare. Thereby, the infrastructure
> of the organization, not least in its external aspect, was finally so
> closely tied to the Third Reich that one could truly speak of a solid
> foundation.[4]

Another deaf leader who supported consolidation under Nazi
leadership was Siepmann, head of the German deaf athletic club,
the Deaf Union for Physical Training. In 1933 he wrote that he
had the "renewal of our German deaf community" in sight as a
"great new mission for the deaf." The division of deaf associations into two church-affiliated groups, an athletic union, and

REGEDE was too much for him. Siepmann wanted "just one association of the German deaf . . . a union," which he saw as "the
crack troops of the German deaf." In this union he envisioned the
training of deaf youth—"our future, the representatives of coming generations"—as a great mission and challenge "in the spirit
of our Führer, Adolf Hitler." [5]

Siepmann considered athletic training, in divisions of gymnastics and team sports, as especially suited to realizing these objectives. Sports needed to be pursued not "so incidentally" as in the
past but "at least once a week." This would simply be "doing one's
duty." Siepmann's remarks reached their zenith in his appeal to
imitate the storm troopers:

> Many of our friends wish to wear the brown shirt of honor, they want
> to be fighters for Adolf Hitler among the storm troopers. Not everyone
> can do this, but one can imitate the troopers by enlisting in the gym-
> nastics and team sports divisions as disciplined, conscientious com-
> petitors. For we are all competitors for our Third Reich. [6]

Siepmann thus laid the foundation for transforming the athletic club into a National Socialist–controlled association, and

Officials of the Reich Union of the Deaf of Germany in 1937 (Fritz Albreghs is on the
right)

Deaf Union of German Girls Athletes from Osnabrück, 1935

further efforts were made to incorporate the remaining independent organizations into REGEDE. As Siepmann ordered, the leaders of the associations sought to enlist deaf youth in the REGEDE union. Enticements, threats, and coercive efforts now began, and appeals were made to the parents of deaf youth.

In May of 1937, Werner Thomas, president of the Berlin Deaf Athletic Association, made an impassioned plea to involve deaf children in Hitler Youth. His remarks, directed at both young deaf people and their parents, appeared in the *Newsletter of the Berlin Deaf Athletic Association (Nachrichtenblatt des Berliner Gehörlosen-Sportvereins)*:

> My inquiries have revealed that . . . of the Leipzig and Dresden Sports Associations almost one hundred percent of the members are doing their duty with joyful hearts as Hitler Youth. It is then all the more shameful that many Berlin athletes still oppose membership. As an old storm trooper of many years, I have had a great deal of valuable experience that training in Hitler Youth and the troopers is very worthwhile for the German people as a whole. There our youngsters will be trained in iron discipline, comradeship and self-sacrifice. There they

will mature into fine, true men, or to put it a better way, into the best National Socialists.

We, as deaf, will never be called to the labor force, to the army and so on. Service in Hitler Youth offers you the last opportunity to go through a hard school.

Top performances in sports are in no way a defense, since serving the interests of Adolf Hitler's Reich takes precedence over everything!!!

In accordance with the appeal of our national athletics leaders from Tschammer and the East, and our association leader, party member Siepmann, I urge you for the last time, dear comrades who are still not more than eighteen years of age, to report to the troop leader G/2 Müller before May 12, 1937. Otherwise, dissociate yourselves from our fine athletic community!

On this occasion I would call to the attention of all Hitler Youth that when one of you is dishonorably dismissed from the movement, he automatically forfeits membership in the athletics club.

Finally I appeal to the respected parents and also to my fellow club members to give their full understanding to the action that I have undertaken in the state's interest. All for Germany! W. Thomas, Club Leader.[7]

Deaf Union of German Girls in 1936—"Integrated" in REGEDE?

Deaf Hitler Youth of the Institution for the Deaf, Osnabrück, 1936

Decades after the collapse of the Nazi dictatorship, deaf people who were persecuted by the Nazis remembered the "one hundred percent National Socialist district leader Werner Thomas, then of Berlin."[8] He was also active as an informer and as a zealous defender of Nazi race ideology, when he harassed his deaf compatriots with provocative expressions and demands such as "let your girlfriend go, she's too good for you! You're not pure and you're even hereditarily unfit."[9] It matches the image of this deaf Nazi functionary (Nazi Party membership No. 237698) that Thomas had hanging in his room an oversized picture of himself "striking a pose in his storm trooper uniform."[10] Thomas even introduced new concepts of Nazi ideology into sign language (see fig. 5.1).

REGEDE's recruitment methods produced results. Membership grew from 3,900 at Easter in 1933 to more than 10,111 by October 1, 1935, and 11,588 by January 1, 1937.[11] Fear of the sterilization law may have augmented these numbers by leading some deaf individuals to become members of REGEDE and thereby

Figure 5.1. Werner Thomas Demonstrating His New Signs for Nazi Concepts. The document is entitled "Speaking Hands." A translated version appears on the opposite page.

Speaking Hands

To Express New Concepts

Hands often say more than words
A gesture that with unusual eloquence expresses the concept of ascendancy. The fingers of each hand form a flower striving toward the light.

This means "OUR . . .
The hand completes a movement from the person addressed to the speaker.

Right . . . FÜHRER"
The concept of the Führer is given a striking signification by the demonstrative gesture of the hand.

Left: WINTER AID
Giving with an open hand
The sense of this great aid effort is so apparent

Right: GREETING THE FÜHRER
The right hand raised over the shoulder means Adolf Hitler

Left: THE NATIONAL GERMAN COMMUNITY
It encompasses all those who recognize themselves as part of the German people and brings them together. The two hands make the idea readily understandable.

The language or rather communication among the deaf is based on the mimed representation of psychological concepts. When hearing and voice are lost, the mental and spiritual comprehension of all processes and concepts increases: heart, eye, and facial expression then contribute much more strongly to the overall world of representation.

The signs and concepts tested in years-long practice and training are passed as a heritage, but our present-day thought world also requires new representations in sign language. When, for example, the expression for Adolf Hitler was given distinct form as a greeting—the palm of the hand raised over the shoulder—it establishes a subtle psychological difference from the prescribed greeting of all Germans, the horizontally extended arm.

Each gesture of the hand communicates a single discrete concept. Anyone who has taken a deeper look into this silent world of communication has recognized that the spoken word is often inferior to the language of the hands, which is drawn from spiritual experience.

members of the Nazi Party. As one deaf person who experienced these events recounted:

> I joined the Nazi Party in 1933. But it was not inner conviction that prompted me to this step, but rather the hope that as a party member I would be protected from the sterilization law. This was also the opinion of the late director of the deaf school in Frankental. I was only a nominal party member. My hope not to fall victim to that law which misapplied the principals of sensible eugenics and showed such contempt for humanity was however not met. Despite the fact that I was a party member, I was sterilized after a twelve-month-long judicial process. Since then my physical and mental suffering has only increased.[12]

Albreghs tried to transform REGEDE into a thoroughly Nazi organization. He organized it hierarchically and supervised it strictly in keeping with Nazi models. Albreghs subdivided the union into nine district inspectorates, which were in turn composed of various district associations; local associations were subsumed in the district associations. Even most staff members wore the brown uniform of the storm troopers, and from Easter 1933 onward, REGEDE's letterhead displayed a radiant swastika (see fig. 5.2).

Altercations among deaf Germans over REGEDE's role between 1933 and 1945 continued long after the war, as shown in an exchange of letters in *German Deaf News (Deutsche Gehörlosen-Zeitung)* between a former REGEDE official and a member of the Old Timers Club of Kassel. The writer of the first letter was a former REGEDE district leader from Hessen-Nassau and a Nazi Party member.[13]

> Prevention is better than cure! Teacher of the deaf Horst Biesold of Bremen has raised the question of the sterilization of the deaf during the Hitler period and has also posed the question of how we can prevent discrimination against the deaf. Most discrimination of the deaf is due to an old prejudice from the time when they were not yet or not sufficiently schooled. Section 51 of the Penal Code declares the deaf not responsible for their actions, although this was relevant to only a minority of them. Sterilization was first practiced in the USA and Sweden! To oppose it openly in Germany was dangerous! The best help came from the ranks of the unschooled members of the Reich Union of the Deaf of Germany.[14]

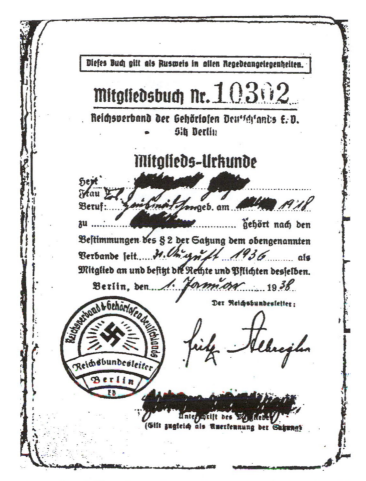

Figure 5.2. A Nazi Party Membership Card with the REGEDE Insignia

The Old Timers Club of Kassel directed its reply to the reference to "help" allegedly given by REGEDE members to deaf persons who were threatened by the sterilization law:

Prevention is better than cure (with regard to the letter to the editor of *DGZ*, No. 5, page 140). Does [the author], who once also wore the brown uniform, count himself among the "unschooled members" of REGEDE of that time? He was far too clever for that! Many of the so cruelly treated deaf have still not forgotten what he said about sterilization to his REGEDE meeting in Herborn in 1936: "The hearing must sacrifice their lives as soldiers. The deaf do not need to be soldiers. But sterilization is a sacrifice like soldiering. We must make this sacrifice!" Would this have been the unschooled or schooled help that REGEDE offered the deaf in the matter of mass sterilization? Or a poor consolation? I can't believe such help was of any value. Even today, all those who were forcibly sterilized feel that their human dignity has been debased. Even today many do not dare to tell everything that was done to them out of a sense of shame. No, mere words do not heal wounds like these. Today people of conscience are concerned that something like this not be repeated. I find it only too necessary that people finally want to do something to make modest compensation to those who were so injured in body and soul.

It is a pity that out of an understandable sense of shame not all will make such claims.

On behalf of the Old Timers Club of Kassel.[15]

Some deaf officials, like their hearing educator models, served Nazi interests. REGEDE leader Albreghs and the administrative head Ballier, both of whom signed the REGEDE membership card (see fig. 5.3) did not hesitate to denounce their "hereditarily diseased" fellows. Five of the 1,215 forcibly sterilized deaf respondents reported that REGEDE had informed on them. One of those affected, who has held important offices in the deaf union from the collapse of the Third Reich until today, remarked on his questionnaire that "Two deaf Nazi party members from the Reich Union of the Deaf of Germany (REGEDE), Albreghs and Ballier" informed on him. He added that Albreghs and Ballier made REGEDE "a strong proponent of sterilization."[16]

Albreghs' beliefs manifest themselves in a commemorative article written for the Second German Congress of the Deaf in Breslau (May 14–16, 1937). In this article he lamented the actions of the German Deaf Workers Union, founded in 1918, which "instead of building up [the deaf community], had destroyed everything in a fratricidal war!"[17] By founding REGEDE in 1927, he hoped to unify Germany's deaf citizens, or at least those who met his political and religious criteria.[18]

Albreghs argued that REGEDE and the unity of deaf Germans was threatened by "the poisonous trinity" of "Jews, Social Demo-

Figure 5.3. REGEDE Membership Card

crats and Communists," which ostensibly had begun "to under-
mine his work."[19] He continually put forth this view of his ene-
mies, and it was intolerable for him that they had been able to establish themselves and "could play such an irresponsible game
with the German deaf community."[20] In his account of history,
the solution to Germany's problems came with the "storm wind
of the National Socialist revolution," with which "Adolf Hitler's
stern brown battalions chased from the throne the parasites on
the body of the people, the bigwigs, and the pack of Jews."[21]

Albreghs' promotion of Nazi racial ideology found its most po-
tent expression in REGEDE's activities, where close collaboration
of the deaf organization with party organs and Nazi institutions
was a matter of course. His deputy in REGEDE was a hearing man,
Edmund Matz, his "storm trooper comrade from R Storm 7/9."
Matz was to be the administrator for deaf affairs in the national
administration of the Nazi Party, division of public welfare.[22]
Albreghs and Matz together pursued the policy of unifying all

Fritz Albreghs, Leader of the Reich Union of the Deaf of Germany

organizations for and of deaf Germans with the premise: "Where resistance arises, it will gradually be eliminated,"[23] and, as party members in Silesia added, "When necessary, harshly and ruthlessly."[24]

Albreghs also cooperated closely with the Nazi teachers' union and its officials, Ruckau, the head of the National Professional Association, and Dr. Maesse, the Reich professional group leader, and others. Albreghs characterized these men as "the most trustworthy comrades and friends, who today as before belong to the strong pillars of the organization."

REGEDE's work with teachers and administrators in encouraging support for the Nazi regime and its racial hygiene program, including the sterilization of deaf people, can be seen in activities reports from the local associations in 1937 (see table 5.1). One regional association, for example, reported that "collaboration with Nazi public welfare is excellent. Almost the entire body of teachers of the deaf are working effectively in our common sense of destiny." REGEDE, Nazi Party leaders, and teachers from the schools for the deaf spoke to deaf audiences on such topics as

Table 5.1 Workshops and Presentations Sponsored by REGEDE Regional Associations in Collaboration with Teachers of the Deaf

Association	Activities	Sponsoring Organization
Regional association 32, Württemberg	Training camp	Party member and senior teacher Zettle
Regional association 6, Franken	Lecture: "The Deaf in the National Political State"	National Socialist Public Welfare
Regional association 16, Main Franken	Lecture on national political themes at each meeting	
Regional association 21, Saar-Pfalz	Marriage counseling, etc.	District Deaf Institution
Regional association 30, Westphalia North	"Approx. 10% of male members belong to the storm troopers"	
Regional association 31, Westphalia South	District professional counselor	Party member Wegge, director of the Provincial Institution for the Deaf, Soest
Regional association 5, Essen	Beneficial promotion by Nazi public welfare. REGEDE got a foothold, despite "great" splintering along denominational lines.	National Socialist Public Welfare
Regional association 11, Koblenz-Trier	A monthly lecture on National Socialism and the union	
Regional association 12, Cologne-Aachen	Collaboration with Nazi public welfare is excellent. Almost the entire body of teachers of the deaf are working effectively in our common sense of destiny.	Teacher of the deaf
Regional association 8, Halle-Merseberg	Counseling center, as the deaf are little familiar with the new laws that affect them.	REGEDE
	Training of members of regional association 8	Teachers of the Deaf
	Lectures	Party member, senior teacher Werner Party member, director Braune

Table 5.1—*Continued*

Association	Activities	Sponsoring Organization
Regional association 23, Saxony	Political enlightenment and training	District speaker of the Nazi Party, local union leader, teachers from the deaf school, Dresden
Regional association 28, Thuringia	Lectures: "What Does National Socialism Demand of you?" "The Struggle Against Degeneration" "Account of the Reich Party Conference on Honor" "Germany in the Struggle Against Jewry and Communism."	"Teachers of the deaf"
Regional association 17, Mecklenburg-Lübeck	Lectures: "The Law for the Prevention of Offspring with Hereditary Diseases and the Deaf" "Gas warfare and protection against gas"	REGEDE
	Each year 6–7 lectures at the local association, Ludwigslust	Teacher of the deaf
	Welfare: "Emphasis will be on counseling and help concerning the implementation of the Law for the Prevention of Offspring with Hereditary Diseases"	Board of Directors of Deaf Welfare, Mecklenberg-Lübeck
Regional association 27, South Hanover-Braunschweig	Leader of the district women's association	Party member, teacher of the deaf Fiedler
Regional association 24	Training and lectures methodically and successfully completed in Breslau and Liegnitz.	Teachers from the institution for the deaf, Silesia
	"Beginning to Mop Up the Individual, Small, Religiously Oriented Clubs," 11 lectures or films	REGEDE

Table 5.1—*Continued*

Association	Activities	Sponsoring Organization
	Themes of race hygiene and the Law for the Prevention of Offspring with Hereditary Diseases	Senior teachers Rother and Krause
	Lecture: "About the Law for the Prevention of Offspring with Hereditary Diseases"	Party member Manko, director of the institution for the deaf, Liegnitz
	Lecture: "Measures of the Law for the Prevention of Offspring with Hereditary Diseases" and the Deaf	
	Lecture: "Hitler Youth, Discipline and Comradeship"	Party member, senior teacher Eisermann
Regional association 9, Hamburg	Recruitment meeting and lecture: "The Incorporation of the Deaf of Germany in REGEDE"	Party member Matz, Berlin
	District union propaganda chief	Party member Paul Jankowski, director of the institution for the deaf
Regional association 3, Danzig	Leadership of the district union since June 1936	Party member Krieger, director of the Danzig institution for the deaf
	"Advice and help for members in dealing with sterilization"	REGEDE
	Lecture: "The Position of the Deaf in the National Socialist State"	District union leader Becker, Königsberg
Regional association 20, East Prussia	Establishment of training evenings	Party member, senior teacher Bewer, Königsberg

Note: Data are from the financial report in *Festschrift 2. Deutscher Gehörlosentages* (1937): 14ff., the commemorative volume of the Second German Congress of the Deaf.

Close Collaboration: Nazi Teachers Union and REGEDE. *Left to right:* Reich Professional Leader Ruckau and Editor-in-Chief Tornow of the National Socialist Teachers Confederation.

"What does National Socialism demand of you?" and "The struggle against degeneration." Another common theme in many regional association meetings was the Law for Prevention of Offspring with Hereditary Diseases and, in Danzig, for example, "advice and help for members in dealing with sterilization." REGEDE's desire to crush local deaf organizations was even a topic. The Silesia association, Regional Association 24, offered a lecture on "Beginning to mop up the individual, small, religiously oriented clubs."

Accounts of REGEDE activities refer frequently to the formation of women's clubs on the district and local levels. Emilie Klüsener-Esch had a substantial involvement in this development, and also in introducing deaf women in general to Nazi ideology. As early as 1911 she had founded a women's division of the Association of the Deaf, but it was not active. She joined the Nazi Women's Organization in 1932, and Albreghs gave her authority to establish the Reich Women's Union within REGEDE.

Association activity logs also offer evidence of lectures and propaganda efforts undertaken by Klüsener-Esch. It is known that she was voluntarily sterilized, although evidently she came from a "hereditarily sound" family (the maternal line could be traced back to 1368). With this personal sacrifice and almost as a model, she tried to convince other deaf women to submit voluntarily to sterilization.[25]

Some educators of deaf students believed that the efforts of Albreghs and his like-minded colleagues to put REGEDE on a National Socialist course did not go far enough, even though the growing influence of Nazi teachers of the deaf on REGEDE policies is evident from the activity logbooks. Senior teacher Knobloch of the Wuppertal-Elberfeld School for the Deaf, for example, busied himself in a variety of activities and, as early as December 1933, wrote to the "Reich Minister and Fellow Party Member," Frick, about his concerns about controlling the German deaf community.[26]

After assessing "with the very greatest interest" Frick's endeavors "to make the German people conscious of the value of

National Socialist Teachers Confederation: Reich Training Course in Race Policy, 1936

good blood," Knobloch came to the point. He asked that Frick direct his attention to REGEDE, "where attentive observation was required so that the deaf and hard of hearing do not have expectations that are impossible to meet and could never be realized by a people intent on reconstruction."[27] Knobloch's letter was forwarded by government counsel Dr. Linden to the Nazi Public Welfare, Division IV, on December 15, 1933, with the request that they look into the matter.[28]

The National Administration of the Nazi Party, N.S. Public Welfare, National Direction, responded on December 20, 1933. This letter is particularly significant, because it indicates the level of control and supervision Nazi Public Welfare exerted over REGEDE.

> With regard to Herr Knobloch's proposal that the Reich union be accorded attentive observation it may be noted that this is already in progress. The Reich union is, in fact, already affiliated with National Socialist Public Welfare as a corporate member and thereby is subordinate to its supervision and control. *It may undertake no measures of consequence without the prior authorization of National Socialist Public Welfare* [emphasis added].[29]

After the "coordination" (*Gleichschaltung*), REGEDE was no longer an independent organization, but one that followed Nazi directives.

6

Deaf Resistance

HERBERT WEINERT, a racial hygienist and teacher of deaf students from Dresden, wrote in the 1930s that "countering" deaf people's "subversive agitation" was a significant aspect of the race hygiene program. He termed such work "a special assignment . . . since [resistance to the sterilization law] always reflects negatively on sterilizations."[1]

Weinert found it "unconditionally necessary" to oppose as strongly as possible what he characterized as "rumors" circulating among the deaf population about sterilizations. As a teacher of deaf pupils, Weinert knew that news and criticism were relayed quickly through sign language and the network of the various deaf organizations, avoiding conventional avenues of communication that were more easily monitored. Weinert expressed his concern about this uncontrolled information exchange: "Rumors circulate . . . and because of the strict solidarity among the deaf they can be transmitted very quickly across great distances."[2]

The question of organizing resistance against sterilization engaged many deaf Germans in the Reich. Maria Wallisfurth's biography of her deaf mother expresses the urgency felt by those threatened by the sterilization law. "They wanted to defend themselves." Wallisfurth wrote. "But how were they to do it? Whoever refused was taken away by the police."[3]

Fascist legislators explicitly permitted the use of force to carry out the sterilization law, well aware of the difficulties that would accompany the law's "voluntary" implementation:

If sterilization has been decreed [section 12, paragraph 1, stated], it is to be carried out even against the will of the person to be sterilized, unless he or she alone has made the application. The responsible physician is to request the necessary measures of the police authorities. Insofar as other measures are not sufficient, the use of physical force is authorized.[4]

Only 17 of the 1,215 deaf people I questioned stated that their sterilization was voluntary. In fact, roughly one-third of the respondents, 393 individuals, ignored the written summons to appear at a given clinic "within two weeks for the surgical intervention necessary for sterilization, under the provisions of the Law for the Prevention of Offspring with Hereditary Diseases." When they failed to appear voluntarily, deaf people were taken to the clinics, most often by the police. Twenty-five respondents, however, stated that either a teacher or principal had taken them to the clinic for sterilization; and nine said that a "public health nurse" had been responsible.

The following documents show officials' use of force and the threat of force to gain deaf compliance with sterilization orders:

State Health Authority for the City and District of Greifswald

No. 3/77/35   Greifswald, July 20, 1935
To: The Office of the Mayor, Local Police Authority, Wolgast
Re: NN of Wolgast, hereditarily diseased

The above named hereditarily diseased person has been sentenced to sterilization by the legally binding decision of the Hereditary Health Court of Greifswald. The order for the operation and for admission to one of the listed hospitals was delivered on June 17, 1935. Thus far NN has avoided the sterilization operation.

I respectfully request, in accordance with the Law for the Prevention of Offspring with Hereditary Diseases, that NN be forcibly conveyed to one of the hospitals named (Surgical Clinic in Greifswald or Dr. Nauck, Greifswald) and that I be informed of the completion of this action.

(signature)
Public Health Officer

The Lord Mayor of the City of Nuremberg
of the Reich Conference of Cities

(stamp) Leader of the City Health Authority
Frau NN
Furrier
Nuremberg
Nuremberg, December 6, 1937
Re: Implementation of the Reich Law for the Prevention of Offspring
with Hereditary Diseases of July 14, 1933
N II 1913 / 5045

In its decision of November 4, 1937 (document Z. XIII 109/37), the Hereditary Health Court of the District Court of Erlangen has ordered your sterilization, since you suffer from hereditary deafness. This decision came into definitive force on November 30, 1937.

You are then directed to present yourself for the medical measures necessary for sterilization *within two weeks* from the day of the issuance of this order. The facility in question is the Municipal Gynecology Clinic of Nuremburg, at Flurstrasse 7.

It should also be noted that sterilization may legally be carried out against the wishes of the subject.

In the event of noncompliance with this official order, you may expect the use of physical force, that is, conveyance by the police authorities to the clinic (in accordance with section 12, paragraph 1, of the Reich Law for the Prevention of Offspring with Hereditary Diseases of July 14, 1933, and article 6, paragraph 5, of the implementation ordinance of December 5, 1933).

The present summons is to be handed over on admission to the clinic.

If you have yourself admitted **at your own expense** to a private institution (hospital or nursing home) that offers full security that reproduction will be precluded, the hereditary health court will **on your application** direct that the performance of the operation be deferred as long as you are a resident of the institution.

Entry into a private institution must, however, take place within two weeks. *On that occasion you should turn the present summons over to the institution.*

Yours truly

Amtsarzt.

Active Resistance

The stories of four individuals demonstrate how deaf people actively resisted the sterilization law.

August Veltmann

August Veltmann is the only deaf person to be awarded a papal order of merit.[5] He received this honor for his courageous opposition to the Nazis and for his determined advocacy on behalf of deaf Catholics in the Third Reich. Veltmann chaired the Catholic Deaf Association in Münster from 1924 until 1945, and I interviewed him in his home when he was eighty-five years old. We discussed his experiences and opposition activities under fascist rule. The interview was conducted in both speech and sign language.

> Q: Mr. Veltmann, did your group, as a Catholic deaf organization, let itself be incorporated in the National Socialist Reich Union of the Deaf of Germany (REGEDE) that was controlled by the Nazi public welfare authority?
>
> A.V.: The entire Catholic deaf union was dissolved by the Nazis. But in Münster we refused to join them from the very beginning. We, too, received demands from REGEDE to become members. But we always declined.
>
> When he seized power, Hitler found, even among deaf persons, some who were willing to follow him, such as the people who founded REGEDE, to which all the deaf associations were supposed to be affiliated. The Catholic Association of Münster, which I represented, rejected the federation and insisted on remaining a Catholic association. REGEDE was not able to catch us.
>
> Q: After the seizure of power in 1933, were you still able to publish your association's newspaper?
>
> A.V.: There was the *Deaf Leader* (*Taubstummen-Führer*), the forerunner of *EPHETA*, which was printed at the Paulinus Press in Trier. Principal Norbert Menke from the deaf school there edited the paper. An honorable man. But soon the Catholic association was dissolved, and Menke was removed from his position at the school. After the war he was "rehabilitated" and became the principal of the school in Cologne. But he was a sick man when I first met him, and he did not live much longer. Yet another victim of the Nazis.

Q: What were you able to accomplish to help your fellow-deaf who were threatened by the Nazi sterilization law?

A.V.: I had extensive correspondence with the Nazi party, which had denied deaf persons the right to marry and wanted to sterilize many of them. Often I was successful in showing that their deafness was due to environmental factors. In that way, some few were spared.

Q: Do you remember any cases in which you were not able to help?

A.V.: In one drastic case, a young man refused the operation. Then one morning the storm troopers drove up in front of the plant and took the man away to the operation by force.

Another case: a young woman was expecting. Since she was afraid that she would be forced to have the baby aborted, she went to relatives in a large city to wait for the delivery.

Then she went to the hospital and ended up on the operating table. What they did there, she still doesn't know. In any case she was made infertile. After the war she went and made inquiries, but they wouldn't say anything.

Q: Which experience between 1933 and 1945 made the most lasting impression on you?

A.V.: It was the Sunday after the tenth of November 1938, after *Kristallnacht*. The Catholic deaf in Münster were holding a meeting on the same avenue as the synagogue. It was still burning. We went there, and I said to my deaf friends, "Look, that is arson directed by the government. After arson comes the prison. What misery! Poor Germany! What more will we have to go through?"

Q: Wasn't such a public statement dangerous?

A.V.: Yes, it certainly was. But I made my statements in sign language without voicing. So only my deaf friends could understand.

Q: Where was there organized resistance in your area of activity?

A.V.: The main associations in the Catholic union that resisted were Münster and Gelsenkirchen, which kept in close touch.

Q: Were you also persecuted because of the stand you took and your resistance?

A.V.: The oppression came from REGEDE. The leaders were the gentlemen from the *German Deaf News* (*Deutsche Gehörlosen-Zeitung*). Several times I was reported on to the Gestapo and was kept under observation because the deaf paid attention to me. Around 1937 or 1938, a senior official from Nazi Public Welfare came to my home. He tried with various enticements such as free uniforms and food allowances to convince me to take over the leadership of the Nazi deaf associations in the Münster area. But I was able to hold that off.

> Q: Did you have to fear denunciation on the part of REGEDE members?
>
> A.V.: Yes, as I said, I was reported to the Gestapo. One example: In 1938 we celebrated the twenty-fifth anniversary of the Catholic Deaf Association in Münster. I gave the formal address. In the speech and in the celebration afterwards you could not express your political opinion. There was always a danger of being betrayed by Nazi followers who were also present.

Documented events from the Provincial Institution for the Deaf in Langenhorst verify Veltmann's statements about Nazi organizations' efforts to pressure deaf Catholic associations, and they show the effort of Nazi institutions to influence church-affiliated deaf education in the Münster area. The Langenhorst Institution was a school for Catholic deaf students in existence since 1841. In 1930, 114 students attended, instructed by 13 teachers, making it the largest Westphalian educational establishment for deaf pupils.[6] In the course of the coordination effort toward fascist educational principles, Catholic education at Langenhorst, and the teaching staff associated with the center before the seizure of power, came under the suspicion of Nazi ideologues.

In December of 1936, the senior president of the Province of Westphalia recommended for the Langenhorst staff a longtime Nazi Party member who was a candidate for training as a teacher of the deaf at the State Institution for the Deaf in Berlin-Neukölln. He argued that the appointment of a teacher from the ranks of long-term Nazi party members was "absolutely necessary because of the conditions" in Langenhorst.[7]

In a communication of March 25, 1937, this official gave additional arguments for the necessity of having a solid party member serve as teacher at the Langenhorst institution. He wrote that Herr Möhle, the teacher candidate whom he was recommending, "was a trusted National Socialist and party member long before the assumption of power." Furthermore, "as the bearer of the National Socialist world view and attitude," Möhle would help "to convert the deaf schools from their purely denominational orientation into National Socialist training institutions."[8] Möhle was admitted to the teacher training college, thus illustrating the strategy of the Nazi education policy to bring denominational schools under the control of the political apparatus.

Hermann Sommer

The turmoil and anxiety that entered the homes of deaf Germans with the enactment of the hereditary health law gripped the seven members of the family of deaf cabinetmaker Hermann Sommer of Kiel. The Kiel medical health center for hereditary and race welfare, in a letter of October 12, 1939, requested that the university audiology clinic in Kiel "examine cabinetmaker Hermann Sommer." The city medical officer appended a handwritten note: "As discussed by telephone, I am sending S. again with the request that his case be dealt with, if at all possible."[9] On February 24, 1940, the university ear, nose, and throat clinic of Kiel delivered its opinion that Sommer was hereditarily diseased, and on April 8, 1940, the Hereditary Health Court in Kiel ordered the personal appearance of Hermann Sommer at 10:30 A.M. on April 18, 1940, in Chamber 106 of the Justice Building at Schützenwall 31/35 in Kiel, "in the matter of his hereditary health case."[10] During the proceedings, a decision was made that Sommer must be sterilized.

Sommer did not let himself be intimidated, even by the summons of the health authority to appear within fourteen days at the surgical clinic in Kiel for sterilization, and despite the warning that "the operation can be performed without your consent in accordance with article 6, paragraph 2, of the amended version of the Hereditary Health Law."[11] Instead, Sommer decided to send a letter to the representative of the Führer, Dr. Leonardo Conti, who had been appointed Reich Physician Leader on April 22, 1939.

The fate of the deaf cabinetmaker was sealed, however, by Conti's inflexible position. The response to Sommer's letter said that "the decision of the hereditary health court of Kiel on April 18, 1940" to require "sterilization of cabinetmaker Hermann Sommer on the grounds of hereditary deafness" was a binding decision. "The clinic's examination has established that Sommer is deaf in both ears, that his sense of balance is fully in order, and that there is no evidence for adventitious injury."[12]

To the thirty-seven-year-old Sommer, father of six healthy, hearing children, this judgment seemed grossly wrong. He filed an appeal in the local court.[13] In its sitting "of June 12, 1940, with the participation of the senior counsel of the provincial court, Dr. Büldt, as chairman, the senior government and medical counsel, Dr. Lenz, and the naval physician, Dr. Warneke, as medical assessor," the superior hereditary health court of Kiel reached the following decision on the Sommer's appeal against the decision of the hereditary health court of Kiel of April 18, 1940: "The objection of the plaintiff, suspected of hereditary disease, against the decision of the hereditary health court of Kiel of April 18, 1940, is dismissed."[14] As grounds for the decision, the court referred to the "medical opinion of the university ear, nose and throat clinic of Kiel dated February 24, 1940." No attempt was made to obtain new information or to conduct genealogical research.[15]

Sommer appealed once more to Conti's office, which responded as follows:

National Socialist German Workers Party

The Representative of the Führer	Munich 33, August 30, 1940
Staff Karlstrasse 21	
Dr. Conti Div. IV/Prof. P/T.	

> Herr Hermann Sommer
> *Kiel-Wellinsdorf*
> Schönbergerstrasse 118

In connection with your submission I have undertaken a comprehensive examination of your hereditary health matter.

I fully understand that the sacrifice that you are called on to make strikes you very hard. I regret, however, not being able to free you from it, since the decision to which you object reflects the sense of the law. The decision of the Hereditary Health Court as well as that of the Superior Court correctly establishes the facts of your hereditary affliction, despite the exemption of your children.

I am unfortunately not in a position to undertake further action.

> Heil Hitler!
> (signature)
> Prof. Dr. Pakheiser

Karl Wacker

On September 17, 1945, during the American occupation of Germany, Karl Wacker's supervisor informed him that "at the request of the American Military Government he was immediately relieved of his duties." A deaf employee of the City Bank of Stuttgart, Wacker was accused of being an active member of the Nazi Party.[16] What had happened?

A Social Democrat, Wacker was true to his party until its official suppression on July 21, 1933. His later membership in the Nazi Party, which caused his problems with the occupation authorities, was instigated by the central REGEDE office in Berlin. In practice, however, during the period of Nazi rule Wacker kept faith with his social democratic convictions and fought for his threatened deaf comrades in Württemburg-Hohenzollern.

Wacker had called the attention of the American Military Government to his resistance efforts in his response to question 115 on the questionnaire that he had completed: "Were you ever detained or limited in your freedom of movement or choice of residence or otherwise in your freedom to pursue business or professional activities for racial or religious reasons or because you actively or passively resisted the National Socialists?" He answered yes and explained: "Because of the sterilization law . . . my family experienced restrictions on its freedom of movement, against which I fought in vain. I also had a great deal of trouble as an advocate of long-standing of the Württemburg deaf against repeated infringements and prejudicial acts."[17] Wacker's reference to his resistance activities was clearly not pursued by the American Military Government, and this oversight resulted in his condemnation as an active Nazi Party member and termination from his employment.

Wacker appealed the occupation authority's decision, and the Third Appeals Chamber of Stuttgart exonerated him on July 5, 1948.[18] It confirmed that "despite his formal membership in the Nazi party he had not simply been passive, but had offered active resistance to the best of his ability."[19] Indeed, in his capacity as chairman of the Association for the Welfare of the Deaf in Württemburg-Hohenzollern, Wacker had not only engaged himself personally on behalf of members who were prosecuted under the sterilization law, but he also openly opposed the work of the Superior Heredity Health Court in Stuttgart. In 1938, the Hereditary Health Court had sent Wacker an explanatory circular about the Law for the Prevention of Offspring with Hereditary Diseases. On August 2, 1938, he wrote the following response:

> I do not require further printed matter, as I will not propagandize among my fellow-sufferers. Your letter of explanation rather gives me the opportunity to state my position. In the past months, objections and complaints have been lodged by numerous deaf persons implicated under the law. These are just normal deaf people pursuing their livelihood. They are capable of earning their own living and are in no way a burden to the state. Why have they, nonetheless, been made to suffer such great pain through sterilization? A decent person could never understand this. In reality these persons, already heavily burdened in psychological terms, have undeservedly been demoted to second-class citizens. These people are not inferiors as your explanatory pamphlet sets out: "Moreover, they have no wish to reproduce." From the legal objections of several deaf persons, I have concluded to my great anger that they must comply under the threat of police force. Many have even been taken away by the police.
>
> As a defender of the deaf, I urgently request you that you take into consideration their capacity for work and do not implicate them under the law. For my part, I will engage my efforts so that the implementation of this inhuman law may be impeded as far as possible. I have committed myself to the welfare of my fellow-deaf and see it as my duty to take a firm stand.[20]

The Superior Hereditary Health Court in Stuttgart reacted sharply a few days later.[21] Their letter to Wacker began by saying "you are hereby informed that the applicability of the sterilization law is sustained." They then issued a warning that resistance would not be tolerated: "There can be no question of an act of clemency with exemption from the sterilization operation," which is "required for the well-being of our people and is also in the best interests of hereditarily diseased deaf persons." The letter went on to argue that sterilization was a "perfectly harmless

Karl Wacker, Born October 16, 1904 (photograph from 1927)

operation," and its only consequence, that is, the inability to have children, "corresponds to the wishes of the hereditarily diseased themselves." The conclusion must have frightened Wacker: "The Gestapo has been informed about you. Further written submissions will be added to the file without answer." [22]

Despite police scrutiny, Wacker continued to fight for deaf people who challenged the sterilization law, as documented by the following "affidavit for Herr Karl Wacker, director of the Home for the Aged Deaf in Winnenden," of December 22, 1946, which gives a firsthand look into the selection and elimination practices of the Nazis.

> In August 1940, I asked the director of the Home for the Aged Deaf in Stuttgart-Botnang (at present in Winnenden), Herr Karl Wacker, to admit my sister, NN, born on DD, 1882, who had been at the sanatorium in Weinsberg, in order to protect her from the threat of the selection process then taking place at the institution and the removal of its inmates.
>
> In consideration of the great danger that threatened my sister, Herr Wacker said that he was quite willing to take her into the home. Because Herr Wacker was known to me as a solicitous defender and advocate of his fellow-deaf and had always involved himself against the unjust prejudice toward the deaf, I thought that nothing would happen to my sister if she got into the home at Botnang.
>
> After about four weeks, Herr Wacker received an inquiry from the Ministry of the Interior, Stuttgart, Department of Public Health, asking whether my sister were in the home for the deaf in Botnang. Herr Wacker recognized at once that my sister was now being sought and would be prosecuted. He immediately asked me to take my sister and find her other accommodation. I did that and got her into a convent in Augsburg, where she still lives today in good health.
>
> My family and I must thank Herr Wacker that my sister did not become one of the many inmates of institutions who lost their lives. [23]

Between August 7, 1938, and the end of the war, Wacker lived in fear of his life, because he was under Gestapo supervision. This did not stop him, though, from continuing his efforts on behalf of other deaf people. It has not been possible to determine why Wacker was not arrested by the Gestapo.

Gertrud Jacob

Gertrud Jacob's story exemplifies the courageous efforts of deaf Germans to resist the effects of the sterilization law.[24] It demonstrates as well the law's capriciousness and the authorities' willingness to ignore evidence presented to them. Most of her story comes from a long interview that took place in London in 1983. She was then seventy-eight years old, well educated, and mentally active. She had lived in Prague, Czechoslovakia, and had been persecuted by the Nazis; she had been a widow since 1982. From her marriage she had two sons. They in turn had four daughters. To illustrate the absurdity of the Nazi hereditary health decisions in her case, she pointed to the fact that her descendants hear normally. The interview was conducted in German accompanied by German Sign Language.

> Q: How old were you at the time you were apprehended by the health authority in Gotha?
>
> G. J.: I was born in 1904. In 1936 the Nazi authorities began their persecution.
>
> Q: How do you explain the intervention of the Gotha health authorities a full two years after the implementation of the Law for the Prevention of Offspring with Hereditary Diseases?
>
> G.J.: From May 1933 to January 1934 I worked in Belgium, in the border area of Eupen, as an *au pair* on a big estate. Then from January to August 1934 I worked as an *au pair* for a couple posted to the consulate in Brussels. That was probably the reason why the Nazi authorities hadn't arrested me.
>
> Q: May I enquire about your reasons for returning to Germany?
>
> G.J.: Of course. First, my parents asked me to come back, and, second, disappointment in a personal relationship prompted me to leave beautiful Belgium. In 1935 I was still able to attend the World Games for the Deaf in London. On my return from London I lived and worked at my parents' place in Gotha.
>
> Q: Who informed on you under the provisions of article 3 to sections 3 and 4 of the ordinance for the implementation of the sterilization law?
>
> G.J.: At that time, no one; I went to the health authority on my own.
>
> Q: Did you want to be voluntarily sterilized?

G.J.: For heaven's sake! I would never have done that voluntarily. No, after I read the Marriage Health Law [The Marriage Health Law of October 18, 1935, *Reich Law Gazette*, 1935, Part I, p. 1246] and without consulting anyone, I went to the health authority to have a marriage fitness certificate issued, so that whatever happened I would have it in my pocket, if I wanted to go abroad again. Still, I tried afterwards to write to Herr Weinert, a teacher of the deaf, to ask some questions. But I never thought that it was a trap.[25]

Q: Did the senior teacher Weinert ask you for a marriage fitness certificate?

G.J.: At that time I sent him a statement from my father in which he described how I became deaf as a result of an accident when I was two years and nine months old. But the two years and nine months wasn't enough for Weinert. He demanded an official certificate. I still have Weinert's letter from 1937. Just read it![26]

Q: Did they issue the marriage fitness certificate that you wanted?

G.J.: No. That's when my persecution began. It was accompanied by indescribable mental suffering.

Q: On what grounds did the health authority refuse to issue the marriage fitness certificate?

G.J.: They referred to the so-called Marriage Health Law and classified me as hereditarily diseased. According to the law at the time, the hereditarily diseased were not to marry.[27]

Q: But you had already established that you became deaf because of an accident when you were two years and nine months old. There can't have been any hereditary disease.

G.J.: That's what I said, too. That's why I was so indignant at the position of the Nazi doctors at the health authority in Gotha.

Q: What did you try to do about it?

G.J.: First of all I tried to get abroad again, to work as an *au pair*. But the Nazi authorities struck out the exit visa in my passport. They told me that I wouldn't be able to leave the country again until after the sterilization. After this setback, I submitted my father's statement and three more affidavits that all confirmed what my father had said. You can read them yourself:

> (Transcript) Gotha, November 19, 1936. Affidavit Richard Jacob, a master stovefitter, affirms that his daughter Gertrud, who was born on December 11, 1904, in my home on Dietrich Eckhardtstrasse 64, was a hearing child and lost her hearing through an accident. While on her way home in the company of her mother, Frau Jacob, the child was struck

on the head by a soccer ball kicked by youngsters playing on Mykoniusplatz. The child's face was very swollen and Gertrud was immediately treated by the ear specialist, Dr. Rosenbaum. [signed] Friedericke Bomberg.

Q: Did the health authorities in Gotha accept the affidavits that you presented and recognize you as hereditarily healthy?

G.J.: No, just the opposite. The medical officer for the Gotha city district made an application that I be sterilized because of hereditary deafness.

Q: What could have been the reason for the Nazi doctor to notify the authorities about you, despite the clear counterevidence? Were your parents known to be opponents of the Nazi regime?

G.J.: No, my parents had not attracted any attention. The health authority in Gotha would have easily been able to find out that my cousin had also gone deaf. It was the recommendation from the Gotha health authority. At considerable trouble, I had been obliged to complete a three-foot-long family tree on the ASTEL model for the Thuringian König family. Without it, the health authority certainly would not have been able to pass a preliminary judgment against me. I have in my possession a letter from my cousin A. K., dated November 4, 1937. At our request, he informed us in the letter that we should know that he lost his hearing due to ear infections. The Erfurt professor had also told my cousin that it was too late to save his hearing. He continued: "In the case of your little Trudie [Gertrud Jacob], the misfortune occurred as a child, but it has nothing to do with the hereditary health authority. Trudie has heard and spoken as everyone knows. You also know quite well that in our family there has been no single case of hearing loss. She and I are the ones to be pitied, even though we have come to our suffering by such different routes." I have also preserved an affidavit from his father G. K. It describes how his firstborn son, A. K., became deaf. I should point out that he also had three brothers and sisters with normal hearing. In addition, by that time my cousin had already had a healthy hearing daughter. So, this was a screaming injustice. They were just trying to construct a hereditary disease. There was also a decision from the hereditary health court in Arnstadt. The session took place on March 28, 1938, in the provincial court house in Gotha.

I was there with my sister S. by request. In the decree from the Hereditary Health Court it said: "The dressmaker G. J., born on November 12, 1904, in Gotha and still a resident there, is to be sterilized." When this judgment was pronounced, I jumped up angrily and shouted at the judges and doctors: "That is terribly unjust! I would rather go and hang myself!" But the panel of judges just withdrew in silence.[28] In the decision, explicit reference was made to my cousin's deafness. In the grounds for the judgment was written—let me read it to you: "The defendant suffers from hereditary deafness. This is confirmed by the assessment of the medical officer and that of the university clinic and polyclinic for ear, nose and throat diseases in Jena dated January 6, 1938." I can still clearly remember that medical evaluation. The examination was conducted by Professor Johannes Zange. It didn't even take five minutes. Zange didn't leave a very favorable impression on me. Otherwise, he was also the medical consultant to the superior hereditary health court in Jena. I still have a newspaper article in which his consultant's activity is praised.

I can also remember a letter from my father to Professor Zange in Jena written on December 18, 1937. In it, he wrote that he had not been able to come to Jena for the examination of his daughter G. J. of Gotha, but that he had been represented by another daughter, S. S. According to the account of Frau S. S., he could not state his agreement with the results, *for what had happened thirty years earlier was a fact and could not be erased by a law. "My daughter heard and spoke! Her hearing suffered badly as a result of an accident"* [29] [speaker's emphasis].

Let me read you some more from the grounds for the decision. The expert opinion, the one that Zange gave, reads: "On the basis of findings made concerning the blood relatives Gertrud Jacob and August König, we come to the conclusion that hereditary deafness is present. The evidence is, firstly, the burden on the family line of two deaf persons in the same generation."

Then there are some medical grounds that don't mean anything to me. But there is another piece of insolence at the end of the statement. I simply have to read this to you, because it just doesn't hold up.

> Also, the statement of parents and relatives that the child heard in the past is, in the case of such small children, to be evaluated with the same caution, since it is difficult even for an experienced ear doctor to prove definitely that the faculty of hearing is present at that age. The statement that the child spoke is to be evaluated in the same way, since the babbling of little children is frequently perceived by relatives as words already being repeated.

You can see, it's laughable. My oldest son was saying individual words at ten months of age; my parents confirmed this for me. I also know that he was already saying "please" and clapping his hands. You can see clearly, the Nazis didn't want to admit the truth, that I was already able to speak. That would have upset their theories of heredity.

Q: Did you challenge the verdict of the hereditary health court?

G.J.: Yes, I knew that there was still the possibility of an appeal, to the superior hereditary health court. I then immediately wrote a letter of objection and sent it to the superior hereditary health court in Jena. Please read the letter.

Q: Was your objection acknowledged?

G.J.: Yes, there was a session of the superior hereditary health court in Jena on May 20, 1938.[30]

> The matter is clear. There are no grounds to defer the decision until Gertrud Jacob gets an additional expert medical opinion. It would reach no other conclusion than those of the assessment of the university ear, nose, and throat clinic in Jena. Gertrud Jacob must then be sterilized. It is inadmissible to refrain from this measure on the grounds of her intellectual comptence and admirable qualities of character. Here it is simply a matter that her unimpeachably identified predisposition to deafness not be transferred to a future generation. Deafness or hearing loss, which are practically the same in her case, is always a severe impairment for a gifted person, and thus the predisposition must also be eradicated.

By a written power of attorney, I had my mother represent me. My sister and her husband were also there.

Q: Now there was no further legal recourse for you. Did you see any way of challenging this unjust verdict?

G.J.: First, I would have to say that my outrage had been replaced by horror and a deep resignation. For nights I was unable to sleep. I was always thinking about it, whether there might not still be some way to get out of it. After some days I decided to take further steps. First I wrote a personal letter to Adolf Hitler. In my despair I thought that I simply had to find the courage to write directly to him. He was the only one who could still prevent the injustice.

As a second step I turned to the district inspector of REGEDE, Herr Arthur Weber. He was a helpful man, not one of the horrible REGEDE Nazis. He took care of getting expert statements from my former teacher, Rittmeier, and my deaf school principal, Schlechtweg, both from Erfurth. In addition, and this I must appreciate as an especially courageous deed, he got me an expert opinion from the head of the university ear clinic in Leipzig, one that had been written up in another case. In doing this, he exposed himself to the danger of being deported to a concentration camp. I still have an original letter from the district inspector of REGEDE, A. Weber.[31] Among other things it states: "In my experience the hereditary health courts set great store by the judgments of teachers and institutions for the deaf." Herr Weber's recommendation was that the head of the deaf school in Erfurth (Director Schlechtweg, ret.) should be consulted, since he could make an objective judgment on the basis of his many years of experience. Herr Schlechtweg was my former teacher, a very qualified man who knew me well as a student. After a brief conversation with my sister we immediately went to him in Erfurth. This was June 30, 1938. After he had heard what I could expect if convicted, he immediately set down the facts about me. In the meantime my situation had become dramatically more critical. On June 27, 1938, I received a summons from the state health authority in Gotha to let myself be sterilized within two weeks.[32] You can understand that I was near despair. It was awful! The letter threatened the use of police force.

Q: In this situation did you see any possibility at all of escaping from your persecution?

G.J.: I bought myself a book with the law text and studied it in the evenings. Suddenly I found a way out, and it was right in the law for the protection of hereditary health—then the Nazis called it the Marriage Fitness Law, I think. In the legislation it states in section 5 that when the fiancé has foreign citizenship, the law is not applicable.[33] The health authority could itself have stated that in the event of marriage to a foreigner the sterilization operation did not need to be performed. But no, they wanted to sterilize first. So I had to find that paragraph myself. You can imagine how happy I was. I regained hope and new courage.

Q: Please forgive me. I don't want to pry into your private life. If you find my question impolite you don't need to answer it. Section 5 of the marriage fitness law that you named wasn't really applicable to you. You weren't engaged to be married, were you?

G.J.: Now I'll have to make my story a bit longer. In 1931 the World Games for the Deaf, the Deaf Olympics if you like, you know this already, were held in Nuremberg. There I made a passing acquaintanceship with a nice, cultivated gentleman from Czecho-slovakia. I didn't think at that time that he would be my future husband. In 1935, we met again by chance at the World Games for the Deaf in London. He knew some German. So we kept in ever closer touch. Thus our common fate was sealed forever. Now when I received the summons from the health authority in Gotha that I had to be sterilized in two weeks, I wrote to my friend in Prague that he should come as soon as possible. He already knew why he should come quickly and he did as I wanted. I should tell you that our marriage plans had met repeated opposition from our families. These objections were of a nationalist kind and centered on the question of whether the hearing impaired of different nationalities should be allowed to get married at all. But because of the active threat of sterilization, suddenly my family in Gotha and his father in Prague agreed to the marriage. So we drafted a letter to the health authority in Gotha and sent it off. Please read it.

Gotha, June 27, 1938
To the Public Health Authority, Gotha

On June 27, 1938, a communication from the Public Health Authority was addressed to my fiancée, Fräulein Gertrud Jacob, Löwenstrasse 13, Gotha, instructing her to present herself for sterilization. Attached you will find my statement sworn under oath that I, NN, am a citizen of Czechoslovakia, who intends to enter into matrimony with Fräulein Gertrud Jacob.

According to section 5 of the Law for the Prevention of Offspring with Hereditary Diseases, sterilization is not applicable if the fiancé is a foreign national. This is true in the present case and I would kindly ask you to nullify the decision.

Respectfully yours,
NN

In that way my dear husband saved me from the grip of the Nazis. I am grateful to him to this day even after his death. And so to fulfill his wishes I continue to live in Czechoslovakia. Whatever I have had to experience in that beautiful country— what will always be for me a foreign country among people speaking a different language—I still long for dear Germany, my old home. It was not easy for me to leave. I also want to tell you that I suffered more fateful blows at the hands of the Nazis. During the period of the Nazi occupation, my father-in-law was taken away to the concentration camp in Mauthausen and was killed there. Also my brother-in-law, my husband's only brother, was summarily shot by the SS after the assassination attempt against Heydrich. So you see, the horrible decision of the Third Reich changed my life, and today I still suffer psychologically from it.

Q: Please let me return to the personal persecution that you experienced. You said that you had sent a letter to Adolf Hitler. Was it answered?

G.J.: After I found the relevant section that offered me the possibility of evading the Nazi authorities, and after my fiancé and I had sent in the certificate that we intended to get married, it really didn't matter to me what form the response from the Reich Chancellery would take. As was to be expected, I did not receive a reply from Hitler himself, but one transmitted by the president of the Superior Provincial Court in Jena.[34] The content was also what you might expect. But now it didn't any longer have any effect on me. Thanks to the generous personal intervention of my future husband, I was saved. But I still wasn't completely free, because the law stipulated a waiting period. Although the health authority was free to make its own resolutions, it had to obtain the decision from the Reich Ministry in Weimar. Moreover, not all who were exposed to the same fate as I managed to escape. They, too, had to bow before the coercion of the sterilization law, despite the fact that they were married to foreigners. We had submitted our papers. But it still wasn't enough. The Gotha registry office required, even before certifying the marriage as legal, that we submit a marriage fitness certificate from the city of Prague and the birth certificates of my fiancé's parents. For a foreigner, it all seemed unbelievable.

Jacob's interview and the documents she provided lead to several conclusions, one of which is that even persons whose deafness was clearly not hereditary were identified and prosecuted under the Law for the Prevention of Offspring with Hereditary Diseases.* The expert opinions of Nazi doctors that supported decisions in the hereditary health courts were perfunctorily drawn up and served primarily to buttress Nazi theories of heredity, sug-

---

*Additional documents relating to Jacobs are available in Appendix 3. *Pub.*

gesting intentional efforts to inflate the number of people who could be sterilized. Counterevidence was rejected as untested. It also appears evident that those affected by the sterilization law were not informed of the possibility of formal legal recourse, and that the only way the law's effects could be avoided was either to have oneself admitted to a private institution or by Jacob's solution, marriage to a foreigner.

7

The Jewish Deaf in Germany

BEFORE WORLD WAR II, the Israelite Institution for the Deaf of Germany at Berlin-Weissensee was a flourishing educational, cultural, and religious center. Approximately one thousand deaf German Jews attended the school.[1] Except for a plaque mounted on the building, there is nothing to recall the life of this institution. At the time of my research, twenty-two former students were still alive and residing in Israel, the United States, and Germany.

The Israelite Institution for the Deaf was founded by Markus Reich, a young Jewish man from Kolin, Bohemia. His life in deaf education began after he made the acquaintance of a deaf man who was educated, well brought up, and could speak. Reich determined that he wanted to "make complete, worthy, happy people of the deaf," and so, in 1865 at the age of twenty-one, he went to Germany, where he hoped he "would learn everything that would qualify him as a teacher of the deaf."[2] Reich studied at the Jewish Teachers Training College in Berlin. The director of the college recognized Reich's exceptional pedagogical gifts, promoted his studies, and exempted him from a year of training. He supported himself through work as a private tutor. From the little he earned, he saved money to procure books about the deaf and deafness. In the years 1870–1871 he worked and studied at the Royal Institution for the Deaf in Berlin, where he took his final examination as a teacher of the deaf and where he noticed that "very often children, especially Jewish children, were denied admission" to the school.[3] Reich then conceived of a plan to establish a Jewish institution for deaf children.

Reich's inspiration for this effort came from two religious sources. First was the "special admonition to support the deaf within the Jewish community," that the Chief Rabbi of London, S. Adler, had made in his 1864 tract *The Morning and the Evening Sacrifice* based on Isaiah 29.18: "Is it not a duty that falls to all of us to take up these children and to protect them on behalf of God, to educate them so that, as the prophet tells us, every day the deaf may hear the word of the book."[4] Second was a passage in the Talmud: "Only the ignorant are truly poor."[5]

Reich turned his plan into a reality, founding in 1873 the Israelite Institution for the Deaf of Germany (*Israelitische Taubstummenanstalt für Deutschland*) in a small house in Fürstenwalde an der Spree. Now along with language training and school

The plaque mounted on the building that was the Israelite Institution for the Deaf in Berlin-Weissensee. It reads, "From this building 146 deaf Jewish citizens were removed by fascist bandits in 1942 and murdered. In remembrance of the dead and as admonition to the living."

The Israelite Institution for the Deaf of Germany, Berlin-Weissensee

studies, he could "preserve and plant in the hearts of the Jewish deaf the religion of their forefathers."[6]

The first years were difficult and filled with privations. Reich was poor, as were most of the twelve children entrusted to him. Following his marriage in 1879, his wife Emma and her sister Anna helped tirelessly in the education of the deaf children. Reich finally decided, in 1884 when facing another fiscal crisis, to form a support organization called "Friends of the Deaf" (*Jedide Ilmim*) for his institution. Well-to-do members of the Jewish community joined together and provided funding, enabling Reich to relocate his school to Weissensee near Berlin, in 1890.

Reich could now "devote himself entirely to the mission of raising and educating his deaf children."[7] The institution continued to expand, and by 1911, he employed four male and two female teachers and had forty-five students. In the same year, work began on rebuilding the institution in Weissensee, supported by the association, which "already counted thousands of members and had a representative in every locality" of Germany.[8] However, Reich did not live to see the completion; he died on May 23, 1911.

Reich's death marked the loss of one of the great men in German deaf education. In a testimonial following his death, one of the school's teachers wrote, "Reich had wholeheartedly entered the world and the being of the deaf. Thus he also used the language of the deaf, sign language, as few hearing persons have ever done. . . . Reich fully mastered sign language and he never let himself be prevented from making use of it whenever it was appropriate, including in teaching. . . . To us teachers, Markus Reich was a true friend and trustworthy counselor."[9]

The entire staff of the institution and in particular the Friends of the Deaf felt obligated to maintain the school in the spirit of its founder and to continue his work after his death. The educational administration and business affairs passed to the hands of Emma Reich, his widow.

The First World War strained the institution. Three teachers were drafted, and the enrollment dropped to thirty-four students. In 1919, Felix Reich assumed the directorship, committed to continuing in his father's spirit. He was able to overcome the difficulties associated with Germany's postwar inflation, thus ensuring the institution's survival.

In order to present the school's educational successes to the outside world, Reich authored numerous publications for the Union of German Teachers of the Deaf. The Friends of the Deaf continued their support. In 1926 the Association of Former Students of the Institution established a publication, *The Link* (*Das Band*), for former students. Reich also encouraged alumni to support the school through the Association for the Advancement of the Interests of the Jewish Deaf with which a special fund and foundation, the Bloch and Meseritz Foundation, were associated. By the 1931–1932 school year, enrollment had reached an all-time high of fifty-nine pupils.[10]

The high quality of the educational training at the Jewish institution was evident in the results of the final vocational examinations of its former students and in the fact that the school's example led the Prussian state to open the first German secondary school for deaf students.[11] German professionals in deaf education acknowledged the successes of the Weissensee school in congratulatory speeches on the occasion of the school's fiftieth anniversary in October 1923.[12] The institution also enjoyed positive recognition abroad, resulting in an increase in the number of students entering the school from other countries. Of the fifty-five children enrolled in 1927, nineteen were deaf Jewish children from abroad.[13]

Throughout its life, the institution set high goals for its students. In describing the school in 1930, Felix Reich wrote that "instruction scarcely differs from that of other institutions, at most in that no definitive rejection of sign language was ever made and that the development of the mind and spirit, and not simply the acquisition of language, was considered the greatest goal." The school also provided classes for gifted children and remedial instruction for those who needed it.[14]

The efforts of the educational leadership and the teaching staff of the institution "to train the spirits and hands of the children so that they could succeed in life, and in addition to give them religious feeling and qualities of character so that they became happy individuals" are reflected in the many different occupations that were taken up by former students. By October 1927, a total of 227 students had attended the institution. Table 7.1 lists the occupations of the school's alumni.

When the Nazis took power in Germany, Jewish deaf people were the first group to be delivered to a power apparatus specifically created for their extermination. Initially it was not from brown-uniformed hearing persons, well known to them from daily encounters, that they suffered harassment, denunciation, curses, and persecution, but from their fellow deaf, the Nazi deaf. Soon after the general seizure of power and with brutal force, the deaf Nazi leaders went to work to expel Jews from the deaf associations. They clearly had no compunction about divesting long-serving, deserving members of their rights, as a notice in the

Table 7.1. Occupations of Former Students
of the Israelite Institution for the Deaf

Occupation	Number
Bookbinder	10
Brushmaker	4
Coachman	1
Dental technician	8
Dressmaker	31
Florist	1
Furrier	4
Gardener	2
Hatmaker	2
Hairdresser	1
Housekeeper	26
Laundress	1
Lithographer	2
Locksmith	2
Mechanic, electrician, watchmaker	10
Milliner	5
Saddler, leatherworker	4
Salesman	1
Seamstress	1
Shoemaker	4
Signpainter	4
Smith	1
Student of physics	1
Tailor	24
Tobacconist	2
Typesetter	14
Typist	1
Woodcarver, cabinetmaker, turner	14
Workman	1
No vocation because of mental impairment	13
No vocation because of poor eyesight	6
Transferred to other schools	26

Dr. Felix Reich (arrow) with Students and Sponsors in front of the Institution, 1929

Jewish Review (Jüdische Rundschau) of August 15, 1933, makes clear:

> We are informed: By order of the Reich association leaders for the German deaf [Albreghs and Ballier], all deaf Jewish members are to be expelled from the associations. This affects in part members who have belonged to their club for decades, have had senior positions of responsibility, and deserve well of the association. In Berlin, for example, 33 deaf Jews were expelled from the General Association for Support of the Deaf, among whom a number of well-deserving members of the board. Quite a large number of the excluded, who had been members for more than 20 years, among whom one deaf woman who had been a member for 57 years, since 1876, were especially hard hit by these measures, since in their advanced age they have lost the right, acquired through earlier contributions, to their monthly subsidy.

Pressure on the deaf Jews increased in the 1930s, and was eventually also exerted by hearing Nazis. The implementation of the sterilization law threw deaf people of Jewish faith into the same state of anxiety and fear as their Christian counterparts. The Union of Orthodox Rabbis of Germany, with its seat in Frankfurt am Main, and the Association of Rabbis of Traditional Law Observance of Germany, with its seat in Altona, urged their members to communicate in their sermons that Jewish religious law did not permit sterilization and that no religious Jew should apply for sterilization on his own or another's behalf, but such admonitions could not check the racist delusions.[15] Some deaf Jews fell victim to the Law for the Prevention of Offspring with Hereditary Diseases and were sterilized.

The increasing repression of the Jews and their exclusion from the social welfare protection system of the state led disabled Jews to form a self-help organization, the Cooperative Association of the Jewish Physically Impaired of Germany, with its seat in Berlin. Subsequently, the preexisting organizations of the Jewish deaf—the Association for the Advancement of the Jewish Deaf in Germany, the Association of Former Students of the Israelite Institution for the Deaf in Weissensee, and the branch associations for the advancement of the interests of the Jewish deaf—joined forces as Co-operative Group 3 (Jewish Deaf) of the new organization.[16]

Felix Reich attempted within his limited means to continue the educational activities at Weissensee, even as teachers were forced to emigrate and some students fled the barbarity with their parents. In August of 1939 Reich tried to get eight of his youngest students to safety in England. Soon after they reached London, Hitler began his assault against Poland, ending Reich's plan to bring out more of his deaf charges from Berlin and Weissensee. Shortly after England's entry into the war, Reich, who had been a front-line officer during the First World War, was arrested and later interned by the British.

The Fate of Those Who Remained

Now a time of terrible suffering began for the Jewish deaf who were still in Germany, a time that only a few would survive. Most were deported and sent to the camps. They were never heard from again. Some went into hiding and survived with the help of non-Jewish Germans. The following brief historical sketch shows the courage of one such German.

In early 1943, the pace of deportations quickened and, along with the thousands of Jews who fell victim to the night raids, there were people wearing the yellow star who were hauled away from their work places. But at this late hour, there were also Germans who would not give in. One of these was Otto Weidt, a little man with a lined face, who ran a small factory on Rosenthalerstrasse in Berlin, where blind and deaf Jews worked. Documents show that over the course of years he employed 165 disabled Jews, hid 65 of them, and looked after their food, shelter, and various amenities. He was arrested eleven times by the Gestapo, and had his premises searched 52 times between 1940 and 1945. Weidt had the heart of a lion and great human compassion. He fought for the life of each Jew who had sought refuge in his house or workshop, but only 27 of those protected by him survived the war years.[17]

Weidt continued to come up with new ways to provide food for those he was caring for. His life was always in danger when he was arranging false papers or when his was moving "his" Jews from one hiding place to another. His bravest act of rescue occurred in January 1943. When he went to his factory in the morning, he found that in the course of the previous night the Gestapo had arrested all the blind and deaf Jews that he employed. At that point all his workers were in a collection center in Greater Hamburgerstrasse, about to be deported. Weidt, never at a loss for a way out, went to the camp. It remains Weidt's secret how he managed to save his disabled workers, yet on a late afternoon in January 1943, a group of deaf, blind, and otherwise disabled Jews trooped through Berlin, happy to be led by Otto Weidt. But their joy at their recovered freedom did not last long, for one after another all the Jews were removed from Weidt's enterprise, among them the Jewish deaf.[18]

A deaf painter from the community of Floss in the Bavarian Forest, David Ludwig Bloch, survived the Dachau concentration camp, escaped to Shanghai, lived there for nine years, and immigrated to the United States. He has incorporated his memories of the Holocaust in a series of oppressive paintings and wood- and lino-cuts.

The story of another survivor, whose mother was a Protestant Christian and whose father was a Jew, shows how race-hygiene-oriented teachers of the deaf dealt with deaf persons who did not fit into their concept of making the German people more purely "Aryan." The deaf man was a member of the Jewish religious community. He described to me how he had attended the Israelite Institution for the Deaf in Berlin-Weissensee. He had had to break off his apprenticeship after one year because of a "mean plot." He made clear later what he meant by that. "The senior teacher, Herr Liepelt, who was a strong Nazi supporter, went one day to my supervisor and told him that I was not of Aryan extraction, but Jewish. Herr Liepelt was known for denouncing Jews, whether they were children, young people, or adults."

Now the betrayed apprentice tried to get by on his own. He always filled out employment applications incorrectly with regard to his religion. When he finally succeeded in getting a job with a company for a longer period, "Liepelt showed up again, now in the capacity of sign language interpreter. He had already persecuted me and betrayed me on the grounds of my religion, and now again, so that I was let go without notice."

With this the trials of this deaf Jew became even greater.

> Because of false statements concerning my religion and because of the sabotage that was going on in factories, as well as the fact that I was descended from Jews and so refused to work in the armaments industry for the war and conquest efforts of the Nazis, I was arrested in 1940, '41, '43, and '45, during which time I was mocked, beaten and mishandled.
>
> I can never forget any of it; it was terrible. The scars on my head from the mistreatment are still visible.

The Nazis had this man under arrest for thirty-three months in different jails. There were also briefer detentions.

> During this time Herr Liepelt was the interpreter and he always brought up the fact that I was of Jewish extraction, a "blood Jew" as he called it. Instead of helping me, he just made everything worse.

8

Sterilization's Legacy

THERE ARE no simple medical criteria by which to measure the consequences of sterilization. After analyzing almost 2,000 accounts of victims of the sterilization law (of which 1,215 are deaf), however, I agree with another scholar's statement that behind the effects of compulsory sterilization lies "the problem of the irreversible violation of physical integrity."[1]

Sterilization Procedures

The usual method of sterilizing men was to sever the sperm duct (vasectomy). As the operation was performed in the transitional area between the groin and the scrotum, that is, outside the abdominal cavity, it was considered relatively inconsequential and was as a rule carried out with local anesthesia, frequently as an outpatient procedure. But the sterilization of women, even in the eyes of those responsible for the sterilization law, was considered a "serious bodily intrusion."[2]

By the 1930s, more than one hundred female sterilization procedures were known.[3] One of these was by way of the vagina. This procedure spared the woman an incision into the abdominal cavity, but it was hardly ever practiced because it was judged too unreliable in terms of the intended "success" of the operation, that is, the future infertility of the woman. For this reason, in almost all cases a laparotomy was practiced, in other words, surgical incision through the abdomen. This operation necessarily involved general anesthesia.

After the abdominal cavity was breached, the most frequently employed methods of sterilization were the crushing, severing, or removal of the Fallopian tubes. Some surgeons opted for the "surest" procedure, however, which was the removal of the uterus. This method was particularly promoted and practiced by Gustav Boeters in Thüringen. Boeters argued that "only the surgically removed, and carefully identified and preserved uterus guarantees the one hundred percent certainty that is desired by the Führer, and can in no instance lead to further recourse to sterilization efforts."[4]

The older methods, simple removal or ligature of the tubes, were seldom practiced because of the high failure rate. The dangerous but bloodless practice of sterilization by X rays became legally permissible in 1936, after an elevated number of fatalities due to other methods had led to unrest and criticism in the general population. This method was employed infrequently before 1939; after that date it was used particularly when the women to be sterilized opposed the operation or were in concentration camps.[5]

The choice of operation method was basically the decision of physicians, who exercised this authority in varying degrees. The fact is that "the sterilization law offered surgeons and gynecologists a broad field for experimentation on human subjects in order to test new operational procedures."[6]

The Trivialization of Surgical Sterilization

Statements by those sterilized contrast starkly with the attempts of Nazi propagandists to trivialize the operation as an inconsequential surgical intervention. Leaflets like that reproduced in figure 8.1 suggested to those affected that the measure was harmless; it was often compared to an appendectomy.

Even some educators of deaf students characterized the "experience of sterilization" as thoroughly positive. In order "to still the anxiety of parents," Herbert Weinert published two statements from parents whose deaf children had been sterilized:

My son Heinz H. has just been sterilized in an operation. As a single mother, I have to welcome wholeheartedly that this was done to my son, if for no other reason than to avoid later mentally inferior offspring. I would also like to note that after this operation my son has suffered no negative effects. On the contrary, in mental terms he does better than before.

I let my congenitally deaf and dumb son, born in 1930, be sterilized for purely eugenic reasons when he was 13 years old. My son got over the operation quite promptly. He does gymnastics, swims, cycles, makes day-long hikes and performs heavy physical work in the third year of his apprenticeship as a baker. He has never complained about pains around the incision or otherwise complained about his abdomen. In his mental development as well we have noted no impairment nor any new demands on us as a result of the sterilization.[7]

A forcibly sterilized deaf woman, who still complains of long-term psychological effects, gave me a note written by a state-

---

An Informative Circular on Sterilization

(pursuant to article 2, paragraph 3, of the ordinance for the implementation of the Law for the Prevention of Offspring with Hereditary Diseases of December 5, 1933, *Reich Law Gazette* 1: p. 1021)

The objective of sterilization, that is, the termination of the reproductive capacity of men and women, is to prevent the further transmission of hereditary disease. Such diseases are congenital feeblemindedness, schizophrenia, manic-depressive insanity, hereditary epilepsy, hereditary St. Vitus' Dance (Huntington's chorea), hereditary blindness, hereditary deafness, severe hereditary bodily malformation, as well as severe alcoholism.

Sterilization is performed as follows: without the removal of the testicles or ovaries, the spermatic cords or Fallopian tubes are tied off, made impassable, or are severed.

The operation is performed by professional physicians in medical facilities designated for this purpose.

No negative consequences for the health of either men or women are to be feared from sterilization. Sexual sensation and the capacity for sexual intercourse are not affected by the operation.

Figure 8.1. Example of Nazi Propaganda Concerning Sterilization

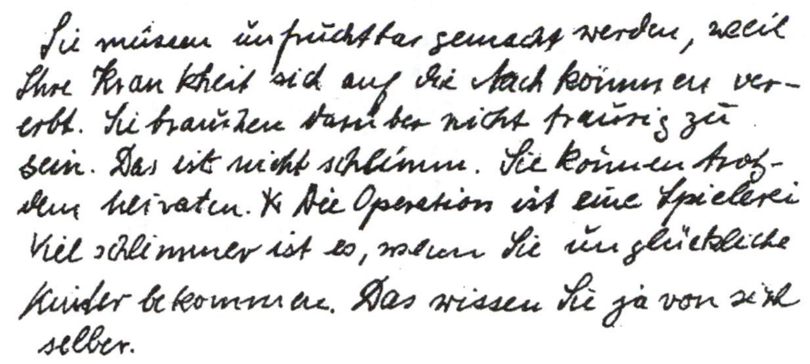

[handwritten German text:]

Sie müssen unfruchtbar gemacht werden, weil Ihre Krankheit sich auf die Nachkommen vererbt. Sie brauchen darüber nicht traurig zu sein. Das ist nicht schlimm. Sie können trotzdem heiraten. X Die Operation ist eine Spielerei. Viel schlimmer ist es, wenn Sie unglückliche Kinder bekommen. Das wissen Sie ja von sich selber.

Contents of the note:

You must be sterilized because your disease would be inherited by your offspring. But you do not need to be sad about it. It's not so bad. You can still marry. The operation is a trifle. It would be much worse to have miserable children. You know that yourself.

Figure 8.2. Letter from a Berlin Doctor Regarding the Sterilization Operation

employed Berlin doctor fifty years earlier, in which he tried to make the operation she was facing more "attractive" (see fig. 8.2).

Nazi doctors attempted to trivialize the operation even though they knew better. This is clear from a letter from the German Federation of Physicians, dated November 7, 1932, and addressed to the Reich Ministry of the Interior. It requested that "a federal law be enacted as speedily as possible, under which sterilization would be permitted for eugenic reasons and regulated."[8] Aware of the complexity of the operation as well as of the accompanying risks and potential long-term consequences, the physicians called for "a cautious approach":

> Too far-reaching an intervention by the state could discredit these good intentions for a long time. Especially in the case of women, surgical sterilization is not completely without risk and, even though in general the patient suffers no harm to her physical and mental well-being and behavior, the decisive elimination of the possibility of reproduction is such a grave intrusion into the personality that it must be surrounded by extensive safeguards.[9]

Even the president of a hereditary health court during the Nazi period raised concerns about the effects of the sterilization operation. In May 1935, the Reich Ministry of Justice criticized the Hereditary Health Court of Münster because that office "had suspended the procedure in seventeen cases." The president of the Hereditary Health Court in Münster justified the suspension of the court process "in view of the particularly favorable domestic conditions" in the case of a deaf woman from the Münster district born in 1896. The senior judge of the court continued: "Consideration has also been made of the fact that in the case of women this is a serious operation."[10]

More recent medical literature also offers evidence that sterilization is "no trifle but rather a grave intrusion into the complexity and depth of our humanity."[11] In a 1965 discussion of possible eugenics laws, the German Federal Attorney General stated that

> sterilization on biological grounds, that is, in consideration of demographic policy [that is, eugenics], is inadmissible, since the ethical views of the general population thus far do not support to any appreciable degree sterilization for biological reasons. The Federal Attorney General's Office calls particular attention to the fact that sterilization—generally the ligature of the Fallopian tubes in the case of a woman—represents a violation of physical integrity with very serious consequences, since the elimination of reproductive capability is a procedure that cannot be reversed.[12]

The Consequences of Sterilizations

A number of deaf people who were sterilized described their feelings and experiences to me. Here are ten typical accounts of their experiences:[13]

> 1. Male, born in 1921:
> On January 30 of this year we watched the TV program about the terrible injustices that the Nazis did to the deaf. It was a monstrous violation of human rights. . . . This program had a great emotional effect on deaf victims of the Nazis. The whole horrible past was brought back to life again. The terrible suffering and complete powerlessness of the deaf during the Third Reich, the hopes for the end of the war, and then complete resignation after many

years of fighting in vain for just compensation for the Nazi atrocities. . . . You also have to remember that the marriage partners of deaf persons who were sterilized were also greatly affected because of the absence of children and the lifelong incompleteness of marital relations (even though it's not mentioned). How great and strong one's love has to be in order to remain faithful! So the spouses of the forcibly sterilized are also to be counted among the victims of the Nazis.[14]

2. Female, born 1918:

   I was forcibly sterilized by the Nazis in July 1938. It was an extremely painful torture, the doctor bored around in the sensitive part of my vagina with his finger. I suffered terrible pain. . . . Throughout my marriage with a deaf husband I have had pains as a result of the operation. Even today the pains are often very intense. Almost always I have pain during intercourse with my husband. While other women have orgasms and experience the joy of lovemaking, the pain from the operation scars kills all pleasure for me. It caused me a lot of grief that I couldn't have a child. I like being a housewife and would have really enjoyed being a mother. All the people whom I get to know well ask me why I don't have any children.[15]

3. Female, born 1914:

   I too belong to the forcibly sterilized. My ancestors had absolutely not transmitted any hereditary diseases. My fiancé at the time also told me that I was not genetically defective. A year later, in 1935, I was very badly disillusioned by the health authority in Osnabrück. About three months after the operation, my fiancé said to me that we had to break up; he couldn't be expected to keep a wife with a "Hitler cut"[16] for the rest of his life.[17]

4. Male, born 1912:

   My wife NN died on DD 1979. She was sterilized and suffered her whole life that she couldn't have any children. She so badly wanted to be a mother . . . Now I, her husband, stand here all alone; if I had had children, I wouldn't feel so lonely in my old age.[18]

5. Female, born 1909:

   My husband was about 24 years old when he was sterilized in 1935. After the sterilization he suffered another eight years, had ruptures on both sides, and also had heart problems. So he had to have all this brought back to mind and he is still psychologically disturbed by it.[19]

6. Female, born 1901:

   I want to write briefly about the forcible sterilization. My mother said no to the Nazi doctor in 1936. But then she died on April 28,

1937. In June, without my knowledge, I was sterilized in XX. After the operation, I was very sick and spent five or six weeks in the hospital. I had a high fever, about 104 degrees, and great pain. In 1938, I had to stay in the hospital from January to the end of March. I was never healthy again. . . . Even today I still have pain in my abdomen. I'm all alone and without help.[20]

7. Male, born 1917:

In 1935, I was an apprentice cabinetmaker. After my adamant refusal, I was hauled away by force by the Gestapo from the workshop in XX and immediately delivered to the hospital in XX. There I was forcibly sterilized. My deaf brother NN was not sterilized, thanks to the Second World War. He had two healthy children. My sister, happily married in XX, also had seven healthy children. I still suffer from it, and question why it was just me who had to suffer a fate with such terrible consequences.[21]

8. Male, born 1915:

After I married my wife, I had a terrible disappointment in our conjugal relations. We had not had intercourse before we married. It was just like holding a doll without feeling in my arms. I couldn't feel anything. I had already been married for a number of years to a woman who had not been sterilized, so that I knew what normal sexual relations were like. They used to say in the papers during the Nazi period: "Marital relations are in no way affected by sterilization." I couldn't suspect that this was just a terrible lie of doctors who had sanctioned sterilization. . . . I have been married to my wife for 28 years, and she is a good and proper housewife. I have not let her see the deep disappointment that I have experienced in our marital relations and I have not mentioned this to her. She doesn't bear any guilt for the fact that sex gives no pleasure but only pain. My wife never wanted intercourse except in complete darkness, never in the daytime, probably so that I couldn't see her pain-filled face. After some years, my wife couldn't bear the pain any longer without complaining, so that I understood why my wife was always so sad and had cried so much. What my wife suffered all those years can't be compensated for with money.[22]

9. Female, born 1920:

When I was fifteen I was brought to XX to be sterilized. Unfortunately, I have no witnesses, just the scar on my abdomen. . . . With time, the abdominal pains were replaced by pains of the heart when my fiancé backed out of the marriage because I could no longer have children. That happened to me three times, so that I withdrew more and more from life. The pain got worse and worse, so that finally an operation was required.[23]

10. Female, born 1920:
    I am writing you now that I am so lonesome without children. My
    husband died in 1981. I am very unhappy. Why were the Nazis so
    cruel as to sterilize me? I wanted to have at most two children. I
    was scarcely 17 years old when I was forced to go to the hospital
    in Königsberg in East Prussia to be sterilized.[24]

On the questionnaire I asked four questions on the subject of
suffering and feelings of pain:

1. Do you still suffer pain from the sterilization operation?[25]
2. Psychological pain?
3. Physical pain?
4. Where is the physical pain located?

Almost half the interviewees responded that they still experience
physical pain from the operation, and more than three-quarters,
76 percent, stated that they continued to have psychological pain
from their forced sterilizations (see table 8.1).

Table 8.1. Responses to Questions 20, 21, and 22

Response	Number	Percentage
Question 20: Do you still suffer from psychological pain? $N = 1215$		
Yes	928	76.38
No	49	4.03
No response	238	19.59
Question 21: Do you still suffer from physical pain? $N = 1215$		
Yes	601	49.47
No	145	11.93
No response	469	38.60
Question 22: Where is the physical pain located? $N = 491$		
Groin/surgical scars	56	11.41
Abdomen	258	52.54
Scrotum	53	10.74
Lower back	54	11.00
General discomfort	49	9.98
Psychological distress caused by pain	21	4.28

The statements of almost 50 percent of respondents that—many years after the fact—they still suffered the physical consequences of forcible sterilization contradict expert medical opinion. For example, in a senior expert opinion on a woman sterilized for racial reasons published in 1958, one scholar argued that "aside from the ability to conceive . . . there appears to be no injury to the health of a physical nature (provided that no complications appear during the operation or in its wake)."[26]

Other German scholars disagree. One has argued that statements about the harmlessness of forced sterilization assume that "infertility as such . . . is neither an illness nor an ailment in the pathological-anatomical sense and thus in the somatic-medical sense." This scholar has reproached his colleagues for not having taken into consideration "the self-evident fact that as a consequence of a sterilization operation there remain at least scars, both those visible externally and those within the abdominal cavity, so that irreversible changes have certainly occurred." The data from my inquiries lead me to conclude that the following statement is correct:

> The extremely commonly expressed medical opinion that a technically faultlessly performed sterilization has no injurious consequences, that complaints lasting past the convalescence period after the operation are to be referred to the patients general physical constitution, must be decisively opposed, since this "received opinion" does not do justice to the makeup of a human being.[27]

Of the 601 respondents who gave a positive response to the question of long-lasting physical injury, 491 made statements about their experience of pain, quite independently of the scientific debate on the matter. They localized the pain most commonly in the abdomen, listing the groin, testicles, and lumbar region as other specific sites of pain (see table 8.1).

Deaf victims' responses to questions concerning their sense of violation support the statement that "it is clearly not the case that there are forcibly sterilized persons who survived this operation without consequences."[28] The fact that only 4.03 percent of respondents reported experiencing no negative psychological con-

sequences, and the information on suffering found in the countless letters that have come in, lead me to reject emphatically the
hypothesis presented by another scholar that forced sterilization
should be judged differently depending on whether it was carried
out for racial reasons or because of health or eugenic considerations.[29] Rather, I agree with the position of a man forcibly sterilized on eugenic grounds. In the following letter he argues that forcibly sterilized Jews and non-Jews should not be judged differently.

> In the forcible sterilization program of the Third Reich there was no
> difference. We were hauled off together, we were sterilized together.
> Together we suffered terribly. Yet, at the end of the war, when the aw-
> ful pain was finally supposed to be at an end, those who had suffered a
> common fate were divided into those qualified to make an application
> for compensation and those unqualified. Was that humane? No, it truly
> was not. It was very inhumane.[30]

Accounts of voluntarily sterilized women show that a significant number of them suffer subsequent psychological distress.[31]
From this, it can be concluded that sterilization performed under
duress, that is, based on a political ideology and realized by a dic-
tatorial government to which those affected are hostile and opposed, must bring in its wake far greater trauma and injury than
voluntary procedures.

Many deaf respondents also have said that without children
their lives have become poorer in respect to several hopes. Almost all expressed anxiety at having to grow old without the supportive love of children, and an uncertain future in isolation and
loneliness.

Another consequence of sterilization was found in responses
to the question "Are you married?" Of the 1,215 deaf respondents,
716 (58.93 percent) answered with either a simple yes or no, and
116 (9.55 percent) gave no response. Another 383 (31.52 percent)
of the forcibly sterilized entered some other answer, though: 184
(15.14 percent) victims reported that they had intentionally chosen their partner because he or she had also been sterilized; 127
(10.45 percent) said they were widowed; and 23 stated without
prompting that they did not get married because of the operation

that they had been forced to undergo. Added to those who replied negatively to the question, this results in 103 persons (8.48 percent) who remained unmarried. In the case of divorced respondents, there were individual replies such as "divorced as a result of the Hitler cut," "divorced because of lack of children," "divorced by the Nazi state." These remarks support the observation that one of the consequences of forcible sterilization is broken marriages.[32]

Case Histories of Young People

A study of the forced sterilization of young people, based on an evaluation of 1,396 questionnaires, or about 10 percent of the estimated 15,000 deaf victims of the sterilization law, indicates that sterilization was particularly traumatic for them.[33] Respondents reported frequently that they did not realize that they were being taken to the hospital for sterilization. One woman recounted, "When I was lying in the hospital, I thought that it was for an examination. When I woke up the next morning, I had been sterilized. I was heartbroken and I cried a lot."[34] Another woman, sterilized at age fifteen, wrote:

> The police came for me at home and took me to the hospital without giving me any reason. After three days without food I was sterilized. The incisions kept breaking open and I had to spend a year in the hospital. This was an unbearable torture for me because I was still very young. I simply couldn't see the meaning of it.[35]

Reported consequences of such operations included broken engagements and celibacy, resulting in some cases from the fact of sterilization, in others from disrupted sexuality (frigidity, pain during intercourse, impotence).

The suffering reported by teenage sterilization victims was disproportionately high. Male victims between the ages of thirteen and eighteen were about 12 percent more likely to report mental suffering than older male victims. The corresponding figure for female victims was about 9 percent. In terms of reported physical pain, the disparities are even greater. About 16 percent more teenage females reported suffering than older victims, and about 19 percent more teenage males than adult males (see table 8.2).[36]

Table 8.2. Responses to Questions 21, 22, and 23 from Victims Sterilized as Teenagers

	Men			Women	
Answer	Number	Percentage	Answer	Number	Percentage
Question 20: Do you still suffer from psychological pain? Are you often sad? Do you feel lonely without children?					
Yes	172	85.15	Yes	195	84.42
No	3	1.49	No	3	1.30
No response	27	13.37	No response	33	14.29
Question 21: Do you still suffer from physical pain?					
Yes	131	64.85	Yes	155	67.10
No	24	11.88	No	30	12.99
No response	47	23.27	No response	46	19.91
Question 22: Where is the physical pain located?					
Groin/surgical scars	38	30.65	Groin/surgical scars	15	9.93
Abdomen	30	24.19	Abdomen	97	64.24
Scrotum	27	21.77	Scrotum		
Lower back	13	10.48	Lower back	28	18.54
General discomfort	21	16.94	General discomfort	17	11.26
Psychological distress caused by pain	8	6.45	Psychological distress caused by pain	17	11.26

There are probably several explanations for the severity of suffering for younger victims of sterilization. As noted, many of those sterilized between the ages of thirteen and eighteen reported that they had been brought to the hospital under the pretext of other treatment and that they were completely surprised by the operation. Protests and resistance were forcibly suppressed, and no explanation for the operation was given. Moreover, the physical pain after the operation experienced by those at the age of puberty was a particular source of anxiety, since such pain affected intimate and taboo-related areas of the body. Many saw the operations as acts of degradation and cruelty, but the full extent of the effects of forcible sterilization became known to these young people only much later.

A sense of shame and inferiority was reported by many older respondents, but was especially apparent in the statements of young victims. Teenagers who were sterilized lacked the support of a firmly established relationship and were at an age when the most important criterion for socialization was "normalcy." These young people felt maimed in their bodies and spirits, and grew up with a sense that their bodily integrity had been violated. One scholar has written that the operations created "disruptions in adaptation and development among young victims" and produced "depression due to uprooting."[37] Another reports that case histories suggest that disruption of the overall personality development of forcibly sterilized young people was closely connected with later frigidity and celibacy.[38]

The impact on human relationships was also apparent to the victims themselves in that the operation left them with a sense of shame and inferiority in comparison with other people. This feeling grew in proportion to their own recognition of the extent of the effects of the operation, and to the reactions of the surrounding world, but also contributed to this reaction because of their withdrawal from their fellow human beings. Severe depression, attempted suicide, and the awareness that their entire lives could have been different were mentioned as consequences of this condition.

The profound and far-reaching psychological and physical consequences of forcible sterilization that were reported by all victims were especially and severely felt by young persons. The traumatic experience of the operation and deflection at an early age from life's natural course led a majority of respondents in this age cohort to outcomes in life which the victims now view with bitterness and despair.

The Sterilization Experience and Nazi Cover-ups

Many of the respondents to the questionnaire made additional comments citing other examples of humiliation, experimentation, and criminal activity that resulted from the sterilization law, and they highlight its psychological effects. For example, fourteen forcibly sterilized deaf respondents reported that after the operation they were admitted to neurological clinics, provincial sanatoriums, and similar institutions because of depression. It is fair to speculate that other subjects were not able to leave these institutions alive because of a "euthanasia" action. In other cases the burden of suffering was so great that it led to suicide. I received detailed accounts of six instances of suicide, yet the actual number must have been much higher. It is interesting as well that of the 662 forcibly sterilized deaf women who responded to the questionnaire, 43, or 7 percent, reported that they had been forced to undergo sterilization despite the fact that they could prove that they had given birth to "healthy" children.

Other deaths in connection with compulsory sterilization have also been reported. One respondent told the story of her classmate, Gertrud L., from the school for the deaf in Trier, who had been sterilized at age fourteen. She was chronically ill for the next four years and finally died in 1938.[39] Another respondent from north Germany wrote that her fellow-sufferer, Grete E., experienced severe psychological distress after her sterilization in 1934, so that she took her own life that same year.[40] A similar tragedy was reported from Hamburg. A deaf woman, Frau Tatjana S., had a daughter in 1934, and in 1937 she was forcibly sterilized. Her daughter gave us the following account of the difficult time that followed.[41]

> The Nazis were cruel and dangerous. They destroyed my mother's abdomen with the sterilization operation. She had continuous bleeding after the operation. The incision didn't heal. All my mother could do was lie in bed. Her suffering lasted for five years. She couldn't eat anything and grew very thin. On June 23, 1942, she died. I was very sad because my mother had to die far too young, just 28 years old. I was only eight years old and saw my mother for only a short time and never had a chance to live together with her. The Nazis were cruel, brutal people.[42]

One of the victims recounted, "I don't know any names, only that a woman died [after sterilization]. She died in my room in September 1939."[43] A student at the Institution for the Deaf in Neuwied, Emma S., also died as a consequence of the operation.[44] But these crimes against deaf persons can no longer be fully documented, and the extent of deaths must be inferred from other sources. Two German scholars have discovered, for instance, a particularly high incidence of death following sterilization operations in Bremen during the first half of 1935.

As early as 1934 government agencies reported that problems accompanied the sterilizations.[45] This concern on the part of the government was not, however, for the fate of the deaf people being sterilized, but was expressed as official anxiety that opposition to the sterilization law might grow stronger both in Germany and abroad. A July 18, 1934, confidential memorandum from the Reich Ministry of the Interior stated:

> In connection with sterilizations performed in conformity with the Law for the Prevention of Offspring with Hereditary Diseases, complications arose in the case of some persons treated and several deaths have occurred. Without any doubt, the heightened occurrence of such incidents will of necessity greatly impede the further implementation of the law.[46]

And in Mecklenburg during the period from March to November 1937, eight deaths were registered among the 304 women who were operated on, representing a mortality rate of nearly 3 percent.[47] Medical journals from 1935 report on female mortality rates of up to 5 percent, however, and an American observer in 1942 put the total number of persons who had died as a consequence of sterilization operations at about 5,000, of which 90 percent were women. Official Nazi government statistics set the mortality rates at 0.5 percent for women and 0.1 percent for men.[48]

There were also far-reaching attempts to suppress the death figures. The effort of the Reich and Prussian Ministry of the Interior is particularly conspicuous in this respect. It announced on July 15, 1935 that "the mortality rates for females who have been sterilized is 0.45 percent, and for men 0.12 percent, for an average of 0.29 percent."[49]

The apprehension of government departments that opposition to the law might grow stronger abroad can be confirmed by documents from Württemberg-Baden and Kiel. A memorandum dated February 27, 1935, from the Württemberg-Baden division of the Reich Ministry of Justice dealt with the question of carrying out sterilizations on persons of German extraction who were living abroad. The woman in question was a resident of Switzerland at the time and was only temporarily being treated in Germany at the Reichenau sanatorium near Konstanz. The author of the memo recommended that the hereditary health court defer the procedure, out of fear of a negative reaction because of "the recent horrifying increase in fatalities in connection with sterilization procedures and in consideration of the attitudes of persons living on the Swiss border toward the sterilization law."[50]

In a confidential memorandum, the Superior Regional Court judge in Kiel informed the Reich Minister of Justice on April 24, 1935, with regard to three judgments passed on hereditary health in his jurisdiction and called attention to "the fatalities . . . that occurred in connection with sterilization cases." The judge was primarily concerned "with the question of how to handle fatal outcomes in hereditary health cases." In detail, he categorized the deaths as follows:

> Two cases from the hereditary health court in Altona, two cases from the hereditary health court in Kiel, and one case from the hereditary health court in Flensburg. . . . In two further cases from the hereditary health court in Kiel, the persons sterilized or to be sterilized took their own lives. Some connection with the sterilization procedure is to be assumed to be pertinent in both cases.

The superior court judge in Kiel also requested an opinion on "how such fatalities should be treated in the event that compensation claims are filed." He categorically excluded legal regulation of compensation on the grounds that "other countries would conclude from such a ruling that there had been an increase in the number of fatalities."[51]

No documentation on deaf victims can be presented in this respect, since I was no longer able to obtain relevant facts during research in the archives or from conversations with survivors. The following letters surrounding the case of a girl who was wrongly diagnosed with "hereditary epilepsy," and who then died from the forced sterilization operation that resulted from the false diagnosis, demonstrate how horrible these events were.[52] In the first letter (fig. 8.3) the father demands an explanation of what happened to his daughter and insists that she did not have epilepsy. The official response (fig. 8.4), admitting that the girl did not have hereditary epilepsy, nevertheless blames her death on a "recent lung inflammation" and concludes that "there are no grounds for assigning culpability in this case."

Deaf victims of sterilization reported five instances of infanticide of newly born children. In one case, a respondent wrote that her infant had been killed immediately after birth, because it was assumed that it was "hereditarily diseased."[53] Another Nazi victim recounted: "The baby was taken away from a deaf woman and after that she died. Around 1937."[54] On the basis of my own research, I know that one newborn was killed because the deaf mother was Jewish.[55]

The questionnaires also raise questions about the sterilization process itself and the care given to deaf victims of the operations. Thirteen men reported independently of one another that they had been sterilized without narcosis or local anesthetic. Among these, two described being strapped to the operating table and being forced to watch the operation in a mirror.[56]

Mannheim, April 22, 1935
An den Kasernen 28
To the Reich Minister of Justice, Berlin

On March 10, 1935, I directed the following communication to the Minister of the Interior in Karlsruhe:

All my objections and appeals, like those of my daughter, have been without result. On February 9, 1935, my daughter was taken away by two woman officers from the vice squad so that she could be sterilized. The day after the operation, my daughter was dead. Who is responsible for this? Who?

I demand a rigorous investigation, so that the guilty may be punished. My daughter was then under medical treatment. Why was an expert opinion not requested from the physician handling the case?

I deny, now as before, that my daughter suffered from epilepsy. No person who knew my daughter would assert that; she suffered only from slight, seconds-long losses of consciousness.

I am convinced that she would shortly have been cured of this complaint, and this, too, was the physician's opinion.

Figure 8.3. Karl Schneider's Letter Demanding an Explanation of His Daughter's Death

President of the Superior District Court

Karlsruhe, Baden, May 20, 1935

Division of Administration
Office of the District Attorney
Nr. 2637
Death of XX in Mannheim
Ordinance of April 27, 1935
To the Reich Minister of Justice
Berlin

With regard to the renewed petition of Karl Schneider of Mannheim on April 22 of this year (Appendix 1), we have the honor to report as follows:

On the application of the District Public Health Officer in Mannheim, the legal process for sterilization was initiated against NN, born in Mannheim on October 8, 1910, and last resident there, by vocation a domestic servant. According to the medical assessment, the patient suffered from hereditary epilepsy. The same diagnosis was made by the physician who was treating her. The sterilization of NN was decreed in the decision on May 4, 1934, of the Hereditary Health Court within the jurisdiction of the Mannheim District Court. On the basis of her prior history and the assessment of the public health officer, the court was convinced that the patient suffered from hereditary epilepsy. The objection of the Schneider family was rejected as groundless by the Superior Hereditary Health Court within the Superior District Court of Karlsruhe on June 26, 1934. For all details, permit us to refer to the documentation of the Hereditary Health Court of the District Court of Mannheim (Appendix 2).

For the performance of the sterilization operation, the patient was referred by the responsible public health officer to the City Hospital in Mannheim (Appendix 3). There, on February 15, 1935, as a result of the medical treatment, NN died (patient file, Appendix 4).

At the behest of the Senior District Attorney of the Provincial Court of Mannheim, a coroner's inquest and autopsy took place on February 16, 1935. Court physicians identified a noticeable thinning of the bone and a hollowed-out depression on the interior of the right frontal bone of the skull, associated with an apparently scarified spot on the subjacent cerebral cortex. In addition, the autopsy revealed a recent inflammation of the lungs as well as inflammation of the bronchial tubes and windpipe. This recent lung inflammation caused the death of NN. Since changes in the vault of the cranium suggested that the basic affliction (epilepsy) was the consequence of an earlier head injury, a special

Figure 8.4. The Official Response to Karl Schneider

examination of the cranium was made. The board of the Institute for Judicial Medicine of the University of Heidelberg established that the alterations to the vault of the cranium were in all likelihood to be adjudged the results of a localized injury to the cranium and brain.

It then appears legitimate to conclude that NN did not suffer from hereditary epilepsy, but that the epileptic seizures were caused by a cranial injury suffered some years earlier. NN should then not have been sterilized on the grounds of hereditary epilepsy. For the details we beg to refer to the appended documentation from the District Attorney's Office in Mannheim (Appendix 5).

It is the expert opinion of the Medical Reviewer of the Ministry of the Interior that there are no grounds for assigning culpability in this case to the physicians of the City Hospital.

The petitioner has filed a similar objection with the Reich Minister of the Interior, to whom the Baden Minister of the Interior is accountable. We then request the return of this documentation at your earliest convenience.

(signatures)

Figure 8.4—*Continued*

Three respondents wrote that they had been tortured in the SS hospital in Breslau.

Other deaf respondents gave repeated accounts of unreasonably long postoperative treatment periods. Materials in the archives of the Mecklenburg State Ministry, Division of Medical Affairs, support the contention that the operations were hardly routine, sometimes requiring long hospital stays. Over a three-month period, the following examples of long stays were discovered:

1. Male patient, born in 1913, 23 days of treatment
2. Female patient, born in 1914, 22 days of treatment
3. Male patient, born in 1902, 26 days of treatment
4. Male patient, born in 1894, 29 days of treatment
5. Female patient, born in 1916, 32 days of treatment
6. Female patient, born in 1913, 23 days of treatment
7. Male patient, born in 1900, 22 days of treatment
8. Male patient, born in 1896, 48 days of treatment[57]

Transcript
The Reich Minister for Public Education and Propaganda
                                        Berlin, June 12, 1935
To: The Reich and Prussian State Minister of the Interior
at Berlin NW 4G, Königsplatz 6

Re: Publicity concerning the implementation of the Law for the Prevention of Offspring with Hereditary Diseases

In response to your communication of June 5, 1935 (Ref. No. IV f 4.05 of May 27, 1935), I would inform you that distribution of the press release which you sent concerning the present status of the implementation of the Law for the Prevention of Offspring with Hereditary Diseases must be deferred for reasons of both internal and external politics. Even though various foreign newspapers have released figures on sterilizations that have been completed to date, the attention paid to these numbers in other countries has thus far been relatively slight. Attention would, however, increase if this communication were now to appear in the German daily press.

I have the express assignment from the Führer to suppress all publicity in the press concerning the effects of the sterilization law. The sterilizations performed under this law deal with procedures that were and still are vital to the well-being of the German people, but the dissemination of general information about them to a wider public is not desirable for sociopsychological reasons. On the other hand, there are no reservations concerning the treatment of these questions in professional scientific publications.

Heil Hitler!
(signed) Dr. Goebbels

Figure 8.5. Letter from Dr. Josef Goebbels Regarding Publicity of Sterilization Procedures

I close with a document in which Dr. Josef Goebbels states that Hitler ordered him "to suppress all publicity in the press concerning the effects of the sterilization law" (see fig. 8.5). Although sterilization procedures "are vital to the well-being of the German people," "dissemination of general information about them to a wider public is not desirable for sociopsychological reasons."

9

Euthanasia and Deaf Germans

THE EXTERMINATION of deaf people in the Third Reich cannot be ignored in this book. Deaf people were a sociocultural minority that Nazi racial hygiene theorists wanted removed from society. Deaf Germans were not "racially intact" or "hereditarily fit," according to German eugenicists. Deaf people's experiences therefore demonstrate a connection between forcible sterilization, the "euthanasia" action against disabled Germans between 1939 and 1945, and the mass extermination of Jews and Romany. This chapter offers evidence for this connection.[1]

In the course of my research on sterilization, I discovered several documents relating to the link between racial hygiene and the extermination of "undesirable" groups. In 1933, Reich Minister of the Interior Frick appointed a commission of experts to oversee population and racial policy. This group became an effective instrument for the realization of his annihilation campaign against people who were deemed "inferior," "burdensome existences," and "unworthy of life." Frick's September 12, 1933, request that Reich SS leader Heinrich Himmler become a member of the commission for population and racial policy, and Himmler's quick acceptance (see fig. 9.1), may be regarded as the first step in the overall extermination strategy of the Nazi race fanatics.

Enthusiasm for measures designed to rid Germany of humans supposedly unfit or "unworthy of life" can been seen in the April 3, 1940, handwritten notes of Senator Vagt, the Bremen representative in the Reich government. Vagt made these notes at a confidential meeting of the German Association of Cities. They recount a discussion of moving residents of medical or psychiatric

160

The Reich SS Führer   Munich, September 29, 1933

To the Reich Minister of the Interior, Dr. Frick
Berlin NW 40
Königsplatz 6
Dear Reich Minster and Party Member Dr. Frick,

I thank you for your invitation of September 12 to join the Expert Advisory Council on Population and Race Policy, and gladly accept the invitation.

As previously understood, I am most willing to make myself available for participation in the work of this important advisory council.

Heil Hitler
(signature)
H. Himmler[2]

Figure 9.1. Heinrich Himmler's Letter to Minister of the Interior Frick

institutions to "primitive lodgings" where "mortality will naturally be substantially greater." Those present at the meeting urged each other to keep these measures quiet for fear that churches would complain or that the United States, which was still officially neutral in the spring of 1940, might be looking for an excuse to join the war against Germany. As was true later, when killings became more and more widespread, the disposal of bodies was an issue of particular concern and detailed discussion.

At the present time there are about 300,000 mentally ill inmates in some 600 sanatoriums and nursing homes. The facilities are urgently needed for other purposes: spare hospitals, air defense, etc. Thirty to 40 percent of the inmates are asocial elements or unworthy of life, in consequence of which the transfer of these elements to primitive lodgings will be carried out, which may cause some unrest in the population.

In these primitive accommodations, mortality will naturally be substantially greater, especially in time of war. Two things are required:
a. to calm the population,
b. not all too many new graves are to be dug at the cemeteries and cremation is then to be preferred (which is equally necessary to prevent the outbreak of epidemics, since most are highly infectious).

It must be assumed that relatives of the deceased will resist such cremation (principally among the Catholics) or at least will request that it be carried out in another locality. In regular cases, the procedure should be as follows: inform the relatives of the death and determine whether they wish an urn to be sent; in the contrary case, deposition of the remains at the nearest cemetery that receives cremations should follow (at no cost to the family). Consequently, cities with cemeteries for cremated remains will then receive urns sent from various localities; the cities will be asked to inform the deputy, Dr. Schlüter of the German Council of Cities, personally how the urns are to be addressed (typical case: Office of the Lord Mayor, Cemetery Administration, in . . .). If this official or others of the cemetery administration have any reservations about these matters, they must immediately be circumvented. The cremations will be paid for; in general and to the greatest extent possible, unnecessary invoices should not be permitted to float around. In every case the Charitable Patient Transport Company should be in contact with the affected city before the transportation of urns.

This whole program must unconditionally be executed with extreme care; there is otherwise a very possible risk that, for example, the United States might take this as a pretext for entering the war!

In conclusion, Reich leader Lord Mayor Piehler urged the greatest secrecy. April 3, 1940. Vagt.

In addition to the procedures outlined in Vagt's notes, Nazi programs targeted groups for "euthanasia" action, commencing in 1939 with action against children. The murdering of children began with a confidential circular from the Reich Ministry of the Interior on August 18, 1939. In this memorandum, physicians and midwives were ordered to report "monstrous births" immediately and also report children up to the age of three who suffered from idiocy, mongolism (Down syndrome), micro- and hydrocephaly, and deformities of the extremities. The completed report forms were to be forwarded by the Reich Committee for the Scientific Registration of Severe Hereditary Ailments to three expert assessors.[3] These physicians entered their decisions as to the life (−) or death (+) of the children on a special form, or recommended further examination or observation.[4] In total, twenty-one "children's wards" were established, in which handicapped children, not only as originally conceived up to the age of three but up to the age of seventeen, were killed by injections of morphium-hydrochloral or luminal, or by starvation. After 1943, the healthy children of Gypsies (Sinti, Roma) and Jews were increasingly killed as well, especially at Hadamar. One historian estimates that five thousand children were killed.[5]

A second part of the Nazi effort to eliminate undesirable people was the T4 program, which killed disabled adults. The abbreviation T4 derived from the address of the central administration, Tiergartenstrasse 4, Berlin-Charlottenburg, whose director was Victor Brack, head of Hitler's chancellery, Central Office II. The extermination organization also had staff of its own that was divided into three organizations: (1) the Reich Cooperative for State Hospitals and Nursing Homes (RAG), who identified people with disabilities; (2) the Public Foundation for Institutional Care, which managed personnel and financial questions; and (3) the Charitable Patient Transport Company (Gekrat), which was responsible for the collection and transfer of disabled people to the observation and killing centers.

The T4 killing action began in October of 1939. In that month Hitler signed a secret order implementing the plan and backdating it to September 1, 1939. The order read as follows:

> Reich leader Bouhler and Dr. med. Brandt are charged with the responsibility of enlarging the competence of certain physicians, designated by name, so that patients who, on the basis of human judgment, are considered incurable, can be granted mercy death after a discerning diagnosis.[6]

In the T4 action at least seventy thousand persons, "who were in no way all incurably ill," were murdered.[7] It should be added that disabled people were killed in gas chambers disguised as shower rooms. Massive protests by the churches and considerable unrest in the population, as well as the reconcentration of all resources, including those for transport, for the campaign against the Soviet Union, contributed to Hitler ordering the suspension of the T4 program on August 24, 1941.[8]

The 14 f 13 action began in the middle of 1941 and affected primarily seriously ill people in the concentration camps under Himmler's supervision. As early as November 1941, a Nazi commission of physicians appeared at the concentration camp in Buchenwald and selected inmates for murder according to criteria of health, race, and political affiliation. Just before this, the camp commander Koch had received a secret communication from Himmler that "all the feebleminded and crippled inmates are to be killed."[9] Inmates thus selected were transferred to the corresponding "euthanasia" centers and there murdered. The number of inmates killed in this way is estimated to be at least ten thousand.

After Himmler had given directions for the large-scale eradication of the Jews in the middle of 1941, the agents of the T4 action, now "unemployed," were transferred to Auschwitz and other mass extermination camps, an undertaking in which they were "most willing."[10]

The term "wild euthanasia" has been used to describe the killing that continued even after Hitler's suspension of T4. This "gentle" death took the form of the starvation of disabled people. Since these activities were no longer centrally directed, an exact or even approximate number of those killed can no longer be determined. Here one must also consider the unknown numbers of those murdered in the occupied countries, especially in Poland and the Soviet Union, and residents of sanatoriums and nursing homes who also fell victim to the Nazi police action.[11] The testimony of two surviving deaf Jews from Poland indicates that deaf people were also counted among these victims.

I was not able to determine the total number of deaf persons who were killed in the "euthanasia" action. Still, some preliminary findings may be presented. Research in the archives of institutions in Schleswig and Homberg revealed fifteen student files with the notation "remanded because of ineducability to . . ." followed by the name of a sanatorium or nursing home, or "not educable, remanded to . . ." followed by the word "family" or "family home" or the name of a sanatorium or nursing home. These measures show that in individual schools for the deaf between 1933 and 1945 remedial programs were no longer offered to students who were academically behind; instead, these children were selected out and delivered for mercy killing.

In response to question No. 25, "Did you know deaf persons (also mentally retarded deaf persons) who were killed by the Nazis?" I received a total of seventy-seven responses. Eleven did not give the name of the person killed, but in these instances other specific information was supplied, for example, "the deaf son of one of my co-workers by the name of Hilde—we worked together in the Hotel Reichshof in Plauen—was taken away and killed. The young man was 17 or 18 years old." [12] In the case of the twenty-seven remanded and exterminated deaf persons known by name, the place of death could no longer be determined. An additional ninteen deaf people were killed in various institutions, such as Schweinspoint, Mosbach in Baden, Emmerdingen, Bunzlau in Silesia, Schleswig, Kalkhausen/Langenfeld, Münster, Sonnenstein über Pirna, Hartheim bei Linz, Meseritz-Obrawalde. Four deaf persons were killed in the "euthanasia" center of Brandenburg/Havel and six in the extermination center of Hadamar near Limburg. Ten communications about euthanasia victims referred to deaf residents of the Pauline Home in Winnenden. One deaf eyewitness gave a credible account that he had seen at least three of his fellow residents taken away in a bus. In addition, one respondent, whose own disturbing life story has already been presented, informed me that her deaf acquaintances, Paul W., Walter Z., Maria R., and Eva S., had been taken from the institution in a bus and were apparently killed.

Where these buses went and what happened to their passengers is apparent in the following July 19, 1940, letter of protest from the Protestant provincial bishop of Württemburg, Wurm, to the Reich Minister of the Interior:

> The patient transport cars that unloaded at the small railway station in Marbach a.L., the buses with darkened windows that carried patients from distant stations or brought them directly from institutions, the smoke rising from the crematorium, which could be seen from a great distance—all this is distressing, the more so since no one gains access to the castle [Castle Grafeneck, one of the "euthanasia" centers].[13]

One historian has written that "in the euthanasia center in Grafeneck from the end of February until mid-December 1940, when the institution was closed—that is, in the space of ten months—a total of 10,654 patients were gassed to death."[14] How many of these victims were deaf and drawn from the Pauline Home at Winnenden will never be determined.

A hearing eyewitness told me that a "150 percent Nazi," one of the teachers of the deaf who was later killed during the war, had forced the sterilization law and "euthanasia" measures onto the home. This witness was unfortunately not prepared to give the name of this Nazi criminal. This same person was also able to recount that the "euthanasia" program was suspended at Winnenden only after the intervention of Bishop Wurm.

Sham registry offices were established at the "euthanasia" centers. They made out death certificates, looked after the disposal of remains, and sent letters of condolence, which were all drafted according to the same pattern, to the survivors of the murdered victims. In all such letters, recipients were informed that the deceased had been transferred to the institution in question "at the direction of the Reich Defense Commissar." Severe influenza, circulatory weakness, heart problems, miliary tuberculosis, and appendicitis were often given as the causes of death. Reference was always made to "official directions connected with war measures" or to the ongoing danger of infection that made necessary the immediate cremation of the bodies. Cremation avoided any possible demands for autopsies. In addition, the notices stated that at the time the institution was closed to visits or that notice of a visit had to be given eight days in advance.

The daughter of one of those killed has written the following account:

My father was in a nursing home in Bavaria. He was not mentally ill but was emotionally disturbed and had neurological ailments. Without prior notification to my mother my father was transferred. It was only shortly after his transfer and his sudden death that my mother found out about it. . . . For this reason I remain convinced today that my father was killed. My mother has never been willing to talk about it, perhaps because of anxiety or shame, I don't know. She died in 1959. . . .

I had to spend my childhood in an orphanage. My mother did not receive a widow's pension or any other kind of support and she had to work for her living. It was only after the war was over that I was able to return home to my mother. I have always suffered psychologically because of it, and also because the home where I lived was in another district and during all those years I was not able to spend one day of my holidays at my mother's side.

I am now 51 years old but I still can't forget these experiences. I would have liked to have had some job training but I couldn't for lack of money. If they had cured my father instead of killing him, I wouldn't have had all these disadvantages. By the way, he was just 47 years old.[15]

When survivors were not satisfied with the standard letter of condolence, a special "physician's consolation" was sent. In these letters, the death was frequently represented as "in reality a true deliverance" from a grievous fate. In order to obscure the operation further, the letters were signed with false names.[16]

The strict secrecy that was mandated for all the activities of the "euthanasia" action was broken by the administrative bodies themselves. For example, the shipment of great numbers of urns and the sudden creation of new burial grounds could not be kept a secret from the population. The following letter illustrates the bureaucratic steps required when ashes were moved.

Local Police Authority Hartheim/Oberdonau, April 5, 1941
IL/16054/Div. Cemetery Administration
To the Cemetery Administration
XX/Oberwesterwald District
Re: Burial of the ashes of NN, born xx, widow of NN, born xx, 1874, in XX, deceased March 22, 1941, in Hartheim, cremated March 23 in Hartheim.
Enclosure: 1 urn.

Accompanying this letter, I forward to you the urn with the ashes of the above-named.

This transfer takes place on the basis of the statement of agreement of the Mayor of XX/Oberwesterwald District, of March 30, 1941. For the burial I would request you to contact Herr XX, xx/Westerwald, directly.

(signature)[17]

The deaf dressmaker, C.W., mother of a hearing daughter, provides an example of a deaf person's fate under Nazi racial hygiene practices. Health authorities seized C.W. when she was thirty years old and ordered her sterilization on July 17, 1937, in Bochum. She was carried off from her work place in Bad Rothenfelde to the Psychiatric Hospital in Münster on April 22, 1940, and was murdered there on June 26, 1940. Her death certificate gave the time of death as exactly twelve o'clock, and the hereditary health court gave the cause of death as a weak heart.[18] Both of these specifics were frequently used to cover up the actual procedures.

A forcibly sterilized deaf woman sent me the following documents concerning the murder of her fifty-seven-year-old mother, and this sad story, told in the bureaucratic language of Nazi civil servants, provides a fitting end to this narration. The remedial training institution in Kalmenhof in Idstein/Taunus mentioned in the first document served as a transit and observation facility established in the "intake zone" of the "euthanasia" centers.[19] From there the victims were forwarded for extermination.

> Kalmenhof Remedial Training Institution, Idstein im Taunus
> July 26, 1941
> To Frau NN, Brambauer/Westphalia
> Xxstrasse xx
>
> By order of the Reich Defense Commissioner, your sister NN, born xx, 1884, in Branbauer was transferred on July 25, 1941, by the Charitable Patient Transport Company, Berlin W9, Potsdamer Platz 1, to another institution whose name and address are not known to me. The receiving institution will send you a corresponding communication. I would ask you to abstain from further inquiries until this notice is received.
>
> If, however, you receive no notification from the receiving institution within fourteen days, I would recommend that you make inquiries with the Charitable Patient Transport Company, giving the relevant personal information and the date of the transfer from Kalmenhof.
>
> Please communicate this information to possible other relatives of the patient if required.
>
> Heil Hitler!
> Director of the Institution[20]

The woman's mother was sent from Kalmenhof to Hadamar, which was in fact a killing center. The next document acknowledges the transfer and warns that visits, telephone calls, inquiries, and even the sending of packages are prohibited.

Provincial Hospital and Nursing Home, August 1, 1941
Hadamar
Ref. No. E 10 -1/53 Bi.
To Frau NN
Brambauer/Westphalia
XX-strasse xx

We inform you that your sister, NN, by ministerial order on the directions of the Reich Defense Commissar has been transferred to our institution and has arrived safely.

At this time visits cannot be permitted for reasons associated with Reich defense and similarly telephone communications cannot be answered.

Any other changes that occur in the condition of the patient or in connection with the ban on visits will be communicated to you at once. The additional work that has been caused by these measures forces us to ask kindly that you abstain from further inquiries as well as from sending packages.

Heil Hitler!
Director of the Institution
(signature)[21]

The final document, announcing the sister's death, also states that the institution is closed to visitors and that the body has already been cremated. Furthermore, the deceased's family is discouraged from requesting her personal belongings and, presumably, remembering that this person "unworthy of life" ever existed. The notification of death from August 18, 1941, and the date of the death, also claimed as August 18, do not correspond to the actual dates of the events, as other historians have been able to demonstrate. The recorded dates between the admittance of the persons to be killed and their execution were consciously separated in order to preclude suspicions.

Provincial Hospital and Nursing Home, Hadamar, August 18, 1941
Hadamar Institution temporarily closed to visits
Ref. No. E 10 -153/Sz
To Frau NN
Brambauer/Westphalia
XX-strasse xx

Dear Frau NN,

Subsequent to our letter of August 1, 1941, we inform you with regret that your sister, Frau NN, born xx, who had to be transferred to

our institution in connection with measures ordered by the Reich Defense Commissar, unexpectedly died on August 18, 1941, as a consequence of pulmonary tuberculosis with an associated attack of miliary
tuberculosis.

Since our institution is designated only as a transit center for those
patients who are to be transferred to another institution in the region
and the stay here serves only to identify carriers of infection, who, as is
well known, are always to be found among such patients, the responsible local police authority has ordered the immediate cremation of
the remains and the disinfection of belongings in order to prevent the
outbreak and transfer of infectious diseases, in accordance with the
relevant portions of ongoing defense measures and pursuant to paragraph 22 of the ordinance to control contagious diseases. In these cases
the agreement of relatives is not required. Belongings brought to the
institution will, after disinfection, be retained as security for the
bearer of costs.

We would inform you kindly to note that damage to personal belongings from the powerful agents employed in disinfecting can very
often not be avoided. Usually both shipment and the drafting of a decision concerning the allocation of the patient's belongings cost more
time and money than the belongings are worth. May we ask you to consider whether it is possible for you to renounce claims to these belongings, so that in the event of damage we can refer them to National Socialist Public Welfare and to otherwise needy inmates of the institution.

In the event that you wish the urn to be buried in a specific cemetery—transport of the urn is without cost—we request you to inform
us, enclosing a statement of agreement with the relevant cemetery administration. Surrender of the urns to private individuals is not permissible by law. If you do not send us this notification within fourteen
days, an alternative burial will be carried out, and we shall also assume
that you abstain from any claim on the belongings, unless we have received a notification to the contrary within this same period.

We enclose a death certificate for submission to the authorities.

Heil Hitler!
(signature)
Encl.[22]

Appendix 1: The Questionnaire

QUESTIONNAIRE
(This questionnaire will be kept by Herr H. Biesold.
Your name will not be released: that is against the law.)

1. Last name_____
2. First name _____
3. Date of birth_____ 4. Place of birth_____
5. Place of residence from 1933 to 1945 _____
   _____
6. Present residence_____
7. May Herr Biesold call on you?* He can sign. _____
8. Which institution did you attend? _____
9. During what period? from 19____ to 19____
10. Occupation_____
11. Were you sterilized?*_____
12. When?_____ 19____
13. Where (city)_____
14. Who reported on you? Underline the correct agency or person below:
    School (institution) for the deaf   family member   relatives
    neighbors   political party (National Socialists)   school doctor
    ear doctor   teacher   supervisor   health authority
15. Are you married?*_____
16. Did the Nazi authorities force you to be sterilized (make threats, say
    that you had to, etc.)?*
17. Who wrote the threatening letter? Underline the correct agency or per-
    son below:
    Party (Nazi)   health authority   school (institution)
    physician at a hospital   law court

Please answer the questions on the other side!

18. Did the police come and take you to the hospital?_____
19. Do you still suffer pain from the sterilization operation?*_____
20. Mental pain (are you often sad, do you feel lonely without children)?*

_____

21. Physical pain?* _____
22. Where does it hurt in your body? _____
23. Below you can write in other comments, tell about other horrible experiences (for example, a Nazi doctor first killed the baby I was carrying).

_____

_____

_____

_____

24. Have you previously applied for compensation?*_____
    When? _____ 19 _____
    Where?_____

25. Did you know other deaf persons (including mentally retarded deaf persons) who were done away with (killed, murdered) by the Nazis? Please include the names of deaf Jews who were deported and killed.
    Last name _____ First name_____
    Previous school/institution _____
    Where were they killed (for example, district hospitals and care facilities in Hadamar, Emmendingen, Münster; Auschwitz concentration camp; etc.)?

    _____

    When were they killed (approximately) _____ 19 ____

Please answer "yes" or "no" to questions followed by a star (*)

Place, Date _____   Signature _____

Comments

Some explanatory comments are required in the case of a few questions whose content will not be immediately understood by many hearing readers.
Question 7: *May Herr Biesold call on you? He can sign.*

This question was asked only on the first one hundred questionnaires that were distributed, in order to get a basic idea of the willingness of the deaf victims to have me call on them. The answers were 87 percent affirmative. The statement "He can sign" is translated from German Sign Language and explains that "the visitor can converse with you in your own language."
Question 14: *Who reported on you?*

This question is in reference to the "application" for sterilization, the notification made to government authorities under the provisions of section 3.4 of the sterilization law. On the returned questionnaires, some deaf persons had written additional titles or names (for example, the mayor, the deaf school principal, or individual teachers).

Question 15: *Did the Nazi authorities force you to be sterilized?*

With this question we hoped to learn of the victims' subjective experience of the coercive nature of the law. In actual fact, the first section of the law refers to voluntary compliance.

Question 16: *Who wrote the threatening letter?*

The ordinance (article 6 to section 12, dating from December 5, 1933) for the implementation of the sterilization law stipulates that "the responsible physician must request the sterilization operation in writing." Preliminary conversations with victims made it clear, however, that other agencies also sent in "requests." This question was intended to determine whether various institutions, among which the schools for the deaf, were actually implicated in the practice of referring the deaf to the authorities for sterilization. The term "threatening letter" was coined during the development of the questionnaire on the basis of the victims' actual experiences at the time. In practice, the summons could, indeed, be perceived as a personal threat, since section 6 stipulated that the relevant persons were to be informed that the surgical intervention could be effected against their wishes and, as prescribed in article 12 of the sterilization law, with the use of physical force.

Question 17: *Did the police come and take you to the hospital?*

In section, 12, paragraph 1, of the sterilization law the legislators provided for the use of physical force as a permissible means to carry out the law. Thus answers to this question may make it possible to document the coercive measures employed by Nazi institutions in the implementation of the law and deaf efforts to resist them.

Question 20: *Mental pain (are you often sad, do you feel lonely without children?).*

Given the complexity of research issues that relate to the long-term consequences of forcible sterilization, we considered this question about the deaf victims' consciousness of psychological trauma to be extremely relevant. Formulating such a question was difficult, since German Sign Language does not employ abstract concepts of "psychology," "psychological," etc. Terms such as "soul" and "spirit," on the other hand, are more at home in a religious context. It then seemed essential to us to make those questioned well aware of the exact content of the question about long-term effects.

Question 23: *Below you can write in other comments, tell about other horrible experiences (for example, a Nazi doctor first killed the baby I was carrying).*

With this phrasing we hoped to learn of the experiences of deaf women who fell victim to the expansion of the sterilization law that was passed on

June 26, 1935, and had their pregnancies terminated. In the Law to Amend
the Law for the Prevention of Offspring with Hereditary Diseases, the Nazis
had added new provisions to section 218 in the interests of racial hygiene:
"If a hereditary health court has legally prescribed the sterilization of a
woman who at the time of the sterilization operation is pregnant, the pregnancy may be terminated with the consent of the woman."

Appendix 2: Questionnaire Data

Table 1. Distribution of Respondents by Sex

	Number of Responses N = 1,215	Percentage of Total
Female	662	54.49
Male	553	45.51

Table 2. Respondents' Year of Birth

Birth Year	Responses N = 1,215	Percentage
1895 and earlier	9	0.74
1896–1900	24	1.98
1901–1905	116	9.55
1906–1910	210	17.28
1911–1915	300	24.69
1916–1920	285	23.46
1921–1925	240	19.75
1926–1930	29	2.39
After 1930	1	0.08
No response	1	0.08

Table 3. Respondents' Place of Residence between 1933 and 1945

Province/District	Responses N = 1,215	Percentage
East Prussia	73	6.01
City of Berlin	90	7.41
Brandenburg	21	1.73

Table 3—*Continued*

Province/District	Responses N = 1,215	Percentage
Pomerania	22	1.81
Posen-West Prussia	1	0.08
Lower Silesia	50	4.12
Upper Silesia	19	1.56
Saxony, Provincial Institution	16	1.32
Schleswig-Holstein	26	2.14
Hanover	58	4.77
Westphalia	144	11.85
Hessen-Nassau	37	3.04
Rhineland	198	16.30
Bavaria	89	7.32
Baden	75	6.17
Thuringia	7	0.58
Saxony	20	1.65
Württemberg	81	6.67
Hesse	28	2.30
Hamberg	31	2.55
Mecklenburg-Schwerin	2	0.16
Oldenburg	28	2.30
Braunschweig	20	1.65
Bremen	14	1.15
Lippe	4	0.33
Lübeck	2	0.16
Saar Region	24	1.98
Sudeten	12	0.99
Austria	3	0.25
No information	20	1.65

Note. The distribution of places of residence is organized by provinces and districts according to *Das Statistische Jahrbuch,* a contemporary annual publication on deaf education (pp. 10ff.).

Table 4. Deaf Institutions Attended by the Respondents

Institution for the Deaf	Responses N = 1,215	Percentage
Königsberg	31	2.55
Rössel	8	0.66
Tilsit	15	1.23

Table 4—*Continued*

Institution for the Deaf	Responses N = 1,215	Percentage
Hufen	1	0.08
Köslin	19	1.56
Stettin	19	1.56
Berlin-Neukölln	24	1.98
City of Berlin	54	4.45
Berlin-Weissensee	4	0.33
Guben	14	1.65
Wriezen	14	1.65
Breslau	22	1.81
Liegnitz	30	2.47
Ratibor	19	1.56
Erfurt	2	0.16
Halberstadt	9	0.74
Halle	6	0.49
Schleswig	29	2.39
Hildesheim	25	2.06
Osnabrück	17	1.40
Stade	9	0.74
Emden	5	0.41
Büren	33	2.73
Langenhorst	24	1.98
Petershagen	24	1.98
Soest	60	4.95
Camberg	23	1.89
Frankfurt am Main	2	0.16
Homberg	26	2.14
Aachen	19	1.56
Brühl	20	1.65
West Elberfeld	20	1.65
Essen	25	2.06
Euskirchen	14	1.15
Kempen	16	1.32
Cologne	31	2.55
Neuwied	35	2.88
Trier	30	2.47
Augsburg	8	0.66
Bamberg	6	0.49
Bayreuth	9	0.74
Dillingen	3	0.25

Table 4—*Continued*

Institution for the Deaf	Responses N =1,215	Percentage
Hohenwart	4	0.33
Zell	1	0.08
Frankental/Pfalz	22	1.81
Munich	7	0.58
Nuremberg	10	0.82
Regensburg	1	0.08
Straubing	12	0.99
Würzburg	7	0.58
Bönnigheim	15	1.23
Pauline Home, Winnenden	7	0.58
Schw. Gmünd (state-run)	19	1.56
Schw. Gmünd (private)	18	1.48
Heiligenbronn	9	0.74
Nürtingen	6	0.49
Wilhelmsdorf	5	0.41
Dresden	4	0.33
Leipzig	15	1.23
Gerlachsheim	23	1.89
Heidelberg	32	2.63
Meersburg	17	1.40
Neckargemünd	4	0.33
Bensheim	10	0.82
Friedberg	16	1.32
Gotha	2	0.16
Hildburghausen	3	0.25
Schleiz	1	0.08
Braunschweig	21	1.73
Bremen	11	0.91
Detmold	3	0.25
Hamburg	26	2.14
Ludwigslust	2	0.16
Lübeck	1	0.08
Wildeshausen	23	1.89
Danzig	4	0.33
Bruck	2	0.16
Vienna XIII	1	0.08
Czernowitz	3	0.25
Prague	1	0.08
Mähr. Schönberg	4	0.33

Table 4—*Continued*

Institution for the Deaf	Responses $N = 1,215$	Percentage
Schneidemühl	2	0.16
Leitmeritz	5	0.41
Marienberg	1	0.08
Ursberg	1	0.08
No information	38	3.14

Note. This ordering also follows that of the statistical annual.

Table 5. Respondents' Year of Entry into the Institution

Year	Responses $N = 1,215$	Percentage
Before 1911	64	5.27
1911	15	1.23
1912	31	2.55
1913	24	1.98
1914	31	2.55
1915	27	2.23
1916	34	2.80
1917	44	3.62
1918	52	4.28
1919	61	5.02
1920	62	5.10
1921	67	5.52
1922	58	4.77
1923	37	3.05
1924	65	5.35
1925	35	2.88
1926	67	5.51
1927	84	6.92
1928	70	5.76
1929	62	5.10
1930	53	4.36
1931	32	2.63
1932	27	2.23
1933	15	1.23
1934	14	1.15
After 1934	9	0.74
No information	75	6.17

Table 6. Occupations of Respondents

Occupation	Responses N = 1,215	Percentage
Homemaker	107	8.81
Tailor/Dressmaker	310	25.50
Seamstress	94	7.74
Artisan	183	15.06
Shoemaker	51	4.20
Foreman	32	2.63
Employee	43	3.54
Unskilled worker	242	19.92
Unemployed	42	3.46
Early pensioner	13	1.07
No information	98	8.07

Table 7. Year When Respondents Were Sterilized

Year	Responses N = 1,215	Percentage
1933	16	1.32
1934	85	7.80
1935	223	18.35
1936	229	18.85
1937	210	17.28
1938	123	10.12
1939	85	7.00
1940	48	3.95
1941	42	3.46
1942	63	5.19
1943	30	2.47
1944	15	1.23
1945	2	0.16
No information	44	3.62

Table 8. Age at the Time of Sterilization

Respondents' Age	Responses N = 1,215	Percentage
9	1	0.08
10	3	0.25

Table 8—*Continued*

Respondents' Age	Responses N = 1,215	Percentage
11	6	0.49
12	21	1.73
13	12	0.99
14	52	4.28
15	91	7.49
16	79	6.50
17	84	6.91
18	57	4.69
19	29	2.39
20	64	5.27
21	47	3.87
22–25	224	18.44
26–30	215	17.70
31–35	130	10.70
36–40	44	3.62
41–45	10	0.82
46–50	2	0.16
No information	44	3.62

Table 9. Place of Sterilization

City/Town	Responses N = 1,215	Percentage
Bonn	10	0.82
Giessen	10	0.82
Hamm	10	0.82
Soest (D)	10	0.82
Solingen	10	0.82
Munich (D)	11	0.91
Paderborn	11	0.91
Schleswig (D)	11	0.91
Siegen	11	0.91
Wuppertal (D)	11	0.91
Düsseldorf	12	0.99
Koblenz	12	0.99
Oldenburg	12	0.99
Dortmund	13	1.07
Schw. Gmünd (D)	13	1.07

Table 9—*Continued*

City/Town	Responses N = 1,215	Percentage
Duisburg	14	1.15
Liegnitz (D)	14	1.15
Essen (D)	15	1.23
Aachen (D)	16	1.32
Breslau (D)	16	1.32
Gelsenkirchen	16	1.32
Heidelberg (D)	18	1.48
Braunschweig (D)	20	1.65
Königsberg (D)	20	1.65
Bremen (D)	21	1.73
Trier (D)	23	1.89
Homburg/Saar	24	1.98
Cologne (D)	24	1.98
Hamburg (D)	28	2.30
Berlin (D)	104	8.55
Other sites (fewer than 10 instances)	634	52.18
No information	41	3.36

Note. For reasons of space, only those cities in which more than ten of the respondents were sterilized are listed. Cities in which an institution for the deaf was located are marked with (D).

Table 10. Agency or Person Who Reported Victims for Sterilization

Reporting Agency or Person	Responses N = 1,591	Percentage
School/Institution	266	21.89
Family	40	3.29
Relatives	13	1.07
Neighbors	8	0.66
Nazi Party	368	30.29
Institutional physician	58	4.77
ENT physician	44	3.62
Teacher	148	12.18
Supervisor	13	1.07
Health authority	558	45.93
No information	75	6.17

Table 10—*Continued*

Reporting Agency or Person	Responses N = 1,591	Percentage
Additions by respondents		
Mayor	16	1.32
Justice department	6	0.49
Reich Union of the Deaf of Germany (REGEDE)	5	0.41

Note. In response to this question, several officials and persons could be named. It was also widespread practice for reports to be made independently by several agencies or persons.

Table 11. Agency or Person Who Wrote the Summons Letter for the Sterilization Operation

Authority	Responses N = 1,462	Percentage
Nazi Party	308	25.35
Health authority	395	32.51
Institution for the Deaf	124	10.21
Hospital physician	64	5.27
Court	316	26.01
Others (13)	12	0.99

Appendix 3: Documents Written by and in Support of Gertrud Jacob

Transcript

Gotha, November 19, 1936

Affidavit

Gertrud Jacob, daughter of master stovefitter Richard Jacob and his wife Frau Frieda Jacob, was born on December 11, 1904, a healthy, strong infant. She began to run and speak at an early age. We lived at that time in a house on Jüdenstrasse 64 with the master painter Johann Bomberg (presently Dietrich Eckertstrasse 64). At the age of two years and nine months the child suffered an accident crossing Mykonius Square on her way home with her mother when her head was struck by the soccer ball of youngsters playing there.

Since the head and face of the child were badly swollen, she was immediately brought to the medical attention of the ear specialist Dr. Rosenbaum, and received electroshock treatments and massage for a full year. The medical findings stated that the auditory nerves, at this childish age still as thin as silk threads, had been deadened by the blow and the shock, and could not fully recover. Some residual hearing was, however, present in the left ear.

That this account in all its details corresponds to the truth is attested to by the signatures of the owner of the house at Jüdenstrasse 64 (Frau Bomberg) and the then co-resident (Frau Kreibe).

signed Richard Jacob   Friedericke Bomberg   Emma Kreibe

Gotha, April 6, 1938

To: the Superior Hereditary Health Court
Jena   By registered mail
Re: Gertrud Jacob, Gotha
    Case No. XIII 57/38

Against the decision of March 24, 1938, delivered March 29, 1938, I hereby
lodge an

Objection

Grounds

It is not accurate that I suffer from deafness, much less hereditary deafness.
I was born November 12, 1904, a healthy and strong child. At the age of two
years and nine months I suffered an accident in that I was struck on the head
by a soccer ball in such fashion that I was immediately brought to the ear
specialist Dr. Rosenbaum for clinical treatment. The treatment occasioned
by the accident took a full year. It is Dr. Rosenbaum's judgment that my auditory nerves, at that age as thin as silk thread, had been deadened by the blow
and shock. He attempted to restore my hearing through electroshocks and
massage.

Evidence
1. The attached testimony of the eyewitness Fritz Riede of Gotha
2. The attached affidavit of Frau Friedericke Bomberg, then owner of the
   ground floor of the house in which I was born and in which my parents
   still lived at the time of the accident
3. The attached affidavit of the then co-resident, Frau Emma Kreibe
4. The deposition of the public health officer, Dr. Sterzing, who likewise
   made a written account of the accident and its consequences when I was
   admitted to the school

Unfortunately I fell ill at the age of nine with diphtheria and had an incision
in the larynx, which also negatively affected my speech.

In 1923, the professor in Jena wanted to operate on me to restore my hearing. Only because he could give me no guarantee that a disfigurement of my
face would not follow the operation, I refrained from taking this step. The
medical assessment was then that my ear was still capable of registering
some degree of sound. This must have been the case, since the doctor would
not otherwise have proposed the operation. Such an operation on deaf ears
would have been without purpose.

I am not deaf in the strict sense of the word, but very hard of hearing. As
a result of the accident, I lost the hearing in my right ear, but I do have some
hearing in my left ear. If the medical assessment that was submitted to the
court states otherwise, I must object to it.

All my blood relations are hereditarily healthy. Unfortunately the August König referred to in the assessment, the son of my mother's brother, had an ear infection just after birth which led to deafness. Whether this is a hereditary defect is beyond my ability to say. He is married to a hereditarily sound woman and has a normal daughter of twelve with good hearing. I enclose a letter from him dated November 4, 1937, for your information. But even if August König has a hereditary defect, it does not mean that his deafness has any connection with my hearing loss; he may have inherited it from his mother's side of the family. In any case, it is an unjust disadvantage for me if his case is associated with the misfortune I suffered from as a result of the accident. The genealogical table for the König family goes back to the seventeenth century but there is no single case of deafness or hearing loss. My grandmother, Amanda König, had ten hereditarily sound children and all were gainfully employed. My great-grandmother Elisabeth König had thirteen hereditarily sound children who were also all good workers.

I do not have the fairly equal residual hearing in both ears that is stated in the decision of March 24, 1938. As previously stated, my left ear is considerably better. Contrary to the statement that objective proof of serious prior trauma is allegedly not to be found, I would explain that the scar on my right ear was unquestionably identified by Professor Zange in Jena as well as by the ear specialists Drs Crusius and Heym of Gotha. Moreover, Professor Zange himself considers this only defective hearing, as he explained to my mother and sister.

Finally, the assessment explains that it seems quite improbable that the blow from a ball to the side of the head could be considered a cause of deafness. But just as it can seem improbable, it can seem probable. In any case, neither case can be unquestionably established on the basis of the assessment, as the law would prescribe as a basis for action. If there is any doubt that the hearing ability of children of two to three years of age cannot be proven, this view needs to be revised in my opinion. If you call a child of this age by name, it will react, as I did according to the information I have from my parents and others. This simple fact establishes that hearing must have been present. The same applies to the baby talk that is mentioned. A child two years and nine months old, if it is not retarded by some illness, can not only babble but also speak normally and can even repeat more difficult words.

In summary, it should be said that the law for the prevention of hereditarily defective offspring is not applicable to me. I refer in this regard to article 1, paragraph 1, of the ordinance of December 5, 1933, according to which the precondition for sterilization is that hereditary disease has been established without question.

Finally, I should not like to omit the fact that I was a gifted student. I attended secondary school with hearing classmates, completed a three-year apprenticeship as a dressmaker with the grade of "very good," learned to care for the sick and for infants, and studied bookkeeping and typing. In addition, I lived at a rooming house for au pairs in Marburg and went from there as an au pair to a doctor's household in Aachen, and later to the home of a consular official in Brussels. Affidavits and other evidence can be presented on request.

It must, of course, be recognized that the law for the prevention of offspring with hereditary diseases is fundamental for a healthy nation. But I believe that there could be nothing worse than if I were charged with hereditary deafness on the basis of the assessment, while I know, supported by the facts and evidence as well as unimpeachable witnesses, that this is not the case. You could say that the whole city of Gotha knows of that accident of thirty years ago and its unfortunate consequences. Before God and on my conscience, I cannot allow that my accident be turned into a congenital affliction by a simple stroke of the pen. I then request that the decision be subjected to a rigorous review and that it be nullified.

Heil Hitler!
(signed) Gertrud Jacob

Gotha, June 16, 1938

to: The Reich Chancellery of the Führer, Berlin
Dear Führer,

I am well aware that your responsibilities are so great and time-consuming that little attention can be given to requests such as mine. Nonetheless, I am writing to you in the hope that you may be able to address yourself to my matters for a few minutes.

For your information I append three documents:

1. The decision of the Hereditary Health Court of Arnstadt, of March 24, 1938
2. A transcript of my objection to this decision, from April 6, 1938
3. The decision of the Superior Hereditary Health Court of Jena, June 20, 1938

In my case there is no further possibility of appeal against this last decision. Yet it must lie within your power, after reviewing the case, to have the case reopened and to give me the opportunity to present myself for a rigorous basic examination. I am firmly convinced that this will yield other conclusions than those reached by Professor Zange. Then the position of the Hereditary Health Court in Jena would also have to be modified.

The reason for my request is that I am fully convinced that the Law for the Prevention of Offspring with Hereditary Diseases should not apply to me. In this, I would emphasize that I, too, recognize and applaud the necessity of this law. But, do believe me, there is nothing worse than being judged under a law when one is firmly convinced that it is inapplicable.

The decision of the Hereditary Health Court is based on two important points. In one instance my relative, August König (not Rudolf), is mentioned prominently. The other is the physician's report from Professor Zange in Jena. August König had ear infections as an infant and is deaf. Based primarily on this fact, Professor Zange declares that my deficient hearing, which now as before is more serious in one ear than in the other, is hereditary. I am firmly convinced that a subsequent thorough examination by another professor would result in an assessment contrary to that of Professor Zange. But this can only happen if you, my Führer, order it.

On all other matters, primarily my prior employment, my letter of appeal of April 6, 1938, gives sufficient information.

In the hope not to have made a vain request, my respects and Heil Hitler!

Transcript [Biesold Archive 1801/14]   Erfurt, 26 Juli, 1938
Dear Herr Weber,

Let me first apologize for not having answered your much appreciated letter at once. Various circumstances prevented me from doing so. Gertrud Jacob was an alert, attentive and good student. She never gave me the impression of one who had been born deaf. I have a vague recollection that she still remembered some words from her first years of life. After an incision in her windpipe because of a life-threatening case of quinsy, her speech became somewhat hoarser. In general, it is not a teacher's business to intervene as any kind of advocate of the deaf with a petition in the course of a judicial process. In this case, the only appropriate person for the courts is the head of the institution. This letter is just my personal opinion to you. Yours truly, Heil Hitler. Fr. Rittmeier.

Stamp; O. Schlechtweg Director of the Institution for the Deaf (ret.)

Erfurt, Pförtehenstrasse 2a

The Jacob family has asked me for information on its daughter who attended the institution here from 1902 to 1920. Since she was a very competent student, I still remember her very clearly. Gertrud Jacob came to the institute with a modest vocabulary, developed her language skills very well, and was as a result the best speaker in the class. This was possible only because she had formerly been able to hear and speak. Erfurt, 30 June, 1938 (signed) Otto Schlechtweg.[Biesold Archive 1801/17]

Notes

Introduction

1. See Henry Friedlander, *The Origins of Nazi Genocide: From Euthanasia to the Final Solution* (Chapel Hill: University of North Carolina Press, 1995).

2. See Raul Hilberg, *The Destruction of the European Jews* (Chicago: Quadrangle, 1961); Sybil Milton, "Holocaust: The Gypsies," in *Genocide in the Twentieth Century: An Anthology of Critical Essays and Oral History*, ed. Israel Charny and others (New York: Garland, 1995), 209–64.

3. See Benno Müller-Hill, *Murderous Science: Elimination by Scientific Selection of Jews, Gypsies, and Others, Germany, 1933–1945*, trans. George R. Fraser (Oxford: Oxford University Press, 1988); Peter Pulzer, *The Rise of Political Anti-Semitism in Germany and Austria* (New York: Wiley, 1964); and Donald Kenrick and Grattan Puxon, *The Destiny of Europe's Gypsies* (New York: Basic Books, 1972).

4. Garland E. Allen, "The Eugenics Record Office at Cold Spring Harbor, 1910–1940: An Essay in Institutional History," *Osiris*, 2d ser., 2 (1986): 232–33.

5. See Stephen Jay Gould, *The Mismeasure of Man* (New York: W. W. Norton, 1981); and Daniel J. Kevles, *In the Name of Eugenics: Genetics and the Uses of Human Heredity* (Berkeley and Los Angeles: University of California Press, 1986).

6. See Friedlander, *Origins of Nazi Genocide*, chap. 1; Robert Proctor, *Racial Hygiene: Medicine under the Nazis* (Cambridge: Harvard University Press, 1988); and Sheila Faith Weiss, "The Race Hygiene Movement in Germany," *Osiris*, 2d ser., 3 (1987): 193–236.

7. Cited in Loren R. Graham, "Science and Values: The Eugenics Movement in Germany and Russia in the 1920s," *American Historical Review* 82 (1977): 1143, note 24.

8. See Friedlander, *Origins of Nazi Genocide*, chap. 2; for an English translation, see Control Commission for Germany (British Element), Legal

Division, British Special Legal Research Unit, "Translations of Nazi Health Laws Concerned with Hereditary Diseases, Matrimonial Health, Sterilization, and Castration (Nov. 8, 1945)."

9. For the most detailed account, see Gisela Bock, *Zwangssterilisation im Nationalsozialismus: Studien zur Rassenpolitik und Frauenpolitik* (Opladen: Westdeutscher Verlag, 1986).

10. Bundesarchiv, Koblenz, R18/5585: "Übersicht über die Durchführung des Gesetzes zur Verhütung erbkranken Nachwuchses."

11. Elisabeth Klamper, ed., *Dokumentationsarchiv des österreichischen Widerstandes, Vienna*, vol. 19 of *Archives of the Holocaust*, ed. Henry Friedlander and Sybil Milton (New York: Garland, 1992), Doc. 50.

12. See Henry Friedlander, "Registering the Handicapped in Nazi Germany: A Case Study," *Jewish History* 11, no. 2 (1997): 89–98; Sybil Milton and David Luebke, "Locating the Victim: An Overview of Census-taking, Tabulation Technology, and Persecution in Nazi Germany," *IEEE Annals of the History of Computing* 16, no. 3 (Fall 1994): 25–39; and Götz Aly and Karl Heinz Roth, *Die restlose Erfassung: Volkszählen, Identifizieren, Aussondern im Nationalsozialismus* (Berlin: Rotbuch Verlag, 1984).

13. See Friedlander, *Origins of Nazi Genocide*; Müller-Hill, *Murderous Science*; Ernst Klee, *"Euthanasie" im NS-Staat: Die "Vernichtung lebensunwerten Lebens"* (Frankfurt: S. Fischer Verlag, 1983); and Michael Burleigh, *Death and Deliverance: "Euthanasia" in Germany, c. 1900–1945* (Cambridge: Cambridge University Press, 1995).

14. Karl Binding and Alfred Hoche, *Die Freigabe der Vernichtung lebensunwerten Lebens: Ihr Maß und Ihre Form* (Leipzig: Verlag von Felix Meiner, 1920), 27.

15. U.S. Military Tribunal, Official Transcript of the Proceedings in Case 1, United States v. Karl Brandt et al., 7304.

16. Gerhard Schmidt, *Selektion in der Heilanstalt, 1939–1945*, 2d ed. (Frankfurt: Edition Suhrkamp, 1983), 67.

17. See Friedlander, *Origins of Nazi Genocide*, chap. 5.

18. Staatsanwaltschaft Hamburg, Anklageschrift gegen Friedrich Lensch und Kurt Struve, 147 Js 58/67, April 24, 1973, 377–78.

19. Sabine Krause, "Wiedergutmachung: Die Nachkriegsgeschichte," in *"Öffne deine Hand für die Stummen": Die Geschichte der Israelitischen Taubstummen-Anstalt Berlin-Weissensee, 1873 bis 1942* (Berlin: Transit, 1993), 170–71.

Chapter 1

1. The need for a reappraisal is discussed in U. Bleidick, "Die Entwicklung und Differenzierung des Sonderschulwesens von 1898 bis 1973 im

Spiegel des Verbandes Deutscher Sonderschulen." *Zeitschrift für Heilpädagogik*, 827.

2. O. Kröhnert, "Geschichte," *Handbuch der Sonderpädagogik*, vol. 3 (1982): 51. See also A. Blau, "Abri von A. Blau über 'Geschicte des Gehörlosenbildungswesens'" in A. Blau, ed., *Enzyklopädisches Handbuch der Sonderpägogik und ihrer Grenzgebiete.* Vol. 1 (Berlin-Charlottenburg, 1969), cols. 1067–74, p. 1073.

3. Ibid.

4. J. A. Gobineau, *Versuch über die Ungleichheit der Menschenracen,* 2d ed. (Stuttgart, 1902).

5. C. Darwin, *Die Abstammung des Menschen und die geschechtliche Zuchtwahl,* 1. Teil (Stuttgart, 1871), 75.

6. W. Doeleke, "Alfred Ploetz (1860–1940) Sozialdarwinist und Gesellschaftbiologe" (Ph.D. diss., Frankfurt, 1975); G. Mann, "Rassenhygiene-Sozialdarwinismus," in *Biologismus im 19. Jahrundert,* ed. G. Mann (Stuttgart, 1973), 76.

7. K. Nowack, *"Euthanasie" und Sterilisierung im "Dritten Reich"* (Göttingen: Vandenhoeck und Ruprecht, 1977), 39.

8. O. Juliusberger, "Zur Frage der Kastration und Sterilisation von Verbrechern und Geisteskranken," *Deutsche Medizinische Wochenschrift* 9 (1912). Reprinted separately.

9. Ibid.

10. G. Hoffmann, "Die Rassenhygiene"; see also B. Bromberger, H. Mausbach, and K. Thomann, *Medizin, Faschismus und Widerstand* (Cologne: Pahl-Rugenstein, 1985), 103.

11. Nowack, *Euthanasie,* 48.

12. The law to establish the compulsory education of deaf children (*Zur Feststellung der Schulpflicht der taubstummen . . . Kinder*), 1911.

13. H. Weinert, "Das Sterilisierungsgesetz," *Blätter für Taubstummenbildung* 1 (1934): 3.

14. E. Schorsch, "Bund deutscher Taubstummenlehrer, Verbandsaufgabe," *Blätter für Taubstummenbildung* 36, no. 5 (1923): 65ff.

15. G. Neuert, "Beruf und Fortbildun der Taubstummen in Baden," *Blätter für Taubstummenbildung* 36, no. 5 (1923): 11.

16. G. Boeters, "Die Unfruchtbarmachung geistig Minderwertiger," in *Sachsische Staatszeitung* (Dresden, July 10–11, August 30–31, 1923).

17. Letter from Boeters to the Reich Public Health Authority (*Reichgesundheitsamt*), December 3, 1923; German Federal Archives, Koblenz, R86/2371.

18. G. Boeters, "Die Verhütung unwerten Lebens (Lex Zwickau)" (1923).

19. From the report of the Reich Public Health Authority to the Reich Ministry of the Interior, October 15, 1923, 3–6.

20. "Principals," the Committee for Population Policy and Racial Hygiene of the Provincial Council for Public Health, December 1, 1923; German Federal Archives, Koblenz, R86/2374.

21. Brief from Professor Bumm to the Reich Minister of the Interior, February 19, 1925; German Federal Archives, Koblenz R86/2374.

22. F. Lenz, "Soziale Notwendigkeiten der Rassenhygiene," *Süddeutsche Monatshefte* (1928): 440.

23. The review appeared in 1926 in *Blätter für Taubstummenbildung* 39, no. 9 (May 1926) and was signed *W. J.*

24. A. Abend, "Was sagt die Rassenhygiene dem Taubstummenlehrer?" *Blätter für Taubstummenbildung* (1925): 104ff.

25. Ibid.

26. Cf. P. Schumann, "Die 'Lex Zwickau' und die Taubstummen," *Blätter für Taubstummenbildung* 39, no. 14 (1926): 225ff.

27. P. Schumann, "Ursachen der Taubstummheit," in *Handbuch des Taubstummenwesens* (Osterwieck, 1929), 16.

28. Ibid., 18.

29. Ibid.

30. Weinert, "Das Sterilisierungsgesetz."

31. Ibid., 1.

32. Ibid., 2ff.

33. Schumann, "Ursachen," 252.

34. H. Maesse, "Einiges zur Frage 'Nationalsozialismus un Arbeit an Taubstummen,'" *Blätter für Taubstummenbildung* 46, no. 11 (1933): 169–70.

35. H. Weinert, "Eheberatung und Familienforschung im Dienste der Taubstummen und Schwerhörigen," *Blätter für die Wohlfahrt der Gehörlosen* 7, no. 1 (1933): 13.

36. Ibid., 15.

37. Ibid.

38. "Zeitschriftenschau," *Die Deutsche Sonderschule* 5, no. 2 (1938): 145. This review of periodicals mentions the journal *Der öffentliche Gesundheitsdienst*, published by Thieme Verlag, Leipzig. Noted in number 19 is Herbert Weinert's "Rassenhyg. Ehevermittlung."

39. H. Weinert, "Bericht über die rassenhygienische Betreuung Gehörgeschädigter in Sachsen," *Die Deutsche Sonderschule* 5 (1938): 807ff.

40. Central State Archives, Potsdam, Reich Ministry of Justice 26–248, item 252.

41. Cited from a transcription of an account by Weinert from February 15, 1935, on "Aufklarungsarbeit . . . in den Ortsgruppen der Gehörlosen und Gehörgeschädigten des Gaues Sachsen," Central State Archives, Potsdam, Reich Ministry of Justice 26–248, item 254.

42. Weinert, "Bericht," 808.

43. Central State Archives, Potsdam, Reich Ministry of Justice item 255.

44. Ibid.

45. Weinert, "Bericht," 807.

46. Ibid., 16.

47. W. Wagner, *Behinderung und Nationalsozialismus—Arbeitshypothesen zur Geschichte der Sonderschule* (Lucerne, 1977), 167.

48. O. Schmähl, *Der taubstumme Mensch* (Berlin, 1933), 106.

49. Ibid., 106ff.

50. Ibid., 107.

51. O. Schmähl, "Der deutsche Gehörlose" in *Festschrift anl. d. 2. Dt. Gl-Tages* (Breslau, 1937), 86.

52. Ibid.

53. Ibid.

54. Ibid., 90.

55. H. Hild, *Sonderpädagogik und Jugendfürsorge im Abwehrkampf* (Camberg, 1932).

56. Ibid., 37.

57. H. Hild, "Sinn und Aufgabe der Taubstummenschule im neuen Staate," *Blätter für Taubstummenbildung* 46 (1933): 233ff.

58. Ibid.

59. Ibid.

60. P. Schumann, "Das Gesetz zur Verhütung erbkranken Nachwuchses und seine Begründung," *Blätter für Taubstummenbildung* 46, no. 17 (1933).

61. Nowack, *Euthanasie.* H. Biesold, "Vergessen oder verschweigen?" *Deutsche Gehörlosen-Zeitung* 12 (1981).

62. See, for example, E. Fischer, "Taubstummheit und Eugenik," *Blätter für die Wohlfahrt der Gehörlosen* 7, no. 1 (1933). Fischer unconditionally advocated the sterilization of deaf people who wished to marry one another.

63. Schumann, "Das Gesetz."

64. P. Schumann, *Geschichte des Taubstummenwesens vom deutschen Standpunkt aus dargestellt* (Frankfurt, 1940), 675.

65. Wagner, *Behinderung,* 166.

66. E. Schorsch, "Umformung!" *Blätter für Taubstummenbildung* 46, no. 10. (1933): 145.

Chapter 2

1. "Die Erkenntnis," 2d ed., cited from P. Schumann, *Handbuch,* 16.

2. Anonymous, *Blätter für Taubstummenbildung* 1 (1888): 448. Under the heading "Miscellaneous," an opinion was voiced on the lecture "on the hereditary transmission of defects that Professor Weismann of Freiburg gave at this year's meeting of natural scientists and physicians in Cologne."

3. F. Bezold, *Die Taubstummheit auf Grund ohrenärztlicher Begutach-*

tungen (Wiesbaden, 1902). Bezold was an ear doctor and professor of ENT medicine at the University of Munich.

4. Bezold, *Die Taubstummheit,* 41.

5. Ibid., 41ff.

6. Bezold, *Die Taubstummheit,* 45.

7. H. Gutzmann, *Sprachheilkunde,* 3d ed. (Berlin, 1924). Cited from P. Schumann, *Handbuch,* 16.

8. *Wirtschaft und Statistik* 7, no. 7 (1927); included here are preliminary statistics from 1925 on the incidence of physical and mental impairment in Germany.

9. M. Werner, "Erbprognose und Sterilisierungsbegutachtung," *Die Deutsche Sonderschule* (1935): 369.

10. P. Schumann, "Die Lex Zwickau," 225ff.

11. L. M., "Die Verbreitung von Erbgebrechen im deutschen Volk" ("The Spread of Hereditary Defects in the German People"). Under the heading "Brief Notices" in *Blätter für Taubstummenbildung* 46, no. 16 (August 1933) is a reference to Verschuer's investigation, which proceeds from the "extremely conservative estimate" of a total of 300,000 hereditarily diseased persons in the German Reich.

12. E. Fischer, "Taubstummheit."

13. K. Wördehoff, "Über die Bedeutung der Vererbung in der Ätiologie der Innenohrschwerhörigkeit" (Ph.D. diss., Würzberg, 1936), noted in *Die Deutsche Sonderschule* (1937): 874.

14. Apparent here are the tragic entanglements that the deaf could also get into. On the one hand, in vol. 76, no. 1 (1942), of the *Monatsschrift für Ohrenheilkunde und Laryngo-Rhinologie,* a deaf author, bravely and at considerable personal risk, attacked Zwanziger, the principal of the school for the deaf in Nuremberg, in his capacity as the Reich group leader of Reich Professional Association V, Special Schools, in the National Socialist German Teachers Confederation, on account of his demands for the reintroduction of the legal terms *taubstumm* (deaf and dumb) and *Taubstummenschule* (school for the deaf and dumb). On the other hand, it is clear from a letter from Professor von Verschuer, director of the University Institute for Hereditary Biology and Race Hygiene in Frankfurt, that this REGEDE official was only too willing to further the objectives of the Nazi hereditary biology program. In the letter Verschuer expresses the hope that "the work begun by Dr. Wilcke, and advanced with your help, can be continued." Reference here is to Wilcke's public lecture when his medical degree was conferred, based on his dissertation from 1939. It should be mentioned that this official was demonstrably able to provide help to others who had been affected by the sterilization law; but we must also mention his murky role in Nazi party activities.

15. W. Wilcke, "Beitrag zur Erforschung der Taubstummheit im Regierungsbezirk Wiesbaden" (Ph.D. diss., Düsseldorf, 1939).

16. Ibid., 18.

17. Anon., "Buchbesprechungen," *Blätter für Taubstummenbildung* (1937): 600.

18. Ibid.

19. Ibid., 601. This reference supports the claim that deaf educators assumed functions that were not foreseen for them in the law (e.g., maintaining lists of those suspected of hereditary disease).

20. S. Seidenberg, "Ohrenärztliche Untersuchungen taubstummer Zwillinge" (Ph.D. diss., Cologne, 1941). The dissertation was examined by Professor Meyer at Gottesberge and Professor Alfred Güttich.

21. Ibid., 1.

22. Ibid., 1.

23. Ibid., 3.

24. If the total of 35,687 deaf Germans (not including the Saar region)—the number recorded in the Reich survey of impairment in 1925–1926—is taken as a base, the 15,000 hereditarily diseased deaf persons forecast by Verschuer would represent 42.03 percent. Verschuer also illustrates the continuity of race hygienic and eugenic thought from the Weimar Republic right up to the present. In the 1920s he released publications in which he called for the sterilization of the disabled. In the Third Reich he was among the leading proponents of race hygiene and then, in the Federal Republic of Germany from 1951, was director of the Institute for Human Genetics in Münster, Westphalia. Characteristically, a study was made at this institute in 1958 on infant euthanasia; see U. Sierck, "Erbgesundheit und genetische Beratung—Spuren der Vergangenheit," *Behindertenpädagogik* 1 (1986).

25. Seidenberg, "Ohrenärztliche," 58.

26. Ibid., 28.

27. E. Emmerig, "Landestaubstummenanstalt München, Jahresbericht 1927–37," *Die Deutsche Sonderschule* (1937): 461. Emmerig was the principal of the provincial school for the deaf in Munich.

28. Emmerig gave a speech on this theme during the congress of the Reich Union for Deaf Welfare on July 11, 1939, in Vienna. That the topic of hereditary biology could be dealt with in the context of a congress on the welfare of the deaf clearly shows that this organization had also fully subscribed to Nazi race ideology. The absurdity of the activities of the Reich Union for Deaf Welfare are evident in the congress proceedings. On the one hand, Emmerig complains about the false information given by the parents of deaf children concerning the causes of deafness, "for fear of referral under the sterilization law" (E. Emmerig, "Hörprüfungsergebnisse, erbbiologisch ausgewertet," in *Tagungsbericht des R.f.G.* [Vienna, 1939], 48) and speculates that "true instances of hereditary influence are to be assumed in the case of at least 40 percent of all deaf persons." On the other hand, the senior teacher and Nazi party member Oberhauser raised the question of whether

new responsibilities could accrue to the organization in the future as a consequence of the sterilization law, since this operation also led to psychological effects that required welfare efforts (*Tagungsbericht,* 23). Oberhauser derived his question from the case study of a young man whose hereditary deafness became evident only after the completion of his education and vocational training. The sterilization operation had such a psychological shock effect on him, that he became unfit for work (*Tagungsbericht,* 23). In addition, the Reich union leader, party member K. Engelmann, called for the closest collaboration among the agencies of the party, in particular National Socialist Public Welfare and the state care institutions. In Engelmann's view, the ideal collaboration of district authorities with the Reich Union for Deaf Welfare would be "a briefing of the lower service agencies of the National Socialist Public Welfare district administrations concerning the nature of the deaf (Deaf is not equivalent to hereditarily diseased"; *Tagungsbericht,* 60).

29. Emmerig, "Hörprüfungsergebnisse," 47.

30. The report for the year 1936 appeared in *Die Deutsche Sonderschule* (1937): 602ff. The school for the deaf in Leitmeritz, Czechoslovakia, was counted among the German-language schools for the deaf in other countries (see *Statistisches Jahrbuch des Bundes Deutscher Taubstummenlehrer, 1931–32,* 26ff.). 130 students attended the school.

31. Emmerig, "Hörprüfungsergebnisse," 47.

32. Promulgated in the *Reich Law Gazette* [RGBL], Part I, 1933, No. 86.

33. Nowack, *Euthanasie,* 64.

34. C. Fouquet, *Euthanasie und Vernichtung 'lebensunwerten' Lebens unter Berücksichtigung des behinderten Menschen* (Solms-Oberbiel, 1978), 52.

35. Wagner, *Behinderung,* 165ff.

36. Nowack, *Euthanasie,* 102.

37. It is beyond the scope of this book to give a proper account of the roles of the Catholic and Protestant churches in Germany and their cooperation in or resistance to the implementation of the sterilization law. Readers are referred to Nowack, *Euthanasie.*

38. Cf. *Deutsche Gehörlosen-Zeitung* 4 (1980): 100; *Unsere Gemeinde* 2 (1980): 9; *Epheta* 3 (1980): 3.

39. Now contained in the Biesold Archive, Library of the Institute for German Sign Language and Communication of the Deaf, University of Hamburg [hereafter Biesold Archive].

40. This same point is made in K. Braun and H. Biesold, TV film "Nazi-Unrecht an Gehörlosen" (Nazi Injustice Toward the Deaf), produced by "Sehen statt Hören" and broadcast January 1981 and January 1982.

41. In all my publications I have tried to make it clear to those concerned that fundamental humanitarian considerations must lie at the base of all sci-

entific inquiry into the effects and long-term consequences of the sterilization law. These humanitarian considerations will (a) support the victims' efforts to win compensation, (b) help draw victims out of their anxiety and
sense of shame, and (c) make it clear to them that this profoundly inhumane
violation of their humanity was an act of Nazi injustice.

42. My sincere thanks are due Frau Herta Giesler, pastor of the deaf in
Bremen, for her ready and willing support.

Chapter 3

1. See U. Bleidick, "Die Entwicklung," 827.

2. G. Lehmann, "Die staatliche Taubstummenanstalt zu Berlin-
Neukölln," in *Taubstummenunterricht und Taubstummen-Fürsorge im
Deutschen Reich,* ed. G. Lehmann (Düsseldorf, 1930), 32.

3. Cf. H. Biesold, "Hörschädigung-Geschichtliche Aspekte," in *Handbuch der Behindertenpädagogik* (Solms: Jarick Oberbiel, 1984).

4. Lehmann, *Taubstummenunterricht,* 35.

5. Ibid., 32.

6. Central State Archives, Potsdam, Rep. 76-VII, 3321, item 4.

7. Ibid.: "Provinzial-Schulkolleg i. d. Brandenburg . . . ," FA 10159/32, of
April 7, 1932, item 56 and overleaf.

8. Central State Archives, Potsdam, Rep. 76-VII, 3321, item 78 and
overleaf.

9. This information comes from research in the Central State Archives,
Potsdam, particularly Rep. 76-VII, Part 5\V, No. 6, vol. 17.

10. "Besprechung der N.S. Taubstummenlehrer," in *XV. Tagung des
Bundes Deutscher Taubstummenlehrer* (Halle [Saale], 1933), 9. Damaschun
wanted to advance the candidacy of Lehmann as executive officer of the
Union of German Teachers of the Deaf, so that as a professional he might
stand above things. But Damaschun was also concerned "that our Führer
must be a Führer in the National Socialist sense."

11. Biesold Archive 484, 849, 891, 1645, 1651.

12. This information has been taken from the preserved minutes book of
the School for the Deaf on Humboldtstrasse in Bremen. The secretary, War-
lich, reported to a meeting of school staff on November 29, 1934, of National
Socialist Training Camp I in Birkenweder, October 14–20, 1934, for teachers at special schools. Lehmann, among others, spoke on these topics at the
camp, which was organized for officials of the National Socialist Teachers
Confederation.

13. Biesold Archive 1651/2.

14. Biesold Archive 1651/7.

15. Biesold Archive 1043/1.

16. P. Bartsch, "Birkenwerder Nachharke," *Die Deutsche Sondershule* (1935): 262.

17. Central State Archives, Potsdam, Rep 76-VII, item 370; the letter has Ref. No. 1043.

18. Central State Archives, Potsdam, Rep 76-VII, item 372 and overleaf; the communication carries number 2498 and is dated February 7, 1938.

19. Central State Archives, Potsdam, Rep 76-VII, 3321, items 233 and overleaf, 234, 237.

20. Central State Archives, Potsdam, Rep 76-VII, 3321, items 309 and overleaf, 310, 325.

21. Central State Archives, Potsdam, Rep 76-VII, item 262 and overleaf; "Annotation E VI" by Dr. Schaefer of the Prussian Ministry for Science.

22. The following is a transcription of Wegge's handwritten notes on the register:

Examined for hereditary health—Determination in the light of the sterilization law

Register of the Provincial Institution for the Deaf in Soest

Registers for previous years list the criteria for decisions [signed] Wegge.

A–Z = Document code according to standards of the Provincial Administration

last column: 1) . . .

2) . . .

23. The relevant text of his deposition is this:

Deposition: Frau NN, born in xx, earlier residing in Königsberg, East Prussia, xx, was forcibly sterilized during the Hitler period through the offices of Senior Teacher of the Deaf, Bewer, also resident in Königsberg. Bewer is known to have been a fanatic Nazi. My home is also in Königsberg, Unterlaak 28, and I have known the applicant since our time at school here.

(Stamp) 16.11.57   Signed Alexander Hundertmark

24. This information is drawn from various compensation documents, including "Regierungspräsidium Nordbaden, Az. I/4a-36460," and from hereditary health court judgments on prosecuted deaf persons.

25. This question is derived from conventional German Sign Language, and refers to the person who made the notification under paragraphs 3 and 4 of the sterilization law, and thus initiated the "selection" process.

26. Letter from E. Singer, January 1, 1951

Baden Association for the Deaf
Provincial Welfare Union for the Deaf
and Hearing-Impaired, Heidelberg

Heidelberg, January 1, 1951

Herr NN, resident in XX,

In response to your request, we can confirm from our own knowledge of the exact circumstances that in 1936 (March 19) you were a victim of the Law for the Prevention of Offspring with Hereditary Diseases. The sterilization operation was performed at that time in the surgical clinic in Heidelberg. Chairman of the Association, (signed) Edwin Singer

27. E. Singer, "Aufstieg," *Neue Blätter für Taubstummenbildung* 1 (1946): 2.

28. Ibid., 4.

29. A. Richter, "Die Landestaubstummenanstalt zu Homberg," in Lehmann, *Taubstummenunterricht*, 80ff.

30. *Statistisches Jahrbuch, 1931*, 22ff.

31. In 1937 the school was moved to Frankfurt am Main, when a police academy was established in the school building.

32. Cf. H. Maesse, "Betrachtungen zum Gesetz zur Verhütung erbkranken Nachwuchses," *Die Deutsche Sonderschule* (1935): 161.

33. Biesold Archive S. 160.

34. Biesold Archive HR/39/34.

35. Biesold Archive HR/39/35. Name omitted for reasons of confidentiality.

36. Cf. *Statistisches Jahrbuch*, 2.

37. Heidbrede was demonstrably a participant in Nazi Training Camp I in Birkenweder, in October 1934, which was organized for officials of the National Socialist German Teachers Confederation; cf. *Die Deutsche Sonderschule*, 272.

38. Cf. Maesse, "Betrachtungen," 161.

39. Biesold Archive SL/20, 1 and 2.

40. See Maesse, "Betrachtungen," 161. Biesold Archive SL/19/1ff.

41. Biesold Archive SL/12.

42. Biesold Archive SL/16/1.

43. Biesold Archive SL/16/2.

44. Biesold Archive SL/17/1.

45. Biesold Archive SL/17/2.

46. Biesold Archive SL 11/181.

47. Biesold Archive 971/2.

48. Biesold Archive 117/2.

49. Biesold Archive 612/3. *Statistisches Jahrbuch*, 59, lists Franz Schmid as director of the St. Josef Private Institution in Schwäbisch Gmünd. The listing of the male teaching staff names Georg Schmid as a senior teacher of the deaf. All other teachers were nuns. Two more nuns taught crafts and worked in the kindergarten.

50. Cf. "Statistische Nachrichten," 55.

51. *Reich Law Gazette* (1933): Part 1, 1022.

52. Biesold Archive 1235/2.

53. Cf. Nowack, *Euthanasie*, 106.

54. Ibid., 110.

55. *Statistisches Jahrbuch*, 96.

56. Biesold Archive WI 83/1.

57. Biesold Archive WI 83/24.

58. Biesold Archive WI 83/52.

59. Ibid.

60. Biesold Archive WI 83/52.

61. Biesold Archive WI 83/55.

62. Biesold Archive WI 83/15, p. 1.

63. Ibid.

64. Biesold Archive WI 83/13, p. 4.

65. Ibid.

66. Handwritten comment, Biesold Archive WI 83/13, p. 1.

67. Biesold Archive 1162/1.

68. Biesold Archive 1162/2.

69. Biesold Archive 1162/5, p. 1.

70. Biesold Archive 1162/1, p. 1.

71. Biesold Archive WI 83/3, p. 1, entries 13 and 19.

72. Biesold Archive WI 83/25.

73. Biesold Archive WI 83/50.

74. Biesold Archive WI 83/58.

75. The brackets and X are entered by hand. In the margin is the handwritten comment, in Müller's handwriting: "Not applicable, since she was admitted to the institution for training, not for custody."

76. Biesold Archive WI 83/14.

77. Biesold Archive WI 83/58.

78. P. Bartsch, "Birkenwerder Nachharke," 262; A. Winnewisser, "Ist angeborene Taubheit immer Erbtaubheit?" *Die Deutsche Sonderschule* (1938): 426; Eisermann, director of the School for the Deaf in Tilsit and Hitler Youth Führer of Reich Banner G, cited from E. Weng, "Weihe eines neuen HJ-Heimes des Reichsbannes Gehörgeschädigte (G) in Tilsit," *Die Deutsche Sonderschule* 11 (1938).

Chapter 4

1. Promulgated in the *Reich Law Gazette* on June 27, 1935.
2. Gisela Bock, *Zwangssterilisation im Nationalsozialismus: Studien zur Rassenpolitik und Frauenpolitik* (Opladen: Westdeutscher Verlag, 1986), 384.
3. Biesold Archive 1071/2.

Chapter 5

1. P. Schumann, *Geschichte,* 675.
2. See section on Karl Wacker in chapter 6.
3. Questionnaire MGIPSIG/99 (revised May 15, 1945): K. Wacker. Military Government of Germany, B. Membership in the Nazi party, Question 2.
4. F. Albreghs, "Von Weimar bis Breslau." *Festschrift anl. d. 2. Dt. Gl-Tages* (Breslau, 1937), 9.
5. H. Siepmann, "Neue grosse Aufgaben für uns Gehörlose." *Blätter für die Wohlfahrt der Gehörlosen* 3/4 (1933): 38ff.
6. Ibid., 40.
7. G/2 indicates a member of the second division of the SA. This newsletter is preserved but in a damaged condition as a result of the war. It is not possible to make a copy.
8. Biesold Archive 891/83, memories of forcibly sterilized deaf Berliners from July 15, 1983.
9. Ibid.
10. Ibid.
11. F. Albreghs, "Von Weimar," 9.
12. Biesold Archive Bd. I, I 03, undated.
13. To preserve the confidentiality of personal information, the name of the signatory is not given. The reader's letter appeared in the *Deutsche Gehörlosen-Zeitung* 5 (1980): 140.
14. Cf. *Festschrift des Reichverbandes,* 32ff.
15. The signatory's name is withheld for reasons of confidentiality. This reader's letter appeared in the *Deutsche Gehörlosen-Zeitung* 7 (1980): 203.
16. Neither Albreghs nor Ballier is still alive.
17. F. Albreghs, "Von Weimar," 4.
18. Ibid., 5.
19. Ibid., 6.
20. Ibid., 6.
21. Ibid., 7.
22. Ibid., 8.
23. Ibid., 9.

24. *Festschrift 2, Deutscher Gehörlosentages*, 62.

25. I owe this information to the research of a school group of hearing-impaired youngsters of the Marcusallee School in Bremen, who successfully competed for the prize in German History 1982–1983 offered by the president of the German Federal Republic with the topic "Forcible Sterilization of the Deaf in the Third Reich." Their tutors were K. Didier, M. Hampe, L. Meyer, all teachers at the Marcusallee special school. The students' work, which I supported, was awarded a fourth prize. See H. Biesold, "'Euthanasie'-und Sterilisationsopfer: Zum Beispiel die Gehörlosen," in *Nicht irgendwo sondern hier bei uns!* (Korber-Stiftung: Hamburg, 1982), 97ff.

26. Central State Archives, Potsdam, Reich Ministry of Justice, Section II, 1782–26–338, item 10.

27. Ibid., overleaf.

28. Central State Archives, Potsdam, Reich Ministry of Justice, Section II, 1782–23.11, item 11.

29. Central State Archives, Potsdam, Reich Ministry of Justice, Section II, 1782–26–338, item 38 and overleaf.

Chapter 6

1. H. Weinert, "Bericht," 808.

2. Ibid.

3. M. Wallisfurth, *Sie hat es mir erzählt*, 2d ed. (Freiburg, 1979), 276.

4. *Reichsgesetzblatt (Reich Law Gazette)* (1933): Part 1, 530.

5. Pope Paul VI, "Pro Ecclesia et Pontifice" (1973).

6. *Statistisches Jahrbuch des Bundes Deutscher Taubstummenlehrer, 1931–32*, 22.

7. Central State Archives, Potsdam, Rep 76-VII, 3321, item 309 overleaf.

8. Central State Archives, Potsdam, Rep 76-VII, 3321, item 325 and overleaf.

9. Biesold Archive 1075/1.

10. Biesold Archive 1075/3.

11. Biesold Archive 1075/6.

12. Biesold Archive 1075/4. This document deals with the decision of the superior hereditary health court of Kiel, July 20, 1940, which relates to the decision of the hereditary health court, first instance, of April 18, 1940.

13. Biesold Archive 1075/4, p. 3.

14. Ibid., p. 1.

15. From what is known today, deafness or hearing loss never occurred among the relatives of the parents of Hermann Sommer nor among those of his wife, Ilse Sommer, who lost her hearing at the age of eight. All five surviving Sommer children are hearing. There are twenty-seven grandchildren and seven great-grandchildren, all hearing.

16. Biesold Archive.

17. Biesold Archive.

18. Stuttgart Court of Appeals III, file 49/60/3651/3 B3205/47. The decision was handed down on July 5, 1948. I have a photocopy of the original documents, but reproduction is not possible due to the poor quality.

19. Ibid., 3.

20. Decision of the Stuttgart Court of Appeals.

21. A copy of this letter was made with the now obsolete "negative process," and further reproduction is not possible. A transcript of the letter exists.

22. Biesold Archive.

23. This affidavit was certified by the district notary public, Ellwangen, on December 23, 1946. A further copy cannot be made since the available copy is a negative.

24. At her express wish, Jacob's birth name has been retained in transcriptions of documents and of the interview. For reasons of personal privacy, however, the names of her relatives have been suppressed. In the interview, the abbreviation G.J. is used.

25. At this point, reference should be made to the work of Weinert, who even before 1933 was engaged in marriage counseling and family research from a eugenics perspective. His intentions have already been made clear, but can be further illustrated by the case of Frau Jacob; hearing-impaired persons who were demonstrably not "hereditarily diseased" were delivered to the machinery of the race hygienists through Weinert's "advisory" and "mediating" activity.

26. Herr Jacob's affidavit is preserved in transcript as Biesold Archive 1801/3. The essential part of Weinert's letter of February 20, 1937, reads as follows:

Herbert Weinert, Klotzsche, Melancthonstrasse 8. Dear Fräulein Jacob. Unfortunately, your father's affidavit, a copy of which you enclosed with your last letter, is scarcely valid for the requirements of a marriage license office, since it is not an official document. I do not doubt its authenticity, but, in the event of a possible marriage union, the question for the health authority is whether you are to be declared hereditarily healthy or hereditarily deaf. Looking ahead, I would like to make some specific suggestions, so that the health authority will not raise objections. The health authority will, in fact, have to approve your application, and issue the requested certificate. But it will probably not be aware that you are requesting the document with a view to a marriage license. This would completely change the situation for the health authority, which has assumed thus far that your application had a purely theoretical purpose. Perhaps in a future application you will state your

true purpose. I think that the matter would then be handled more ex-
peditiously. (BA 1801/7)

27. An excerpt from the Law for the Protection of the Hereditary Health
of the German People (marriage health law) of October 18, 1935 (*Reich Law
Gazette* 1935, Part I, p. 1246), confirms Frau J.'s account. In section 1, point
1, it states that "a marriage may not be joined . . . [there follows an explanation of exclusionary conditions under the letters a to c; d then reads:] if one
of the betrothed suffers from hereditary disease in the sense of the Law for
the Prevention of Offspring with Hereditary Diseases."
    28. Biesold Archive 1801/9. A copy of the decision of the Hereditary
Health Court of Arnstadt from March 28, 1938, has been preserved.
    29. Biesold Archive 1801/1. I have a copy of the passage from the news-
paper, *Thüringer Gauzeitung*, of December 12, 1940. Zange's service is evaluated on the occasion of his sixtieth birthday under the heading "Kultur-
spiegel." The last sentence of the third paragraph states that "Prof. Zange is
active as a medical evaluator for the Thuringian Superior Hereditary Health
Court."
    30. Biesold Archive 1801/11, the decision of the Superior Hereditary
Health Court of Jena, Wg 237/38, of June 3, 1938. In this decision, too, hereditary predisposition is raised as an issue: "Your cousin is also deaf." The objection of Frau J. that her cousin was late-deafened as a result of illness is dismissed without being tested, with the comment "there can be no question
of an adventitious impairment in his case." The judgment of the ear specialist, Dr. Rosenbaum (then deceased), that is cited in the appeal, is not discussed. There could be no recognition among Nazi race doctors of the opinion of a Jewish doctor. It is simply ignored with the following comment: "If
Dr. Rosenbaum did make the statement attributed to him in the appeal, it
will not stand up to the scrutiny of a professional physician." In any case,
"true professional physicians" found no evidence in this judgment for
demonstrable prior possession of spoken language by this "hereditarily diseased person." "The incipient linguistic development that Gertrud Jacob
displayed until the time of her accident will not be judged here. The clinical
findings and the case of her cousin leave no doubt." This is how the decision
was reached. The concluding part of the decision is reproduced unabridged
in order to support further the claim that counterevidence of any kind was
always dismissed untested, with race-hygienic phrasing.
    31. Biesold Archive 1801/16. In the response of the REGEDE district su-
pervisor, Arthur Weber, from July 28, 1938 (ref. GBI 582/38), he informs his
"fellow-sufferer" that he is enclosing "an expert opinion from the director
of the university ear clinic in Leipzig for her information." "You can draw
your own conclusion whether there is any purpose in your addressing yourself to Leipzig. I would ask you to treat the expert opinion as highly confiden-

tial, as otherwise, as I earlier told you, I would have to make an acquaintance with the concentration camp."

The expert opinions of the senior teacher of the deaf, Rittmeier, and the director of the institution for the deaf, Schlechtweg, are found in appendix 3 [Biesold Archive 1801/14 and 1801/17]. Both of these professional educators independently attest to Gertrud Jacob's acquisition of spoken language and thus invalidate the hereditary factor in the grounds of the hereditary health court decision. The stand taken by the teacher, Rittmeier, at the end of his submission, is further evidence of the "half-hearted advocacy" of educators of the deaf. On the other hand, the courageous position of Schlechtweg shows that educators could indeed create opportunities to save deaf students from the clutches of Nazi institutions.

32. Biesold Archive 1801/13.

33. Section 5, point 1, of the marriage health law states: "The prescriptions of this law are not applicable if both the engaged have or the male partner has foreign citizenship" (*Reich Law Gazette* 1935, Part 1, p. 1246).

34. Biesold Archive 1801/18 is a copy of this letter from the senior president of the provincial court of Jena, dated July 3, 1938 (ref. Az. 3133-J 62/38). The letter states that the "submission to the Führer and Reich Chancellor of June 16, 1938, was referred by the Reich Minister of Justice" to the senior president of the provincial court of Jena "for administrative handling." The letter expresses regret "not to have been able to deal with the matter to your satisfaction." It continues: "According to what you have presented, there are otherwise no grounds to take up the appeal again, which would have to be effected through the hereditary health court." The reason why Hitler himself did not grant an exemption cynically follows, with almost the same race-hygienic phrases that figured in the grounds of the decision of the superior hereditary health court of Jena, dated May 20, 1938 (cf. BA 1801/11): "The Führer and Reich Chancellor will not intervene with a pardon, since the decree that a person is to be sterilized is in no way a punishment. The decree is rather for the maintenance of the national collectivity and in the interests of the racial improvement of the German people, and individual citizens will be required to make the sacrifice that is asked of them, because there is an imminent danger that their offspring will also suffer from the affliction, and that their descendants will at least carry the seed of the impairment with which they are afflicted."

Chapter 7

1. I was able to establish the following data: number of congenitally and adventitiously deaf of the Jewish faith in the German Reich (excluding Baden and Württemberg, and the Saar Region) according to their own statement

= 531 + (assuming 10.91 percent of total German population for Baden and Württemberg = 58) = 589 + (1.10 percent for the Saar = 6) = 595. To be added are 88 students who described themselves as Jewish, for a total of 683. The remaining 317, in my estimate, would consist of persons who were very hard of hearing, were late deafened, or had multiple disabilities.

2. F. Reich, "50 Jahre Israelitische Taubstummenanstalt und ihr Gründer Dir. M. Reich," in *Beiträge zur Fortbildung und Unterhaltung der Taubstummen* (1923), 6.

3. Ibid., 7.

4. S. Adler, *The Morning and the Evening Sacrifice* (London, 1864), 13ff.

5. Nedarin, 41a.

6. F. Reich, "Der Mosaische Religionsunterricht," in *Handbuch des Taubstummenwesens* (Osterwieck, 1929), 450.

7. F. Reich, "Die Israelitische Taubstummenanstalt für Deutschland zu Berlin-Weissensee," in *Taubstummenunterricht*, ed. G. Lehmann (Dusseldorf, 1930), 43.

8. E. Reich, "Taubstumme Entstummen!" *Jüdische Rundschau*, 1st supplement (April 26, 1934).

9. M. Meyer, "Markus Reich als Direktor," in F. Reich, "50 Jahre," ed. F. Reich (1923), 9ff.

10. Enrollment Statistics from the Israelite Institution for the Deaf

Year	Number of Students	Explanation
1873	4	Founding year
1889	12	Last year at the Fürstenwalde facility
1890	22	First year at Weissensee
1911	48	Reconstruction at Weissensee, Markus Reich dies
1916	34	First World War
1919	43	28 boys and 15 girls
1920	48	31 boys and 17 girls
1921 (no new admissions)	48	31 boys and 17 girls
1922–25	53	33 boys and 20 girls
1926 (no new admissions)	48	26 boys and 22 girls
1927	55	32 boys and 23 girls
1930	58	35 boys and 23 girls
1931/32	59	36 boys and 23 girls

11. E. Reich, 1934.

12. From Nos. 40–44, Annual Reports for 1923–1927 of the Association Friends of the Deaf—*Jedide Ilmim* (Berlin-Weissensee, 1927).

13. Countries of origin for students enrolled in 1927:

Berlin	11	Württemberg	1
East Prussia	2	Saar Region	1
Pommerania	1	Lithuania	4
Thuringia	2	Poland	8
Westphalia	4	Czechoslovakia	2
Frankfurt am Main	8	Yugoslavia	1
Hessen-Nassau	2	Belgium	1
Rhineland	2	Mexico	1
Bavaria	2	Palestine	1

14. F. Reich, "Die Israelitische Taubstummenanstalt," 43.

15. Central State Archives, Potsdam, Reich Ministry of Justice, 26–250, item 161.

16. *Jüdische Rundschau* (September 28, 1934).

17. H. D. Leuner, *Als Mitlied ein Verbrechen war (When Compassion Was A Crime)* (Wiesbaden, 1967), 101ff.

18. Ibid., 102.

Chapter 8

1. H. Kretz, "Folgen der Sterilisation," 1341.

2. Gütt, Rüdin, and Ruttke, *Das Gesetz zur Verhütung erbkranken Nachwuchses vom 14. Juli 1933 nebst Ausführungsbestimmungen* (Munich, 1936), 224.

3. Bock, *Zwangssterilisation,* 374.

4. Ibid.

5. Ibid., 375.

6. Wissmann, 1936, 2176–79; Boeninghaus, 1935, 9–20; cite from Rothmaler, 1991, 188.

7. H. Weinert, "Zwei Äusserungen zur Sterilisation," *Die Deutsche Sonderschule* (1934): 578.

8. Central State Archives, Potsdam, Reich Ministry of Justice, 15.01, 26–248, item 101. Otherwise, the physicians of the German Union of Physicians Associations in their concern called for a special law that would heighten existing security. Forcible sterilization was expressly rejected.

9. Ibid., item 101 overleaf.

10. Ibid., 148/15, dated May 8, 1935.

11. P. Petersen, *Sterilisation* (Stuttgart, 1981), 3.

12. H. Kretz, "Folgen der Sterilization," 1298ff.; Kretz quotes the Federal Attorney General's office from *Deutsche Richterzeitung* (1965), 22.

13. Statements reflecting the syntactic patterns of German Sign Language have been edited by the author. These quotations are not arbitrarily

selected from among the several hundred pieces of correspondence with forcibly sterilized deaf persons.

14. Biesold Archive 931/5.

15. Biesold Archive 1453/3.

16. In German Sign Language the concept of sterilization is usually expressed by two signs, HITLER and CUT. The use of a single sign—right thumb extended from a closed fist [A handshape] and drawn from left to right across the abdomen—is frequently accompanied by the mouthed word *Hitlerschnitt* (HITLER CUT).

17. Biesold Archive 408/1.

18. Biesold Archive 155/1.

19. Biesold Archive BbI II, 133/80

20. Biesold Archive BbI, 879/82.

21. Biesold Archive BbI II, 241/80.

22. Biesold Archive BbI II, 1453/82.

23. Biesold Archive BbI II, 1471/82.

24. Biesold Archive BbI II, 1202/81.

25. A formal editorial error occurred in the questionnaire. Questions 1 and 2 were originally conceived as a single question: "Do you still suffer pain from the sterilization, psychological pain?" But the incorrect division into two questions did serve as a control factor in evaluating responses to question 3.

26. K. Kolle, "Die Opfer der nationalsozialistischen Verfolgung in psychiatrischer Sicht," *Der Nervenarzt* 29, no. 4 (1958): 153.

27. Kretz, "Folgen der Sterilisation," 1341.

28. Ibid.

29. Kolle, "Die Opfer," 154.

30. Biesold Archive 931/4.

31. M. Ekblad, *The Prognosis after Sterilization on Social-Psychiatric Grounds* (Copenhagen, 1961), cited from Kretz, op. cit., p. 1302; T. von Uexküll, *Lehrbuch der psychosomatischen Medizin,* 2d ed. (Munich, 1981), 717ff.

32. Ibid., 1343.

33. Susanne Fortlage; Nowack, *Euthanasie,* 102.

34. Biesold Archive, 1437.

35. Biesold Archive, 516.

36. Of the total of 1,396 respondents, 433 had been sterilized between the ages of thirteen and eighteen. Of the 131 male and 155 female respondents who responded to the question about physical pain affirmatively, 124 men (94.66 percent) and 151 women (97.42 percent) gave more precise indications of their experience of pain.

37. Kolle, "Die Opfer," 155.

38. Kretz, "Folgen der Sterilisation," 1302.

39. Biesold Archive 722.

40. Biesold Archive 290 and 366.
41. Statements have been translated from German Sign Language.
42. Biesold Archive 1506/2 f.
43. Biesold Archive 796/732.
44. Biesold Archive 869/743.
45. See N. Schmacke and H.-G. Güse, *Zwangssterilisiert verleugnet vergessen, zur Geschichte der nationalsozialistischen Rassenhygiene am Beispiel Bremen* (Bremen, 1984), 122ff.
46. Central State Archives, Potsdam, Reich Ministry of the Interior, II 1079d/7.7, item 4.
47. State Archives, Schwerin, Mecklenburg Main Provincial Archive, 11131 (via the Central State Archives, Potsdam).
48. Bock, *Zwangssterilisation,* 376.
49. Central State Archives, Potsdam, Reich and Prussian Ministry of the Interior, IVf 3506 III/1079.
50. Central State Archives, Potsdam, Reich Ministry of Justice, IVb 4279.
51. Central State Archives, Potsdam, Reich Ministry of Justice, 6234, item 72 and overleaf.
52. Central State Archives, Potsdam, Reich Ministry of Justice, 6234, item 2b.
53. Biesold Archive 1041/1042.
54. Biesold Archive 949/914.
55. Biesold Archive 1114.
56. Biesold Archive 182/170.
57. State Archives, Schwerin, Mecklenburg Main Provincial Archive, 11131. In this sampling, notifications of the public health authorities concerning sterilization in accordance with section 11, paragraph 2, of the sterilization law and article 8 of the implementation ordinance were screened. The following archival materials were employed: 13, 77, 89, 124, 126 (via the Central State Archives, Potsdam).

Chapter 9

1. See also the relevant works of C. Fouquet (1978), K. Nowack (1978), E. Klee (1983), B. Müller-Hill (1984), and B. Bromberger, H. Mausbach, and K. Thomann (1985).
2. Central State Archives, Potsdam, Reich Ministry of the Interior, 26228/1, item 12 overleaf. For more information see K. Dörner, "Nationalsozialismus und Lebensvernichtung," *Vierteljahreshefte für Zeigeschichte* (1967): 137.
3. Professor Catel, Professor Heinze, and Dr. Wentzler.
4. Nowack, *Euthanasie,* 77.
5. Ibid., 78.

6. Cited from Nowack, *Euthanasie,* 79, in original; translation from Friedlander, *Origins of Nazi Genocide,* 67.

7. Nowack, *Euthanasie,* 80.

8. C. Fouquet, *Euthanasie und Vernichtung "lebensunwerten" Lebens unter Berücksichtigung des behinderten Menschen* (Sohms-Oberbiel: Jarick Oberbiel, 1978), 65ff.

9. Nowack, *Euthanasie,* 84.

10. Ibid., 85.

11. See E. Klee, *Euthanasie im NS-Staat* (Frankfurt: S. Fischer, 1983), 367ff., 401ff.

12. Biesold Archive 1705.

13. K. Kupiul, *Quellen zur Geschichte des deutschen Protestantismus (1871–1945),* (Göttingen, 1960), 300ff.

14. E. Kogon, *Nationalsozialistische Massentötungen durch Giftgas* (Frankfurt: S. Fischer, 1983), 60/327.

15. Biesold Archive 1504/82.

16. Klee, *Euthanasie im NS-Staat,* 138.

17. Biesold Archive Eu 12/3.

18. Biesold Archive 1617/2, 939/5.

19. See Klee *Euthanasie im NS-Staat,* 267.

20. Biesold Archive 353/2.

21. Biesold Archive 353/3.

22. Biesold Archive 353/4.

Author's Bibliography

Abend, A. "Was Sagt die Rassenhygiene dem Taubstummenlehrer?" *Blätter für Taubstummenbildung* (1925).

Adler, S. *The Morning and the Evening Sacrifice.* London, 1864.

Albreghs, F. "Von Weimar bis Breslau." *Festschrift anl. d. 2. Dt. Gl-Tages.* Breslau, 1937.

Bartsch, P. "Birkenwerder nachharke." *Die Deutsche Sonderschule* (1935). Library of Congress preservation microfilming program: Washington, D.C.: Library of Congress photoduplication service; 35 mm microfilm reels.

Bastian, T. *Von der Eugenik zur Euthanasie.* Bad Wörishofen, 1981.

Baur, E., E. Fischer, and F. Lenz. *Menschliche Erblichkeitslehre und Rassenhygiene,* Vols. 2–3. Munich: J. F. Lehmann, 1932.

Bayer, W., K. Häfner, and Kisker. *Psychiatrie der Verfolgten.* Berlin, 1964.

Bezold, F. *Die Taubstummheit auf Grund ohrenärztlicher Begutachtungen.* Wiesbaden, 1902.

Biesold, H. "Sind 5.000-DM Entschädigung für Zwangssterilisierte genug?" *Deutsche Gehörlosen-Zeitung* (1981): 2.

———. "Vergessen oder verschweigen?" *Deutsche Gehörlosen-Zeitung* (1981): 12.

———. "'Euthanasie' und Sterilisationsopfer: Zum Beispiel die Gehörlosen." *Nicht irgendwo, sondern hier bei uns!* Hamburg: Körber-Stiftung, 1982.

———. "Vergessen oder verschweigen? Gehörlose Nazi-Opfer klagen an." *Behindertenpädagogik* 3 (1982).

———. "Härteentschädigung für Zwangssterilisierte." *Recht und Psychiatrie* 2 (1983). Rehburg-Loccum: Psychiatrie-Verlag.

———. "Sterilisation im Hitler-Reich." *Hörgeschädigten Pädagogik* 2 (1984).

———. "Deutsche Gehörlosenbildung im Faschismus." In *Zum Verhältnis von Pädagogik und Sonderpädagogik.* Lucerne, 1984.

———. "Hörschädigung-Geschichtliche Aspekte." *Handbuch der Behindertenpädagogik.* Solms-Oberbiel, 1984.

212   Author's Bibliography

Binding, K., and A. Hoche. *Die Freigabe der Vernichtung lebensunwerten Lebens, ihr Ma und ihre Form.* Leipzig, 1920.

Blau, A. "Geschichte des Gehörlosenbildungswesens." In *Enzyklopädisches Handbuch der Sonderpädagogik und ihrer Grenzgebiet,* edited by A. Blau. Vol. 1: 1067–74. Berlin, 1969.

Bleidick, U. "Die Entwicklung und Differenzierung des Sonderschulwesens von 1898 bis 1973 im Spiegel des Verbandes Deutscher Sonderschule." *Zeitschrift für Heilpädagogik.* 824–45.

Bock, G. *Zwangssterilisation im Nationalsozialismus: Studien zur Rassenpolitik und Frauenpolitik.* Opladen: Westdeutscher Verlag, 1986.

Boeters, G. "Die Unfruchtbarmachung geistig Minderwertiger." *Sächsische Staatszeitung* (July/August) 1923.

Braun, K., and H. Biesold. Nazi-Unrecht an Gehörlosen. Produced by Sehen statt Hören. Munich: Bavarian Television. Television broadcast, 1982.

Bromberger, B., H. Mausbach, and K. Thomann. *Medizin, Faschismus und Widerstand.* Cologne: Pahl-Rugenstein, 1985.

Büchner, F. *Vom geistigen Standort der modernen Medizin.* Freiburg, 1957.

Darwin, C. *Die Abstammung des Menschen und die geschlechtliche Zuchtwahl, 1. Teil.* Stuttgart, 1871.

Denker, A. *Taubstummheit.* Halle, 1919.

Doeleke, W. "Alfred Ploetz (1860–1940): Sozialdarwinist und Gesellschaftsbiologe." Frankfurt: Unpublished doctoral dissertation, 1975.

Dörner, K. "Nationalsozialismus und Lebensvernichtung." *Vierteljahreshefte für Zeitgeschichte* 15 (1967).

———. *Der Krieg gegen die psychisch Kranken.* Rehburg-Loccum: Psychiatrie-Verlag, 1980.

Ekblad, M. *The Prognosis after Sterilization on Social-Psychiatric Grounds.* Copenhagen, 1961.

Emmerig, E. "Landestaubstummenanstalt München, Jahresbericht 1927–37." *Die Deutsche Sonderschule* (1937). Washington, D.C.: Library of Congress preservation microfilming program. Microfilm reels; 35 mm.

———. "Hörprüfungsergebnisse, erbbiologisch ausgewertet." *Tagungsbericht des R.f.G.* Vienna, 1939.

Fischer, E. "Taubstummheit und Eugenik." *Blätter für die Wohlfahrt der Gehörlosen* 7, no. 1 (1933).

Fouquet, C. *Euthanasie und Vernichtung "lebensunwerten" Lebens unter Berücksichtigung des behinderten Menschen.* Sohms-Oberbiel: Jarick Oberbiel, 1978.

Fuhrmann, W., and F. Vogel. Genetische Familienberatung. 3d ed. Berlin, 1982.

Gamm, H.-J. "Der Faschismuskomplex und die Sonderpädagogik." *Zeitschrift für Heilpädagogik* 34, no. 12 (1983): 789–97.

————. *Führung und Verführung, Pädagogik des Nationalsozialismus.* 2d ed. Frankfurt, 1984.

Gaupp, R. *Die Unfruchtbarmachung geistig und sittlicher Kranker und Minderwertiger.* Berlin.

Gobineau, J. A. *Versuch über die Ungleichheit der Menschenracen.* 2d ed. Stuttgart, 1902.

Grele, R., et al. "Oral History—Geschichte von unten." *Literatur und Erfahrung* 10 (1982).

Güse, H.-G., and N. Schmacke. *Psychiatrie zwischen bürgerlicher Revolution und Faschismus,* 2 vols. Kronberg: Athenäum-Verlag, 1976.

Gütt, A., E. Rüdin, and F. Ruttke. *Das Gesetz zur Verhütung erbkranken Nachwuchses vom 14. Juli 1933 nebst Ausführungsbestimmungen.* Munich, 1934.

Gutzmann, H. *Sprachheilkunde.* 3d ed. Berlin, 1924.

Hauner, M. *Hitler, A Chronology of His Life and Time.* London, 1983.

Hild, H. *Sonderpädagogik und Jugendfürsorge im Abwehrkampf.* Camberg, 1932. Duplicated.

————. "Sinn und Aufgabe der Taubstummenschule im neuen Staate." *Blätter für Taubstummenbildung* 46 (1933): 233.

Hoffman, G. "Die Rassenhygiene in dem Vereinigten Staaten von Nordamerika." *Deutsche Medizinische Wochenschrift,* 1985.

Holste, U. "Gebärdensprache im Brennpunkt internationaler empirischer Forschung." *Hörgeschädigtenpädagogik* 1 (1982).

Jantzen, W. *Behinderung und Faschismus, in Konstitutionsprobleme materialistischer Behindertenpädagogik.* Lollar, 1977.

————. "Behindertenpädagogik, gestern, heute und morgen." *Handbuch der Behindertenpädagogik,* 280–93. Munich: Kösel, 1979.

Juliusburger, O. "Zur Frage der Kastration und Sterilisation von Verbrechern und Geistes kranken." *Deutsche Medizinische Wochenschrift* 9. Stuttgart: Georg Thieme Verlag, 1912.

Klee, E. *Euthanasie im NS-Staat.* Frankfurt: S. Fischer, 1983.

————. *Dokumente zur Euthanasie.* Frankfurt: Fischer Taschenbuch, 1985.

Kogon, E., et al. *Nationalsozialistische Massentötungen durch Giftgas.* Frankfurt: S. Fischer, 1983.

Kolle, K. "Die Opfer der nationalsozialistischen Verfolgung in Psychiatrischer Sicht," *Der Nervenarzt* 29, no. 4 (1958).

Kramer, H. *Die Erkenntnis und Heilung der Ohrenkrankheiten.* 2d ed. Leipzig, 1836.

Krause, W. "Kein Geld für die Gehörlosen." *Der Stern* 16 (1981): 266ff.

Kretz, H. "Folgen der Sterilisation: Zur Frage der Entschädigung Zwangssterilisierter nach dem Bundesentschädigungsgesetz." *Medizinische Klinik* 62 (1967): 34, 35.

Kröhnert, O. *Die sprachliche Bildung des Gehörlosen.* Weinheim, 1966.

————. "Geschichte." In *Handbuch der Sonderpädagogik,* vol. 3, 1982.

Kupiul, K. *Quellen zur Geschichte des deutschen Protestantismus (1871–1945).* Göttingen, 1960.

Lehmann, G., ed. *Taubstummenunterricht und Taubstummen-Fürsorge im Deutschen Reich.* Düsseldorf, 1930.

Lenz, F. "Soziale Notwendigkeiten der Rassenhygiene." *Süddeutsche Monatshefte,* 1928.

Leuner, H. D. *Als Mitleid ein Verbrechen war.* Wiesbaden, 1967.

Maesse, H. "Taubstummenbildung und-fürsorge im nationalsozialistischen Staat." In *Die Deutsche Sonderschule* 1 (1934): 21.

————. "Einiges zur Frage 'Nationalsozialismus und Arbeit an Taubstummen.'" *Blätter für Taubstummenbildung* 46 (1933): 11.

————. "Betrachtungen zum Gesetz zur Verhütung erbkranken Nachwuchses." *Die Deutsche Sonderschule* (1935): 161.

Maier, W. *Das Problem der Leiblichkeit.* Tübingen, 1964.

Mann, G. "Rassenhygiene-Sozialdarwinismus." In *Biologismus im 19. Jahrhundert,* ed. G. Mann. Stuttgart, 1973.

Meyer, M. "Markus Reich als Direktor." In *50 Jahre Israelitische Taubstummenanstalt und ihr Gründer Direktor M. Reich,* ed. F. Reich, 1923.

Neuert, G. "Beruf und Fortbildung der Taubstummen in Baden." *Blätter für Taubstummenbildung* 36 (1923): 5.

Nowack, K. *"Euthanasie" und Sterilisierung im "Dritten Reich."* Göttingen: Vandenhoeck und Ruprecht, 1977.

Paul, H. *Psychische Spätschäden nach politischer Verfolgung.* 2d ed. Basel, 1967.

Petersen, P. *Sterilisation.* Stuttgart, 1981.

Peukert, D., and J. Reulecke. *Die Reihen fast geschlossen Beiträge zur Geschichte des Alltags unterm Nationalsozialismus.* Wuppertal: Hammer, 1981.

Peukert, D., and J. Reulecke. "Die Reihen fast geschlossen." In *Beiträge zur Geschichte des Alltags unterm Nationalsozialismus.* Wuppertal, 1981.

Pfefferle, F. "Untersuchungen über die Kinder der Taubstummenanstalt Heidelberg, Stand 15.3.1937." *Die Deutsche Sonderschule* (1937). Washington, D.C.: Library of Congress preservation microfilming program; 35 mm microfilm reels.

Pschyrembel, W. *Klinisches Wörterbuch, mit klinischen Syndromen.* 2d ed. New York: de Gruyter, 1975.

Reich, E. "Taubstumme Entstummen!" *Jüdische Rundschau,* 1st Supplement (April 26, 1934).

Reich, F. "50 Jahre Israelitische Taubstummenanstalt und ihr Gründer Dir.

M. Reich." *Beiträge zur Fortbildung und Unterhaltung der Taubstummen* 30 (1923).

———. "Der Mosaische Religionsunterricht." In *Handbuch des Taubstummenwesens*. Osterwieck, 1929.

———. "Die Israelitische Taubstummenanstalt für Deutschland zu Berlin-Weissensee." In *Taubstummenunterricht*, ed. G. Lehmann.

Reichmann, E., ed. *Handbuch der kritischen und materialistischen Behinderten-pädagogik und ihrer Nebenwissenschaften*. Solms Oberbiel: Jarick Oberbiel, 1984.

Richter, A. "Die Landestaubstummenanstalt zu Homberg." In *Taubstummenunterricht*, ed. G. Lehmann, 1930.

Romey, S. "Faschismus." In *Handbuch der kritischen und materialistischen Behinderten-pädagogik und ihrer Nebenwissenschaften*, ed. E. Reichmann. Solms-Oberbiel: Jarick Oberbiel, 1984.

Roth, K. H. *Erfassung zur Vernichtung: von der Sozialhygiene zum "Gesetz über Sterbehilfe."* Berlin: Verlagsgesellschaft Gesundheit, 1984.

Schallmeyer, W. *Vererbung und Auslese in ihrer soziologischen und wissenschaftlichen Bedeutung*. 1910.

Schmacke, N., and H. G. Güse. *Zwangssterilisiert verleugnet vergessen, zur Geschichte der nationalsozialistischen Rassenhygiene am beispiel Bremen*. Bremen: Brockkamp, 1984.

Schmähl, O. *Der taubstumme Mensch*. Berlin, 1933.

———. "Der deutsche Gehörlose." In *Festschrift anl. d. 2. Dt. Gl-Tages*. Breslau, 1937.

———. "Der gegenwärtige Stand der Taubstummenbildung in Niederschlesien." In *Festschrift anl. d. 2. Dt. Gl-Tages*. Breslau, 1937.

Schorsch, E. "Bund deutscher Taubstummenlehrer, Verbandsaufgabe." *Blätter für Taubstummenbildung* 36 (1923): 5.

———. "Umformung!" *Blätter für Taubstummenbildung* 46 (1933): 10.

Schumann, P. "Die Unfruchtbarmachung geistig Minderwertiger." *Blätter für Taubstummenbildung* 30 (1923): 20.

———. "Die 'Lex-Zwickau' und die Taubstummen." *Blätter für Taubstummenbildung* 39 (1926): 14.

———. "Ursachen der Taubstummheit." In *Handbuch des Taubstummenwesens*. Osterwieck, 1929.

———. "Das Gesetz zur Verhütung erbkranken Nachwuchses und seine Begründung." *Blätter für Taubstummenbildung* 46 (1933): 17.

———. *Geschichte des Taubstummenwesens vom deutschen Standpunkt aus dargestellt*. Frankfurt, 1940.

Seidenberg, S. "Ohrenärztliche Untersuchungen taubstummer Zwillinge." Ph.D. diss., 1941.

Siepmann, H. "Neue grosse Aufgaben für uns Gehörlose." *Blätter für die Wohlfahrt der Gehörlosen* 3/4 (1933).

Sierck, U. *Die Wohltäter-Mafia, vom Erbgesundheitsgericht zur humangenetischen Beratung.* Hamburg, 1984.

———. "Erbgesundheit und genetische Beratung—Spuren der Vergangenheit." In *Behindertenpädagogik* 1 (1986).

Singer, E. "Aufstieg." *Neue Blätter für Taubstummenbildung* 1. Neckargemund: Bechinger, 1946.

Stengel, H. *Humangenetik.* 3d ed. Heidelberg, 1979.

Stoeckenius, M., and G. Barbuceanu. *Schwachsinn unklarer Genese.* Stuttgart, 1983.

von Uexküll, T. *Lehrbuch der psychosomatischen Medizin.* 2d ed. Munich, 1981.

Wagner, W. "Gefährdetes Leben und Schule." In *Gefährdetes Leben, Bericht über eine Arbeitstagung* 56 (1964). Frankfurt: Evangelische Akademie in Hessen und Nassau.

———. *Behinderung und Nationalsozialismus Arbeitshypothesen zur Geschichte der Sonderschule.* Lucerne, 1977.

Wallisfurth, M. *Sie hat es mir erzählt.* 2d ed. Freiburg, 1979.

Walter, E. *Handbuch der Taubstummenbildung.* Berlin, 1895.

Weinert, H. "Eheberatung und Familienforschung im Dienste der Taubstummen und Schwerhörigen." *Blätter für die Wohlfahrt der Gehörlosen* 7 (1933): 1.

———. "Das Sterilisierungsgesetz." *Blätter für Taubstummenbildung* 1 (1934).

———. "Zwei Äusserungen zur Sterilisation." *Die Deutsche Sonderschule* (1935): 578.

———. "Rassenhygienische Ehevermittlung." *Der öffentliche Gesundheitsdienst* (1937): 19.

———. "Ehevermittlung für Erbkranke." *Die Deutsche Sonderschule* (1938): 5.

———. "Bericht über die rassenhygienische Betreuung Gehörgeschädigter in Sachsen." *Die Deutsche Sonderschule* (1938): 5.

Welker, O. "Taubstummgehörlos?" *Monatsschrift f. Ohrenheilkunde und Laryngo-Rhinologie* 76 (1942): 1.

Weng, E. "Weihe eines neuen HJ-Heimes des Reichsbannes Gehör-geschädigte (G) in Tilsit." *Die Deutsche Sonderschule* (1938): 11.

Werner, M. "Erbprognose und Sterilisierungsbegutachtung." *Die Deutsche Sonderschule* (1935): 362.

Wilcke, W. "Beitrag zur Erforschung der Taubstummheit im Regierungsbezirk Wiesbaden." Unpublished doctoral dissertation. Düsseldorf, 1939.

Winnewisser, A. "Ist angeborene Taubheit immer Erbtaubheit?" *Die Deutsche Sonderschule* (1938): 3.147, 4.245, 5.300, 6.407.

Witte, B. S. "Die Wahl der Sicherheit: Freiwillige Sterilisation des Mannes, Vorurteile und Urteile." *Sexualmedizin* 3 (1974).

Wördehoff, K. "Über die Bedeutung der Vererbung in der Ätiologie der Innenohrschwerhörigkeit." Ph.D. diss., Würzburg, 1936.

Zankl, H. *Humangenetik.* Berlin, 1980.

Selected Bibliography in English

Alexander, Leo. "Medical Science under Dictatorship." *New England Journal of Medicine* 241, no. 2 (1974): 39–47.

Aly, Götz, Peter Chroust, and Christian Pross. *Cleansing the Fatherland: Nazi Medicine and Racial Hygiene.* Translated by Belinda Cooper. Baltimore: Johns Hopkins University Press, 1994.

Annas, George J., and Michael A. Grodin, eds. *The Nazi Doctors and the Nuremburg Code: Human Rights in Human Experimentation.* New York: Oxford University Press, 1992.

Allen, Garland E. "The Eugenics Record Office at Cold Spring Harbor, 1910–1940: An Essay in Institutional History." *Osiris*, 2d. ser., 2 (1986): 225–64.

Bell, Alexander Graham. *Family Papers Documenting Bell's Interest in Eugenics and in the Education of the Deaf.* Washington, D.C.: Library of Congress Manuscript Division. Microfilm.

Browning, Christopher R. *Fateful Months: Essays on the Emergence of the Final Solution.* New York: Homes and Meier, 1985.

Burleigh, Michael. *The Racial State: Germany, 1933–1945.* New York: Cambridge University Press, 1991.

———. *Death and Deliverance: "Euthanasia" in Germany c. 1900–1945.* New York: Cambridge University Press, 1994.

———. *Confronting the Nazi Past: New Debates on Modern German History.* New York: St. Martin's Press, 1996.

———. *Ethics and Extermination: Reflections on Nazi Genocide.* New York: Cambridge University Press, 1997.

Caplan, Arthur L. *When Medicine Went Mad: Bioethics and the Holocaust.* Totowa, N.J.: Humana Press, 1992.

Caplan, Arthur L., H. Tristram Engelhardt, Jr., and James J. McCartney. *Concepts of Health and Disease: Interdisciplinary Perspectives.* Reading, Mass.: Addison-Wesley, Advanced Book Program / World Science Division, 1981.

Clay, Catrine, and Michael Leapman. *Master Race: The Lebensborn Experiment in Nazi Germany.* London: Hodder & Stoughton, 1995.

Cocks, Geoffrey. *Treating Mind & Body: Essays in the History of Science, Professions, and Society under Extreme Conditions.* New Brunswick, N.J.: Transaction Publishers, 1998.

Control Commission for Germany (British Element). Legal division. British Special Legal Research Unit. "Translations of Nazi Health Laws Concerned with Hereditary Diseases, Matrimonial Health, Sterilization, and Castration." Mimeograph, 1945.

Edelheit, Abraham J., and Hershel Edelheit. *Bibliography on Holocaust Literature.* Boulder, Colo.: Westview Press, 1986.

Falk, Richard A, Gabriel Kolko, and Robert Jay Lifton. *Crimes of War: A Legal, Political-Documentary, and Psychological Inquiry into the Responsibility of Leaders, Citizens, and Soldiers for Criminal Acts in Wars.* New York: Random House, 1971.

Friedlander, Henry. *The Origins of Nazi Genocide: From Euthanasia to the Final Solution.* Chapel Hill: University of North Carolina Press, 1995.

Friedlander, Henry, and Sybil Milton, eds. Berlin Document Center. *Archives of the Holocaust Series.* Vol. 11. New York: Garland Publishing, 1995.

———. *The Holocaust: Ideology, Bureaucracy, and Genocide: The San Jose Papers.* Millwood, N.Y.: Kraus International Publications, 1980.

———. Archives of the Holocaust: An International Collection of Selected Documents. New York: Garland Publishing, 1995.

Friedman, Ina. *The Other Victims: First-Person Stories of Non-Jews Persecuted by the Nazis.* Boston: Houghton Mifflin, 1990.

Gallagher, Hugh Gregory. *By Trust Betrayed: Patients, Physicians, and the License to Kill in the Third Reich.* Arlington, Va.: Vandamere Press, 1990.

Grossmann, Atina. *Reforming Sex: The German Movement for Birth Control and Abortion Reform, 1920–1950.* New York: Oxford University Press, 1995.

Hastings Center. *Biomedical Ethics and the Shadow of Nazism: A Conference on the Proper Use of the Nazi Analogy in Ethical Debate, April 8, 1976.* Edited by Peter Steinfels and Carol Levine. New York: Hastings on Hudson, 1976.

Heberer, Patricia. "'If I Transgress My Oath': The Story of the Hadamar Trial." Master's thesis, Southern Illinois University at Edwardsville, 1989.

Hillel, Marc, and Clarissa Henry. *Of Pure Blood.* Translated by Eric Mossbacher. New York: McGraw-Hill, 1976.

James, Eldon R, ed. *The Statutory Criminal Law of Germany.* Prepared by Vladimir Gsovski. Washington, D.C.: Library of Congress, 1947.

Kater, Michael H. *Doctors under Hitler*. Chapel Hill: University of North Carolina Press, 1989.

Katz, Jay. *Human Sacrifice and Human Experimentation: Reflections at Nuremberg*. Yale Law School Occasional Papers; second series, no. 2. New Haven, Conn.: Yale Law School, 1997.

Kevles, Daniel J. *In the Name of Eugenics: Genetics and the Uses of Human Heredity*. Cambridge, Mass.: Harvard University Press, 1995.

Kintner, Earl W., ed. *The Hadamar Trial: Trial of Alfons Klein, Adolf Wahlmann, Heinrich Ruoff, Karl Willig, Adolf Merkle, Irmgard Huber, and Philipp Blum*. London: William Hodge, 1949.

Kühl, Stefan. *The Nazi Connection: Eugenics, American Racism, and German National Socialism*. New York: Oxford University Press, 1994.

Leuner, Heinz David. *When Compassion Was a Crime*. Weisbaden: Limes Verlag, 1967.

Lifton, Robert Jay. *The Nazi Doctors: Medical Killing and the Psychology of Genocide*. New York: Basic Books, 1986.

Mendelsohn, John, ed. *The Holocaust: Selected Documents*. 18 vols. New York: Garland Publishing, 1982.

Miller, Marvin D. *Terminating the "Socially Inadequate": The American Eugenicists and the German Race Hygienists, California to Cold Spring Harbor, Long Island to Germany*. Commack, N.Y.: Malamud-Rose, 1996.

Pernick, Martin S. *The Black Stork: Eugenics and the Death of "Defective" Babies in American Medicine and Motion Pictures since 1915*. New York: Oxford University Press, 1996.

Proctor, Robert. *Racial Hygiene: Medicine under the Nazis*. Cambridge, Mass: Harvard University Press, 1988.

Pross, Christian, and Götz Aly. *The Value of the Human Being: Medicine in Germany 1918–1945*. Berlin: Arztekammer Berlin, 1991.

Roland, Charles, Henry Friedlander, and Benno Müller-Hill, eds. *Medical Science without Compassion: Past and Present*. Hamburg: Hamburger Stiftung für Sozialgeschichte des 20. Jahrhunderts, 1992.

Snyder, Louis S., ed. *The Third Reich, 1933–1945: A Bibliographical Guide to German National Socialism*. New York: Garland Publishers, 1987.

Thornton, Larry Patrick. "Weeding the Garden: Euthanasia, National Socialism, and Germany 1939–1945." Ph.D. diss., University of Illinois at Urbana-Champaign, 1991.

Tucker, William H. *The Science and Politics of Racial Research*. Urbana: University of Illinois Press, 1994.

Tutorow, Norman E., ed. *War Crimes, War Criminals, and War Crimes Trials: An Annotated Bibliography and Source Book*. New York: Greenwood Press, 1986.

Weindling, Paul. *Health, Race, and German Politics between National Unification and Nazism, 1870–1945.* New York: Cambridge University Press, 1989.

Weiss, Sheila Faith. *Race Hygiene and National Efficiency: The Eugenics of Wilhelm Schallmayer.* Berkeley: University of California Press, 1987.

Index

Page numbers in italics indicate photographs, page numbers followed by *f* indicate figures, page numbers followed by *t* indicate tables

Abend, A., 19
abortions, forced, 113; case of Fanny Mikus, 87–90; diagnosis of "hereditary feeblemindedness" and, 85; emotional effects of, 85, 87; Law for the Prevention of Offspring with Hereditary Diseases and, 5–6, 84; length of pregnancy and, 85*t*; number of, 84; Pauline Home in Winnenden and, 85, 86*f*
Adler, Rabbi S., 131
Albreghs, Fritz, 91, *92, 98,* 100–2, *102,* 106, 107
anti-Semitism: racial, 2, 3
Archive for Racial Science and Social Biology, 14
Association for the Advancement of the Interests of the Jewish Deaf, 133
Association for the Advancement of the Jewish Deaf in Germany, 137
Association of Former Students of the Israelite Institution for the Deaf in Weissensee, 137
Association of Rabbis of Traditional Law Observance of Germany, 136–37
Asylum for the Deaf in Winnenden, 73–82
athletic associations, 91–93
"Audiological Studies of Deaf Twins" (Seidenberg), 31–32
Auschwitz, 10, 164

Baden Association for the Deaf in Heidelberg, 54
Ballier (REGEDE official), 100

Bauer, E., 18–19
Beck, K., 54
Berlin Deaf Athletic Association, 93
Berlin-Neukölln Training Institute for Teachers of the Deaf, 42–48
Bernburg killing center, 10
Bewer (school director), 53
Bezold, F., 28–29
Binding, Karl, 8
Blätter für Taubstummenbildung (Journal for Deaf Education), 16, 27, 28, 30
blind persons: sterilization of, 5
Bloch, David Ludwig, 138
Bloch and Meseritz Foundation, 133
Blood Protection and Reich Citizenship Laws, 35
Boeters, Gustav, 16–17, 18, 141
Bouhler, Philipp, 7, 9
Brack, Victor, 7, 163
Brandenburg killing center, 10, 165
Brandt, Karl, 7, 9
Breslau Educational and Training Institution for the Deaf, 24
Buchenwald, 164
Büldt (doctor), 116
Bumm (professor), 17, 18
burial urns: transport of, 167

Catholic church: opposition to sterilization, 70–71
Catholic Deaf Association in Münster, 112–15
Catholic deaf schools, 68–73
Chancellery of the Führer, 7

Charitable Foundation for Institutional Care, 9

Charitable Patient Transport Company, 163

children, deaf: effects of sterilization law on, 81, 82*f*; physical and psychological effects of sterilization on, 68, 150–52; resistance to sterilization, 46, 68–69; T4 killing operations and, 9. *See also* teacher-collaborators

children, disabled: "euthanasia" actions and, 162–63; T4 killing operations and, 8–9, 10, 11

children, Jewish and Gypsy: murder of, 163

City of Berlin school for the deaf, 41

concentration camps, 163–64

condolence letters, 167

congenital feeblemindedness: forced abortions and, 85; Law for the Prevention of Offspring with Hereditary Diseases and, 5, 35; sterilization and, 74, 76, 79

Conrad (school director), 69–73

Conti, Leonardo, 115

"Contribution to the Investigation of Deafness in the Administrative District of Wiesbaden" (Wilcke), 30

Cooperative Association of the Jewish Physically Impaired of Germany, 137

Co-operative Group 3, 137

cremation, 161–62, 166

Darwin, Charles, 14

Das Band (The Link), 133

Davenport, Charles, 2, 3

deaf collaborators, 102–6, 107. *See also* Reich Union of the Deaf of Germany

deaf institutions: number of sterilization victims from, 34, 35*t*; private, sterilization of students and, 68–83; regional, sterilization of students and, 41, 42–67, 82–83; studies on heritability of deafness and, 32–33, 34*t*. *See also individual institutions*

Deaf Leader (newspaper), 112

deafness: heritability of, German research on, 28–34

deaf organizations: Catholic, 112–15; consolidation under Nazi authority, 91–93; Jewish, 133, 137; women's, 106–7. *See also* Reich Union of the Deaf of Germany

deaf persons: denunciations of, 6–7, 23–24, 41 (*see also* teacher–collaborators); "euthanasia" actions and, 160–70; resistance to sterilization (*see* deaf resistance); sterilization of (*see* sterilization); T4 killing operations and, 9, 163, 164. *See also* Jewish deaf; victims of sterilization

deaf resistance: active, 46, 112–29; Catholic deaf organizations and, 112–15; by Catholic students, 68–73; extent of, 109; Jacob, Gertrud and, 121–29; passive, 83, 110; Sommer, Hermann, 115–16, 202 n. 15; Veltmann, August and, 112–15; Wacker, Karl and, 117–20

Deaf Union for Physical Training, 91

Deaf Union of German Girls, *94*

Deaf Union of German Girls Athletes, *93*

denunciations: of deaf persons, 6–7, 23–24, 41; of deaf resistors, 114; of disabled persons, 6–7, 23–24; of Jewish deaf, 134, 136, 139. *See also* teacher-collaborators

depression, as a result of sterilization, 152–53

Deutsche Gehörlosen-Zeitung (German Deaf News), 98, 113

Deutsche Medizinische Wochenschrift (German Medical Weekly), 15

Dillingen school. *See* District Instructional and Vocational Institution for Deaf Girls

Dirr, Mother Agreda, 71–73*f*

disabled persons: denunciations of, 6–7, 23–24; issues of restitution and, 11–12; marriage laws and, 6; Nazi efforts to define and identify, 6; Nazi policies of exclusion and, 2; Nazi racial hygiene policy and, 4–7; T4 killing operations and, 7–11. *See also* children, disabled

District Instructional and Vocational Institution for Deaf Girls, 68–73

divorce, as a consequence of sterilization, 150

Dresden State Institution for the Deaf, 69

Eglfing-Haar state hospital, 9
Emmerig, E., 32–33, 195 n. 28
Engelmann, K., 196 n. 28
eugenics: in America, 3, 15; in contemporary thought, 195 n. 24; on deaf persons, 160; development of racial hygiene policy and, 16–18 (see also racial hygiene policy); in Germany, 3–4; history and development of, 2–3, 13, 14–15; "positive" and "negative," 3; teachers of the deaf and, 16, 18–24; in teacher training programs, 43–45
"Eugenics in the United States of America" (Hofmann), 15
"euthanasia" actions: cremation of bodies and, 161–62, 166; linked to racial hygiene policy, 160; medical experimentation and, 8; murder of children, 162–63; murder of concentration camp inmates, 164; murder of medical and psychiatric patients, 160–62; Nazi efforts at secrecy and cover up, 166–70; number of victims, 164–66; "wild euthanasia," 11, 164. See also Nazi killing programs; T4 killing operations
"euthanasia" centers, 165–66
"Examinations of the Children at the Institution for the Deaf in Heidelberg" (Pfefferle), 33, 34t
exclusion laws (U.S.), 3
Eyrich (doctor), 76, 77

Fallopian tube ligation, 141
Federal Committee for Public Health Service, 22
Fischer, Eugen, 3, 18–19, 29
Frick, Wilhelm, 107–8, 160, 161f

Galton, Francis, 2
gas chambers: in T4 killing operations, 10, 163
German Association of Cities, 160–62
German Deaf News, 98, 113
German Deaf Workers Union, 100
German Federal Attorney General, 144
German Federation of Physicians, 143

German Medical Weekly, 15
German sign language, 95, 96–97f, 208 n. 16
German Union of Physicians Associations, 207 n. 8
Germany, postwar: contemporary eugenics thought in, 195 n. 24; restitution of victims and, 11–12
Gestapo, 113, 120, 138
Gmelin, Walter, 78
Gobineau, Joseph Arthur de, 14
Goebbels, Josef, 159
Gotha health authority, 121–24
Grafeneck killing center, 10, 165–66
Grotjahn, Alfred, 4
Grundriss der menschlichen Erblichkeitslehre und Rassenhygiene (Bauer, Fischer, and Lenz), 18–19
Günther, Hans, 4
Gypsies: children, murder of, 163; killing centers and, 10, 11; Nazi policies of exclusion and, 1–2

Hadamar killing hospital, 10, 163, 165, 168–70
Hartheim killing center, 10
health authorities: teacher-collaborators and, 49, 50f, 59–60, 61, 64–65, 74, 75–79, 80–81
Heidbrede (school director), 62–67, 199 n. 37
Heidelberg Institution for the Deaf, 33–34, 54–58
hereditary disease: German research on, 28–34; Law for the Prevention of Offspring with Hereditary Diseases and, 5, 35–36; sterilization and (see sterilization)
hereditary disease questionnaires, 16, 22, 66–67f
"hereditary feeblemindedness." See congenital feeblemindedness
hereditary health courts: on effects of surgical sterilization, 144; in Kiel, 115, 116; Nazi medicine and, 115, 116, 123–25, 128–29; in Stuttgart, 118, 120; teacher-collaborators and, 75–76, 77, 79, 81
Hild, Hans, 25–26
Hill, Friedrich, 13–14

Himmler, Heinrich, 160, 161*f,* 163, 164
"History of the Deaf from the German
　Perspective" (Schumann), 27
Hitler, Adolf: Jacob, Gertrud and, 125,
　128, 205 n. 34; race hygiene concept
　and, 4; suppression of publicity about
　sterilization, 159; T4 killing opera-
　tions and, 7, 8, 9, 10, 163
Hitler cut, 208 n. 16
Hitlerschnitt, 208 n. 16
Hitler Youth, 93–94, *95*
Hoche, Alfred, 8
Hoffmann, W., 54
Hofmann, G., 15
Hogen (doctor), 69, 70*f*
Homberg Institution, 58–62, 164
hospitals: Hadamar killing hospital, 10,
　163, 165, 168–70; T4 killing opera-
　tions and, 8–9, 10, 11. *See also* "eu-
　thanasia" centers
Hundertmark, Alexander, 53

immigration policy (U.S.), 3
Indiana: sterilization program in, 15
infanticide, 8–9, 156
Israelite Institution for the Deaf of Ger-
　many, 130–34, 135*f, 136,* 137, 206 n.
　10, 207 n. 13
Israelitische Taubstummenanstalt für
　Deutschland. *See* Israelite Institution
　for the Deaf of Germany

Jacob, Gertrud, 121–29, 204 n. 30, 205 n.
　31
Jena Superior Provincial Court, 128,
　205 n. 34
Jewish deaf: denunciations by deaf Nazi
　leaders, 134, 136; denunciations by
　teachers, 139; Israelite Institution for
　the Deaf of Germany, 130–34, 135*f,*
　136, 137; Law for the Prevention of
　Offspring with Hereditary Diseases
　and, 136–37; Nazi repression and,
　134, 136, 137; number of, 205–206 n.
　1; Otto Weidt and, 138; survivors,
　138–39
Jewish Review (periodical), 136
Jews: children, murder of, 163; killing
　centers and, 10, 11; marriage laws

and, 6; Nazi policies of exclusion and,
　1–2; sterilization and, 149
Journal for Deaf Education, 16, 27, 28,
　30
Jüdische Rundschau (Jewish Review),
　136
Juliusburger, O., 15

Kalmenhof Remedial Training Institu-
　tion, 168
Klüsener-Esch, Emilie, 106–7
Knobloch (teacher), 107–8
Koch (Buchenwald camp commander),
　164
Königsberg Provincial Institution for the
　Deaf, 53

Langenhorst Provincial Institution for
　the Deaf, 114–15
laparotomies, 140–41
Law for the Prevention of Offspring
　with Hereditary Diseases: collabora-
　tion of teachers with (*see* teacher-col-
　laborators); definition of hereditary
　disease in, 5, 35–36; forced abortions
　and, 5–6, 84; foreign reaction and,
　154–55; Jewish deaf and, 136–37;
　Marriage Health Law and, 126–27;
　number of victims, 34, 35*t,* 36; origins
　of, 4–5, 35; postwar Germany on, 11–
　12; Reich Union of the Deaf of Ger-
　many and, 106; resistance to (*see* deaf
　resistance); significance of, 34–35;
　teachers of the deaf and, 16, 20, 24–
　27; use of force and, 46, 109–11. *See
　also* racial hygiene policy; steriliza-
　tion
Law for the Protection of the Hereditary
　Health of the German Nation, 6,
　204 n. 27. *See also* Marriage Health
　Law
Law for the Restoration of the Profes-
　sional Civil Service, 35
Law to Amend the Law for the Preven-
　tion of Offspring with Hereditary Dis-
　eases, 84
Lehmann, Gotthold, 42–48, 197 n. 10
Leitmeritz Institution for the Deaf, 33,
　196 n. 30

Lenz (doctor), 116
Lenz, Fritz, 3, 4, 18–19
Lex Zwickau, 16
"'Lex Zwickau' and the Deaf, The" (Schumann), 29
Liepelt (teacher), 139
Linden, Herbert, 7
Link, The (periodical), 133

Maesse, H., *44*, 60–61, 82–83, 102
Marcusallee School, 202 n. 25
Markus, Emma, 132, 133
marriage counseling, 21–22, 203 n. 25
Marriage Health Law, 6, 35, 122, 126–27, 204 n. 27, 205 n. 33
mass exterminations. *See* Nazi killing programs
Matz, Edmund, 101–2
medical community: concept of mass killing and, 8; concepts of heredity and "moral deficiency" in, 13–14; eugenics and, 14; support for sterilization programs, 16–17, 18. *See also* health authorities; Nazi medicine; physicians
medical experimentation, 8, 141
Menke, Norbert, 112
mentally ill: "euthanasia" actions and, 160–62; Law for the Prevention of Offspring with Hereditary Diseases and, 5, 35; sterilization of, 5
Meseritz-Obrawalde state hospital, 11
Mikus, Fanny, 87–90
Möhle (teacher), 114–15
Morning and the Evening Sacrifice, The (Adler), 131
Müller (superintendent), 75–82
Munich Provincial Institution for the Deaf, 32
Münster Institution for Human Genetics, 195 n. 24
Münster Psychiatric Hospital, 168

Nachrichtenblatt des Berliner Gehörlosen-Sportvereins (Newsletter of the Berlin Deaf Athletic Association), 93–94
Naecke, Paul, 15
National Professional Association, 102

National Socialist Teachers Confederation, 21, 24, 45, *47*, *107*, 197 n. 12
National Union for the Welfare of the Deaf, 91
"Nazi Injustice Toward the Deaf" (television program), 87
Nazi killing programs: 14 f 13 action, 163–64; disposal of bodies and, 161–62; fear of U.S. reaction to, 161, 162; against Jews and Gypsies, 10, 11, 163; linked to racial hygiene policy, 160. *See also* "euthanasia" actions; T4 killing operations
Nazi medicine: abuse of sterilization patients, 156; collaboration with hereditary health courts, 115, 116, 123–25, 128–29; collaboration with killing programs, 164; collaboration with teachers of the deaf, 25, 54, 61–62, 76–77, 83; cooperation with T4 killing operations, 8–9, 10, 11; human experimentation and, 8, 141; trivialization of surgical sterilization, 143, 148. *See also* health authorities
Nazi party: membership card, *99f*; Reich Union of the Deaf of Germany and, 91–102; teachers of the deaf and, 47–48, 75, 114–15; Wacker, Karl and, 91, 117
Nazi Public Welfare, 91, 108, 196 n. 28
Nazi regime: concept of racial purity and, 1–2; eugenics movement and, 3–4; "euthanasia" actions, 160–70; exclusion of disabled persons, 2; exclusion of non-Aryan peoples, 1–2; Nuremberg race laws, 1–2, 6, 35; racial hygiene policy of, 4–7 (*see also* racial hygiene policy); Reich Union of the Deaf of Germany and, 91–102; research on hereditary disease and, 28, 29–34; suppression of publicity about sterilization, 159. *See also* Law for the Prevention of Offspring with Hereditary Diseases; Nazi killing programs; Nazi medicine
Nazi Teachers' Union, 102–6, *106*, 107
Nazi Women's Organization, 106
"negative" eugenics, 3
Neuert, G., 16

Newsletter of the Berlin Deaf Athletic Association, 93–94
Nuremberg race laws, 1–2, 6, 35

Oberhauser (teacher), 195–96n. 28
Old Timers Club of Kassel, 98, 99
Operation T4. *See* T4 killing operations
Osnabrück Institution for the Deaf, 95
Outline of Human Genetics and Racial Hygiene (Bauer, Fischer, and Lenz), 18–19

Pauline Home in Winnenden, 73–82; "euthanasia" actions and, 165–66; forced abortions and, 85, 86*f*
Petershagen Provincial Institution for the Deaf, 49
Pfannmüller, Hermann, 9
Pfefferle, F., 33, 34*t*
Pfingsten, Georg, 62
physicians: Jewish, 204n. 30; T4 killing operations and, 8–9, 10, 11; trivialization of surgical sterilization, 148. *See also* health authorities; medical community; Nazi medicine
Plötz, Alfred, 14
Poland: "wild euthanasia" in, 11, 164
"positive" eugenics, 3
pregnancy: length of, forced abortions and, 85*t*
psychiatric patients. *See* mentally ill
Public Foundation for Institutional Care, 163

questionnaires. *See* hereditary disease questionnaires

Race Policy Authority, 22
racial hygiene concept: in contemporary thought, 195n. 24; origins of, 13, 14–15. *See also* eugenics
racial hygiene policy: defining and identifying disabled persons, 6; denunciations of disabled persons, 6; hereditary disease questionnaires and, 16, 22; linked to Nazi killing programs, 160; marriage laws and, 6; origins of, 4; Reich Union for Deaf Welfare and, 195–96n. 28; Reich Union of the Deaf

of Germany and, 102–6, 194n. 14; sterilization law and, 4–6, 34–35; teacher-collaborators and, 24–27, 62–67, 82–83; T4 killing operations and, 7–11, 163, 164. *See also* Law for the Prevention of Offspring with Hereditary Diseases; sterilization
racism: German anti-Semitism and, 2, 3; German eugenics and, 3, 4
REGEDE. *See* Reich Union of the Deaf of Germany
Reich, Felix, 133, 134, *136*, 137
Reich, Markus, 130–33
Reich Committee for the Scientific Registration of Severe Hereditary Ailments, 8, 162
Reich Cooperative for State Hospitals and Nursing Homes, 9, 163
Reich Ministry of the Interior, 7, 154, 162
Reich Professional Group of Teachers of the Deaf and Hard of Hearing, *44*
Reich Union for Deaf Welfare, 195–96n. 28
Reich Union of Pastors of the Protestant Deaf, 37, 38*f*, 39*f*
Reich Union of the Deaf of Germany (REGEDE), 30, 83, *92*; Catholic deaf organizations and, 112, 113–14; collaboration with racial hygiene policy, 102–6, 194n. 14; denunciation of resistors, 114; incorporation into Nazi Public Welfare, 91, 108; insignia, 99*f*; Jacob, Gertrud and, 125–26; Law for the Prevention of Offspring with Hereditary Diseases and, 106; membership card, 101*f*; membership figures, 95; members of, sterilization and, 95, 98–100; Nazi influence in, 91–102; women's clubs and, 106–7; workshops and presentations sponsored by, 103–5*f*
Reich Women's Union, 106
religious deaf schools: Catholic, 68–73. *See also* Israelite Institution for the Deaf of Germany
Rittmeier (teacher), 126, 205n. 31
Rönigk, Oskar, 58–62
Rosenbaum (doctor), 204n. 30

Royal Institution for the Deaf, 130
Ruckau (teachers' union leader), 102, *106*
Rüdin, Ernst, 3, 4, 15

Schaefer (Reich Minister), 48
Schafft, Hermann, 58
schizophrenics, 5, 35
Schlechtweg (school director), 126, 205 n. 31
Schleswig Institution for the Deaf, 62–67, 164
Schmähl, Otto, 24–25
Schmid, Franz, 68, 200 n. 49
Schmid, Georg, 68, 200 n. 49
Schumann, P., 19–20, 21, 26–27, 29
Schürmann (teacher), 46–47
Schwäbisch Gmünd school. *See* St. Joseph Private Institution for the Deaf
Seidenberg, S., 31–32
Siepmann, H., 91–93
sign language, 95, 96–97*f*, 208 n. 16
Singer, Edwin, 54, 56–58, 198–99 n. 26
social Darwinism, 14
Society for Racial Hygiene, 14
Soest Provincial Institution for the Deaf, 41, 46, 48–52
Sommer, Hermann, 115–16, 202 n. 15
Sonnenstein killing center, 10
Soviet Union: "wild euthanasia" in, 11, 164
"Speaking Hands," 96–97*f*
"Special Education and Youth Welfare in the Context of National Defense" (Hild), 25
St. Joseph Private Institution for the Deaf, 55, 68, 200 n. 49
starvation: in "euthanasia" actions, 8, 163, 164
State Institution for the Deaf at Berlin-Neukölln. *See* Berlin-Neukölln Training Institute for Teachers of the Deaf
sterilization: in America, 15; Berlin-Neukölln Training Institute and, 45–46; Boeters, Gustav and, 16–17, 18; Catholic opposition to, 70–71; District Instructional and Vocational Institution for Deaf Girls and, 68–73; early proponents of, 15; German Federal Attorney General on, 144; German Public Health Department on, 17–18; in German sign language, 208 n. 16; Heidelberg Institution and, 54, 56–57*f*; Homberg Institution and, 59–62; Jewish deaf and, 136–37; Königsberg Provincial Institution and, 53; mortality from, 153–54, 155–56, 156–58*f*; number of victims, 34, 35*t*, 36; Pauline Home in Winnenden and, 73–82; physical and psychological effects of, 56–57*f*, 68, 140, 144–53, 196–97 n. 41; postwar Germany on, 11–12; for racial reasons, 149; Reich Union of the Deaf of Germany members and, 95, 98–100; resistance to (*see* deaf resistance); Schleswig Institution and, 62–67; Soest Provincial Institution and, 48–52; St. Joseph Private Institution and, 68; teachers of the deaf and, 22–23. *See also* Law for the Prevention of Offspring with Hereditary Diseases
"Sterilization Law, The" (Weinert), 20
sterilization procedures, 140–41; abuse of patients, 156, 158; Nazi suppression of information about, 158; postoperative treatment periods, 158; trivialization of, 18, 52*f*, 141–44
Stuttgart Hereditary Health Court, 118, 120
suicide, 153
survivors: Jewish deaf, 138–39; restitution and, 11. *See also* victims of sterilization

Taubstummen-Führer (*Deaf Leader*), 112
teacher-collaborators: Bewer (school director), 53; collaboration with health authorities, 49, 50*f*, 59–60, 61, 64–65, 74, 75–79, 80–81; collaboration with Nazi medicine, 25, 54, 61–62, 76–77, 83; collaboration with racial hygiene policy, 24–27, 62–67, 82–83; Conrad (school director), 69–73; denunciations of Jewish deaf, 139; Heidbrede (school director), 62–67, 199 n. 37; Hild, Hans, 25–26; Lehmann, Gotthold, 42–48,

teacher-collaborators (*continued*)
197 n. 10; Müller (superintendent),
75–82; in private institutions, 68–82;
in regional institutions, 42–67, 82–83;
Rönigk, Oskar, 58–62; Schmähl, Otto,
24–25; Schmid, Franz, 68, 200 n. 49;
Schmid, Georg, 68, 200 n. 49; Schumann, P., 19–20, 21, 26–27, 29;
Singer, Edwin, 54, 56–58; trivialization of surgical sterilization, 18, 52*f*,
141–42; Wegge (school director), 48–
52, 198 n. 22; Weinert, Herbert, 16,
20–24, 109, 122, 141–42, 203 n. 25,
203–4 n. 26
teachers of the deaf: eugenics and, 16,
18–24, 43–45; as Nazi party members, 47–48, 75, 114–15; Reich, Markus, 130–33; Reich Union of the Deaf
of Germany and, 102–6, 107. *See also*
teacher-collaborators
teacher training: eugenics and, 43–45;
Nazi party membership and, 47–48
teenagers, deaf: Nazi murder of, 165;
physical and psychological effects of
sterilization on, 68, 150–52, 196 n. 28
T4 killing centers, 10–11. *See also* "euthanasia" centers
T4 killing operations, 7–11, 163, 164.
See also "euthanasia" actions
Thomas, Werner, 93–95, 96–97*f*
Tornow (teachers' union leader), *106*
torture, 158
"Transformation!" (Schumann), 27
Treblinka, 10
tubal ligations, 141
twin studies, 31–32

Union of German Teachers of the Deaf,
16, 45, 133, 197 n. 10
Union of Orthodox Rabbis of Germany,
136–37
United States: eugenics movement in, 3;
sterilization programs in, 15
uterus: removal of, 141

Vagt (senator), 160–62
vasectomies, 140
Vatican: opposition to sterilization, 70–
71

Veltmann, August, 112–15
Verschuer, Otmar von, 4, 29, 194 n. 14,
195 n. 24
victims of sterilization: abuse of, 156,
158; depression and, 153; interviews
with, 36–37, 40; issues of restitution
and, 11–12; medical experimentation
and, 141; mortality and, 153–54, 155–
56, 156–58*f*; number of, 34, 35*t*, 36;
physical and psychological distress of,
56–57*f*, 68, 140, 144–53, 196 n. 28,
196–97 n. 41; postoperative treatment
periods, 158; Reich Union of Pastors
of the Protestant Deaf and, 37, 38*f*,
39*f*; suicide and, 153; survey information from, 40–41, 208 n. 36. *See also*
survivors

Wacker, Karl, 91, 117–20
Wagner, J.-E., 68
Wallisfurth, Maria, 109
Warneke (doctor), 116
Weber, Arthur, 125–26, 204–5 n. 31
Wegge (school director), 48–52, 198 n. 22
Weidt, Otto, 138
Weinert, Herbert, 16, 20–24, 109, 122,
141–42, 203 n. 25, 203–4 n. 26
Werner, M., 29
Wesendahl, Josef, 30–31
Wilcke, W., 30, 194 n. 14
"wild euthanasia," 11, 164
Winnenden Home for the Aged Deaf,
120
Winnenden Pauline Home, 73–82, 85,
86*f*
women's deaf associations, 106–7
Wördehoff, K., 30
Wurm (bishop of Württemburg), 165,
166
Württemburg-Hohenzollern Association
for the Welfare of the Deaf, 118

X rays: in sterilization, 141

Zange, Johannes, 124, 204 n. 29
Zwanziger (school director), 194 n. 14
Zwickau Law, 16